Published by The Reader's Digest Association Limited.

First Edition Copyright © 1995
The Reader's Digest Association Limited,
Berkeley Square House, Berkeley Square, London W1X 6AB

Copyright © 1995
The Reader's Digest Association Far East Limited
Philippines Copyright 1995
The Reader's Digest Association Far East Limited

Consultant editor: Lizzie Boyd

Typeset in Century Schoolbook

PRINTED IN SPAIN

ISBN 0 276 42211 2

Opposite: The gardens at romantic Crathes Castle in the Grampians
date from the early 18th century. Immaculately clipped topiary yew hedges
divide the gardens into separate enclosures, each with its own
distinctive personality.

Overleaf: Rousham House and garden by the River Cherwell
in Oxfordshire is an enduring memorial to the 18th-century landscapist
William Kent, and virtually untouched by the passing of time.

Pages 6-7: Warmed by the Gulf Stream, Inverewe in the austere Scottish
Highlands is a paradise of near-tropical plants. In early summer, the sunken
rose garden is ablaze with scented blooms and frothing catmint.

Reader's
Digest

PUBLISHED BY THE READER'S DIGEST ASSOCIATION LIMITED
LONDON NEW YORK MONTREAL SYDNEY CAPE TOWN

SUCCESSFUL GARDENING

GARDENS
TO VISIT

CONTENTS

Gardens to visit

Gardening in the British Isles is more than a hobby, it is a national compulsion. And although a rich history, varied soils and a mild climate have all contributed, the instinct to nurture and adorn underlies this very British passion. Indeed, few people would consider their home complete without a garden, be it a humble cottage plot or a formal parkscape.

Much toil, and much science too, lies behind the nation's heritage. It was from Britain that many of the world's greatest plant hunters set out, gathering seed from the frozen Himalayas and steamy Amazonian rainforests. Today, the fruits of their labours grace small town gardens and rolling country acres alike.

British gardens are testament to an age old tradition of love, labour and experiment. Tastes and styles may change, but the love of gardening flourishes as strongly as ever. Another tradition also flourishes: for generations now, the owners of Britain's finest gardens – more than 100 of which are described in this book – have opened their gardens to the public and given pleasure to countless millions.

Abbotsbury Dorset

Palm trees are not the first things a visitor might expect to find growing among the thatched cottages of Dorset. Yet, situated to the west of Abbotsbury village, on the road to Chesil Beach, is a 20-acre paradise of subtropical trees and shrubs. Here, rhododendrons, camellias, hydrangeas and magnolias grow in splendid profusion. Their rounded clusters are diversified not only by the upthrust of huge Chusan palms, but also by ginkgo and sword-leaved cordylines.

The gardens form part of the Fox-Strangways estate and were originally those of Abbotsbury Castle, an 18th-century summer residence built by Elizabeth, Countess of Ilchester. The building itself was destroyed by fire in 1913, and its replacement was demolished in 1936. The gardens though have remained. They were severely

▲ **Tropical Dorset** A palm tree sets the tone for this lush corner of the subtropical gardens at Abbotsbury, where exotic plants flourish in the mild climate protected by the high walls of an old 'gardener's bothy'.

damaged by storms in 1990, but much new planting has taken place, including the New Zealand and Himalayan Glade.

The climate in this corner of England is exceptionally mild. The soil is heavy and acid loam. Many of the old plantings came from China and the Himalayas, originally specimens grown from seeds collected by such indefatigable Far Eastern plant hunters as George Forrest (1873-1932) and E. H. Wilson (1876-1930).

An old walled garden forms the centrepiece of the estate, containing such glories as the golden false acacia (*Robinia pseudoacacia* 'Frisia') and a Caucasian wing nut (*Pterocarya fraxinifolia*), which is said to be the largest in Britain. On the West Lawn nearby is a fine Fulham Oak, so called because it is a variety of *Quercus* x *hispanica* raised at the Fulham Road, London, nursery of James Veitch & Sons. To the east is the Woodland Garden, where ponds and streams glimmer amid lush, jungle-like banks; woodland trails include the Hydrangea Walk and the Azalea Path.

A new visitor centre, with plant shop and refreshment area, has recently been added, along with a children's playground. But the character of the whole remains determined by venerable specimens grown to enormous size: the old camellias and magnolias especially, which are seen at their finest in late spring. Peacocks strut the lawns, exotic cousins for the graceful white birds which haunt Abbotsbury's famous swannery nearby. This was established by Benedictine monks in the 14th century or earlier in the waters of the Fleet, behind Chesil Beach.

Alton Towers Staffordshire

The great garden at Alton Towers is one of the largest and most fantastic landscape follies in Europe. It was the brainchild of Charles Talbot, 15th Earl of Shrewsbury, a nobleman of immense wealth whose mania for building and landscape is said to have matched in extent that of 'mad' King Ludwig of Bavaria, who decorated his kingdom with fairy-tale castles. For most of his life the earl lived at his palace at Heythrop in Oxfordshire. But he also owned some 10,000 acres of farmland in Staffordshire's picturesque Churnet Valley. And there, in 1812, at the age of 60, the earl decided to indulge his interest in landscape design.

Over the next 15 years, while the original bailiff's house, Alveton Lodge, was being transformed into a Gothic-style palace by a succession of no fewer than eight architects, an army of labourers and gardeners was brought in to sculpt the rugged countryside with terraces, pools, canals and winding paths. The planting of trees and shrubs was not enough to improve the vistas. There had to be architectural features too – temple, pagoda, grotto and splashing fountain – all the picturesque effects in which early 19th-century landowners delighted.

Incredible variety

At Alton Towers an incredible variety of such features was introduced. Entire dead trees were even planted for dramatic effect. In the immature garden their impact must have been garish – even outrageous.

With the passing of time, however, the woods and shrubs have ripened to full-blown maturity, diminishing the shock of the architectural fantasies. Softened by foliage, the follies no longer intrude.

Other notable structures include a fine, seven-domed conservatory, designed by Robert Abraham, the Corkscrew Fountain and a hilltop Gothic Tower. The most fanciful creations, though, remain gloriously bizarre. There is, for example, an imitation Stonehenge, bearing little resemblance to the famous circle on Salisbury Plain since it is constructed in a straight line. In addition, the garden is graced by a Swiss cottage, the size of a warehouse, in which lived a blind

▲ **Alton Towers** A row of yew arches in a quiet corner of Alton Towers awaits the daily rush of holidaymakers who come to visit the extraordinary combination – Europe's premier theme park, with attractions that include 'thrill rides' and the magnificent secluded garden. It is all based upon a dream landscape created by the Earl of Shrewsbury at the beginning of the 19th century.

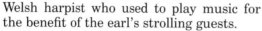

▲ **Fantasy world** In its heyday Alton Towers was one of the grandest houses in Europe, set in fantastically landscaped gardens. The house is now a ruined shell open to the public, but the magnificent gardens are totally unspoilt.

▲ **Chinese pagoda** Designed by Robert Abraham (1774-1850), this airy, three-storey Chinese pagoda at Alton Towers is sited on one of the small islands in the lakes. It is really a fountain spurting water 21m (69ft) into the air; tinkling bells hang from the octagonal roof, creating an enchanting effect.

Welsh harpist who used to play music for the benefit of the earl's strolling guests.

The 15th Earl of Shrewsbury died in 1827, but the house and garden were extended and further embellished by his nephew, John, the 16th Earl. It was he who gave the name Alton Towers to the mansion and its grounds, and he also erected the Corinthian-style memorial to his uncle, which crowns a knoll above the chain of small lakes.

Yet there is much more to admire at Alton Towers than the unique collection of ornamental follies. The lawns are interspersed with fine rose beds, and the garden is renowned for its rhododendrons, which bloom in vivid masses in June. From the memorial, a splendid rock garden, one of the finest in Britain, tumbles down the hillside.

Backing the central chain of lakes are acres of beautiful woods where many miles of winding pathway lead among oaks, cedars, sycamores, horse chestnuts and Wellingtonias. The many ornamental specimens include the fern-leafed beech (*Fagus sylvatica* 'Laciniata') and the magnificent tulip-tree (*Liriodendron tulipifera*) whose large leaves, turning bright butter yellow, contribute to the wonderful autumn mosaic of tones.

Anglesey Abbey
Cambridgeshire

The house is old, a Tudor mansion built from the ruins of a 12th-century priory. And the gardens, too, have an air of antiquity, laid out in the grand manner with the confidence and spacious scale of earlier eras. Their impression of age, though, is illusory, for Anglesey's broad avenues and bosky groves, its elegant statuary and urns – all were established in the present century. The grounds are a testament to creative ingenuity and flawless taste combined. And the wonderful diversity of scenes were all coaxed from the same uncompromising landscape – of fenland loam spread broad and level under the vast East Anglian sky.

▲ **Anglesey Abbey** Nothing at Anglesey Abbey, now a National Trust property, is quite what it seems. The gardens, which look as though they were created in Georgian times, were laid out just before the Second World War. The Coronation Avenue, flanked by massive and stately horse chestnuts and impassive stone statuary, commemorates the coronation of King George VI in 1937.

Anglesey Abbey in Cambridgeshire was founded in 1135, probably by Henry I. Its inhabitants were Augustinian priors who carried out their offices at the house for four centuries before the abbey was closed during the Dissolution of the Monasteries in the 1530s. Thereafter, the abbey was rebuilt as a secular residence which passed through the hands of many different owners. And in 1926 it was bought in partially ruined state by Huttleston Broughton, the son of an industrial magnate, who in 1929 became Lord Fairhaven.

The grounds were enormous, comprising well over 100 acres of rough parkland and farming country. There were a few fine old trees; close to the house, for example, was a splendid copper beech, and a weeping silver lime (*Tilia petiolaris*), which was to remain Lord Fairhaven's favourite in the garden. These and a few other mature plantings he kept – otherwise, the canvas was bare.

Dramatic focus

Lord Fairhaven had space in abundance to work with. The problem was the lack of natural drama in the terrain. And this he resolved through subtly contrasted plantings, balancing formal beds and clipped hedges with generous profusions of natural foliage. Above all, he achieved interest through the thoughtful disposition of fine statues and urns. Executed in stone, marble or metal, they remain a focus for the eye in practically every vista.

The most spacious symmetries are found to the south and west of the house, and the prelude is quite delightful. From the front drive a beautiful expanse of grassland, known as the South Glade, curves round the sunny southern face of the house. It is a mass of cowslips in spring.

The glade narrows at its end, hemmed by hornbeams and with the romantic Jubilee Avenue running off to left and right. This is planted with a frothy profusion of white-flowered narcissi, a colour theme that continues into May when the wild banks are snow-drifted with cow parsley. The focus for the eye is a great stone urn, set by Lord Fairhaven to mark the 800th anniversary of the priory's founding.

A little further along, the glade issues into a walk with a very different aura. This is the great Coronation Avenue, an immense green way which runs ruler straight for half a mile into the distance, flanked to each side by horse chestnuts ranked three trees deep. The avenue was laid out in 1937 to commemorate the coronation of King George VI and Queen Elizabeth. The perspectives are huge. At one point, cross vistas lead the eye south to a statue of Apollo Belvedere; and north to a circular temple.

The grand effects are only part of Anglesey's attraction. Returning towards the house you come to the secluded Narcissus Garden, where a statue of the

▲ **Fenland spring** Creating landscape surprises in the flat Cambridge fens is not easy, but it has been achieved at Anglesey Abbey by the clever blending of majestic specimen trees and dramatic patches of naturalised spring bulbs. The grounds, normally closed to the public during the winter months, are open for Snowdrop weekends in February.

mythical youth may be seen mirrored in a pool. Beyond it is the Hyacinth Garden, Anglesey's great springtime showpiece, where 4,500 bulbs are planted out in formal beds every year to create a scented paradise of blue and white.

A short walk brings you back to the front drive, where you may begin to explore the eastern grounds. A winding path leads through a wooded dell to the Dahlia Garden, cunningly conceived as a curved corridor of beech hedges which enclose a multicoloured crescent of flowers. Statues of Pan and Apollo embellish the walk.

Situated beside the Dahlia Garden is one of Anglesey's most imaginative features. This is the Herbaceous Garden, devised by Major Vernon Daniell in 1937 as one grand semi-circle framed by a towering beech hedge. The long sweeping curve of flowers is broken only by recessed seats and clipped box trees in leaded tubs. The borders, seen at their best in June and July, are massed

▲ **Growing inspiration** It has long been a tradition at Anglesey Abbey to celebrate national occasions by establishing some new, grand feature in the gardens. This group of pillars was erected in the middle of a vast lawn in 1953 to commemorate the coronation of Queen Elizabeth II; they contain a copy of the statue of the Boy David by the 17th-century Italian sculptor Bernini.

with lupins, scented paeonies, salvias and huge delphiniums. Less familiar species include the white-flowering sea kale (*Crambe cordifolia*) and the aromatically leaved burning bush (*Dictamnus albus*) with its white or pink flowers borne on upthrusting spikes. A statue of a Saxon deity provides a stabilizing element in the riot of colour.

From the masterpieces of formal plantsmanship, a beguiling path strikes out to the north where the setting is more rural. It reaches the millstream of the Lode, lined with poplars on its far bank, and winds on through natural woodlands past the willow-fringed Quarry Pool.

Another of Anglesey's grand formal walks – Emperor's Walk – leads back south from the north-eastern boundary wall. Conceived in 1953, it takes its name from 12 marble busts of Roman emperors which line one side of the green way.

Halfway down you come to a circular bay, adorned with statuary, and if you turn right you arrive at a curious temple. With classi-

cal pillars and Chinese-style roof, it was built to enclose a huge porphyry urn. The bowl is 1.9m (6ft 4in) wide, making it the largest single piece of the crystalline rock which exists in England.

Beyond it the path cuts through the Warrior's Walk, a narrow way lined with spruce trees which runs parallel to the broader Emperor's Walk. The path returns to the front drive of the house by way of a magnificent arboretum. The specimen trees are informally planted on a swathe of greensward, merging to the north with regularly spaced lime avenues.

The collection is fittingly varied for a garden as diverse in character as Anglesey. A circuit recommended by the National Trust takes in all of the features mentioned. Yet even this does not do full justice to the range of scenes and moods. There is, for example, a pinetum to the east, containing a collection of conifers; and Pilgrim's Lawn south of Coronation Avenue, where trees and shrubs are grown chiefly for their foliage tones.

Arley Hall Cheshire

A Saracen's head has been the crest on the Warburton coat of arms since 1218, when Geoffrey Warburton lopped one off as a gory trophy of the Crusades. The 'mighty Warburton' is one of Cheshire's great families and their first hall at Arley was built in 1469. The gardens, then, have an impressive lineage – they have been in the hands of one family for over 500 years.

Arley's soil is an acid Cheshire clay which requires good drainage and aeration if it is not to revert to the swampy condition noted by an early 19th-century visitor. And the estate found its saviour in 1831 when it passed to Rowland Egerton-Warburton, who nurtured the property over the next 60 years until his death.

Rowland Egerton-Warburton rebuilt Arley Hall as a romantic Jacobean-style mansion. He closely supervised the work of his architect, George Latham, and devoted equal personal attention to the creation of his 'garden fair'. Though relics of earlier eras were incorporated in the design – existing walled kitchen gardens, for example, and a fine old 15th-century tithe barn – much of what is seen today is the work of Rowland and his wife, Mary.

In the surrounding parkland they cleared views, planted new woodlands and laid out new drives. To separate the 12-acre garden from the park they made a ha-ha with a 201m (220yd) terrace known as the Furlong Walk. This became a much-trodden way, and towards the end of his life, when Rowland became blind, he used to walk it guided by a wire with bells to warn when he approached either end.

Many of the plants growing in the Herbaceous Borders can be seen in a painting of

▲ Herbaceous borders
The double herbaceous borders at Arley Hall were laid out in 1846, as the first ever established in England. Old-fashioned perennials predominate and are at their most exuberant in early and mid summer. A grassy path between them leads to a classic-style pavilion flanked by massive buttresses of clipped yew.

▲ Walled garden The original walled kitchen garden at Arley Hall, probably dating from the 15th century, is now a secluded haven of tranquillity and heady summer scents. Behind high brick walls supporting trained fruit trees is an intimate garden designed around a formal lily pool, with gravel walks between symmetrical beds of herbaceous perennials, billowing clouds of lady's mantle and bush roses in delicate colour schemes.

1889, made by George Elgood. Viscountess Ashbrook, who has cared for the gardens since 1939, has been careful to preserve the old flowers as well as introduce some new varieties. Though splendid in high summer and lit with the orange and yellow warmth of heleniums, dahlias and solidagos in autumn, the borders are perhaps at their loveliest earlier on. As the viscountess wrote in *The Englishwoman's Garden*: 'In early June the border has its "blue period" and I prefer this to any other season. The varied blues of delphinium, campanula, and "Johnson's Blue" geranium are magical against the velvety green of the young growth on the yew hedges.'

Green pillars
The most striking and unusual feature of the gardens at Arley also dates from the time of Rowland Egerton-Warburton. This is an avenue of evergreen or holm oak (*Quercus ilex*), planted in about 1840. The tree is Mediterranean in origin and normally spreads to about 18m (60ft). The 14 specimens at Arley, however, have been clipped in cylindrical shape and stand like huge green pillars of some great, unroofed temple.

The Furlong Walk, Herbaceous Borders and Ilex Avenue form a rough triangle to the south-west of the hall. In the middle is a half-timbered tea cottage used in Victorian times for tea parties in the garden. Round about are irregular plantings of shrub roses which form exuberant displays in the summer. The June-flowering *Rosa sancta* is a particular enchantress, petalled a delicate pink and thought to be among the most ancient garden roses known.

Lady Ashbrook made several important modifications to the 19th-century design. The Furlong Walk, for example, originally ended at a winding pool and alpine rock garden designed by Mrs Rowland Egerton-Warburton. This secluded corner has been replanted with azaleas, rhododendrons and other flowering shrubs.

Though necessity has determined some of the changes at Arley, others have been effected for sheer pleasure. In 1969, for example, Lady Ashbrook established a herb garden where, among thymes, bergamots, marjorams and a host of other delights, the eau de Cologne mint was to prove one of her special favourites: 'far superior to the bottled stuff.' There is fragrance in the air at Arley, for Lady Ashbrook also planted a scented garden stocked with shrubs and flowers selected specifically for their fragrance: lilies, heliotropes, mignonettes, dwarf lavenders and pink floribunda roses.

Barnsley House
Gloucestershire

Approach the garden by the village of Barnsley and you bring one impression with you. It is of the warm Cotswold stone which abounds in this corner of Gloucestershire, lining cottage fronts and drystone walls with shades of soft grey and honeyed yellow. Barnsley House partakes of the mellow aura. Coming up the drive you encounter a creeper-clad building so clustered with mounds of 150-year-old clipped box around one ground-floor window that the very walls seem rooted in the soil.

The house was built in 1697, and there were many well-established trees when Mr and Mrs David Verey took up residence in 1951. But Mrs Rosemary Verey, now a distinguished writer on gardening, began as an enthusiastic amateur. Following Mr Verey's death in 1984, Mrs Verey moved into a small house in the grounds, and continues to tend the garden.

An avid reading of 16th- and 17th-century gardening manuals has produced many inspired touches. By the old kitchen door is a geometrical herb garden rich in time-honoured aromas of camphor, rue, lovage, thyme, sage, teucrium and filipendula – even woad. Facing the main lawn is a delightful knot garden. At the four corners, clipped variegated hollies stand sentinel.

Long vistas abound in this 4-acre garden. The yew walk, flanking a path of old Cotswold stone, interplanted with rock roses (*Helianthemum*), for instance, meets a long grassed allée at right-angles. Look left and the eye travels to an 18th-century 'temple' (brought from Fairford Park in 1962) with a lily pool to catch its reflections. Look right and a specially commissioned fountain provides focus for the eye. Explore the allée and a more secret vista opens up, leading through a narrow gap in a hedge to a statue of a veiled huntswoman. This is cunningly contrived – blink as you walk and you miss it.

An avenue of pleached limes runs parallel to the grassed allée and issues into a laburnum tunnel. This becomes bewitchingly beautiful in early June as the golden cascades of laburnum meet upthrust mauve heads of *Allium aflatunense*.

Barnsley's garden is for all seasons. In winter, scented shrubs flower near the house. Spring colour arrives as early as February, when golden winter aconites spread in sheets under the tall trees bordering the drive. After the vivid displays of summer, foliage and form come into their own. Mixed beds around the yew walk are mosaics in autumn, picked out with silver-leaved plants and variegated ivies. Among them subtle touches catch the eye: here a creamy swathe of *Nicotiana affinis*, there the twinkling of a late viola or dianthus. In October, among the last blooms of the roses, one incident of vehement colour arrests every passer-by. It is a planting of sensational pink asters 'Elma Potschkii' grouped by luminous blue *Salvia patens*, and 1.8m (6ft) tall *Nicotiana sylvestris*.

▲ **Jewel in the Cotswolds** Romantic Barnsley House is the centrepiece in 4 acres of a landscape in miniature. Enchanting vistas, with hidden surprises such as a statue, a fountain and the façade of an 18th-century 'temple' as focal points, lead the eye ever on. Sentinel junipers guard a lily pond that darkly reflects the calm Cotswold sky. The kitchen garden is a delight of small neat potager beds and trained fruit trees.

▲ **'Delight in simple things'** Rudyard Kipling lived at Bateman's (opposite) from 1902 until his death in 1936. His children grew up there – the boy and girl who figure in *Puck of Pook's Hill*, a story set in the surrounding countryside – and he loved the place dearly. When he first saw the 17th-century house, he wrote: 'We went through every room and found no shadow of ancient regrets, stifled miseries, not any menace, though the "new" end of her was 300 years old . . .'

Bateman's East Sussex

Rudyard Kipling was 36 when he discovered Bateman's. The author of *Kim* and *The Jungle Books* was already prospering in his career and had spent some three years searching with his wife for a new home. And when they came upon the fine old Jacobean house, built in 1634, at Burwash in Sussex they knew that they had found it, declaring, by Kipling's own account: 'That's her! The Only She! Make an honest woman of her quick!' The year was 1902, and Bateman's was to be Kipling's home until his death in 1936. It is now a National Trust property.

Kipling and his wife created a 10-acre domain designed to blend in with the low Sussex hills around. They had acquired some existing features which lent a mature charm to the garden. There was, for example, an old 'Maiden's Blush' rose by the front door, a flower which has bloomed in English gardens since the 15th century. It is a full-petalled Alba rose, opening from creamy buds to the palest pink blooms with exquisite sweet scent. South of the house was the bole of a huge 300-year-old white willow and, near by, well-established rows of pleached lime trees.

But the Kiplings gave the garden its present shape. To suit the character of the house, they divided the acres up into compartments with formal yew hedges and paths flagged with local stone. The main area extends to the south of the house,

▲ **Kipling's roses** The formal rose garden at Bateman's was laid out by Kipling, with paved walks and statuary. In high summer, brightly coloured bush roses fill the air with sweet scents. In the house, the living rooms and the study remain much as they were in Kipling's days.

▲ **Bateman's** Kipling felt that 'a proper gardener's work' was best accomplished on the knees, and he should have known, since he designed and planted much of Bateman's garden himself, including the yew hedges, the pool, wild garden and pleached pear walk. Now a National Trust property, the house and garden are open on specified days from April to October. The flour mill is in operation on Saturdays during the season.

where Kipling designed a rectangular pool for the children to bathe in. It was not merely a utilitarian feature though. At one end he placed a seat backed by low stone walls and a curved hedge of clipped yew; at the other a paved rose garden.

At Bateman's you never stray far from associations with the writer's life and work. From the south garden, for example, you can see Pook's Hill, famed through Kipling's Puck tales. By the yew hedge which bounds the garden is a sundial on which the writer inscribed 'It is later than you think'. Beyond is a natural garden which stretches down to the trout stream of the Dudwell, and secluded among trees is a pets' cemetery where several much-loved cats and dogs are buried.

The bridges crossing the stream lead to an old watermill which features in several of Kipling's Sussex stories, and which nowadays grinds corn for flour. It is intimately connected with the history of the house, for in 1903 the writer had it equipped with turbine and generator, which provided the electricity at Bateman's for 25 years.

A pleasing riverside path follows the stream's course among banks which are radiant in spring. Daffodils, narcissi and anemones grow in profusion, with the yellow blooms of skunk cabbage (*Lysichiton americanus*) and the huge overhanging umbrellas of *Gunnera manicata*. The many unusual trees include two startlingly gnarled and twisted hazelnut trees (*Corylus avellana* 'Contorta').

To the north of the house, the chief attraction is a walled flower garden. Its wrought-iron gates (bearing the initials RK) lead to an enchanting pleached pear walk laid out by Kipling. Clematis intermingles with the trees while lily-of-the-valley carpets the beds in which they are planted. And to the north-west, near the car park, is an extensive and quite exceptional herb garden.

Bedgebury National Pinetum
Kent

The Weald of Kent is known more for the fragrance of its orchards than for the resinous scent of pines. Yet at Bedgebury, in the Garden of England, is the most comprehensive collection of conifers in Europe.

The National Pinetum covers 250 acres of rolling country near the red-tiled Kentish village of Goudhurst. The great woodland garden was created in 1924 as an extension of the Royal Botanic Gardens at Kew. The purpose of the pinetum is chiefly scientific. The 400 species, and a further 2,000 varieties of conifer, were planted for botanical study. But presentation of sheer visual delights has also played its part in the planning.

The pinetum was established jointly by the authorities at Kew and the Forestry Commission. What they had acquired was a tract of pleasantly undulating country, dipped by two small valleys with a ridge of higher land between. The ground varies in elevation between 60-90m (200-300ft) and each of the valleys is threaded by a stream. Marshall's Lake, where wild ducks abound, is situated at their confluence.

The entrance to the pinetum leads to several Japanese dogwoods (*Cornus kousa*), katsuras (*Cercidiphyllum japonicum*) and sweet gums (*Liquidambar styraciflua*), deciduous trees native to North America whose leaves blaze with scarlet in autumn. Immediately, you are made aware of Bedgebury's varied attractions. Around the pinetum are a large number of other broad-leaved trees and shrubs included for their pictorial effect.

Spruce valley

A bridge leads across the western stream to Dallimore Avenue. The broad way runs as far as Marshall's Lake. This is Spruce Valley, with notable specimens including fine Brewer's weeping spruces (*Picea breweriana*), recognizable by their spreading branches from which hang long pendulous branchlets.

At the end of the walk, at the lake's edge, is an impressive plantation of swamp cypresses (*Taxodium distichum*), their rusty autumn tones mingling with the deeper reds of Chinese dawn redwoods (*Metasequoia glyptostroboides*). The swamp cypress, a native of the Everglades in Florida, is unique among conifers in that it grows readily standing in water.

Back from the lake, on the summit of the ridge separating Bedgebury's two valleys, is one of the pinetum's finest effects. This is

▼ **Bedgebury National Pinetum** The trees at Bedgebury National Pinetum have been imported from all over the world and planted there in order to study their potential usefulness in afforestation schemes, for timber, or for some other practical purpose. Ornamentation is a secondary consideration, but no one would realise it from a stroll through the magnificent planned rides and family groupings of conifers. When the light falls true, the soft greens, greys and golds of the trees combine in a symphony of pastel hues.

the spacious Cypress Avenue, planted in 1935 with the hybrid Leyland cypress (x *Cupressocyparis leylandii*). In less than 60 years the trees have grown to heights of 37m (120ft) or more. For the sheer drama of lofty elevation, however, they are surpassed by a nearby group of silver firs from North-West America. The largest of these were planted in 1925 and have reached well over 30m (100ft). Tallest of all is a giant fir (*Abies grandis*) over 3m (10ft) in girth and more than 46m (150ft) high.

The cone-bearers represented at Bedgebury have been garnered from temperate regions the world over. There are cedars, larches, hemlocks, sequoias and monkey puzzles. The rarities include examples of the deciduous Chinese golden larch (*Pseudolarix amabilis*), which turns orange in late autumn.

Bedgebury is open to visitors every day of the year. Though it suffered storm damage in 1987, it still has a great deal to show at all seasons. You may come in spring and summer to admire the flowering species, in autumn for the foliage tones. And even in winter Bedgebury remains a marvel. When snow hangs from the great firs and Marshall's Lake is a leaden sheet, the woods have an aura of magnificent, almost Siberian, austerity.

Belton House Lincolnshire

Formal gardens, an elegant orangery and a fine Restoration home – everything at Belton House speaks of ancestral wealth and style. Standing proud in its 600 acres of rolling parkland, the building was the home of the Brownlow family for 300 years and is now a National Trust property.

The garden north of the house is in the Dutch style. From the stepped terrace you look down an immaculate gravel path flanked by columnar yews and symmetrically patterned parterres planted with roses and edged with lavender. To the left, beyond a frame of trees grown more naturally, are manicured green lawns, and beyond is the Italian garden with a central round pool and fountain, clipped yews and flower beds planted in red and yellow.

Behind rises the tall and finely proportioned orangery, designed in 1819 by Sir Jeffry Wyatville and standing on the site of Belton's early manor house (mentioned in the Domesday Book). In reality, it was not built for orange cultivation; it is a camellia house, erected to shelter the delicate Far Eastern plants in an age when their nurture was still fairly new to Europe.

To the right, set somewhat back from the orangery, is the little church of St Peter and St Paul, which predates the great house by many centuries but forms an indissoluble feature of the garden's views. Many changes have been made to the little Norman church; Sir Jeffry Wyatville designed the chapel in 1816, and there are imposing monuments to the Brownlow family.

Urns and statuary complete the serene composition of the formal gardens. Away to the east are more naturally landscaped acres of parkland, where lakeside and woodland trails have been laid out. The park, though not the house and garden, is open to the public throughout the year.

▲ **Bicton Park** The formal gardens at Bicton in Devon were laid out in the French grand manner in 1735 when most English gardens were yielding to park landscaping under the influence of 'Capability' Brown. Le Nôtre chose a design with strong similarities to his famous work at Chateau Pomponne near Paris. The centrepiece is a sunken garden with a huge formal pool and a fountain, surrounded by charming bronze statuary.

Berkeley Castle
Gloucestershire

'How far is it, my lord, to Berkeley now?' asks Bolingbroke in Shakespeare's *Richard II*. Steeped in history and romance, the 12th-century battlements of Berkeley Castle loom in high drama above the Severn Vale. Edward II was foully murdered there, and the walls were breached by Cromwell. But apart from one great void in the ramparts which testifies to the Roundhead siege, the fortress has survived as one of the best preserved in the country.

The 6-acre terraced garden faces south and east, overlooking the lovely water meadows of the Doverte Brook. Today the castle's mighty buttresses shelter not armoured soldiery but a wide range of interesting plants. They thrive in the reflected warmth of the old stonework, some even seeding themselves in the ancient mortar.

The terraces were skilfully planted in this century by Captain Rob Berkeley. The shrubs and flowers which surge from the borders include yuccas, fuchsias, acanthus and red-hot pokers, while sheltered in one particularly warm corner is an especially fine, tender cestrum. Mature climbers cluster the castle walls. There are roses, clematis, hydrangeas and wisterias, and two magnificent *Magnolia delavayi* smothered with creamy-white flowers in June.

Bicton Park Devon

Avenues of chestnut or lime are common enough features in Britain's great gardens. But at Bicton in Devon you find something more unusual – an avenue of monkey-puzzle trees (*Araucaria araucana*), planted in 1840 and still flourishing, leads to the nearby Bicton College of Agriculture. Trees grow to great heights in this 50-acre garden, and among its gigantic conifers is the tallest monkey puzzle in Britain (over 27m/88ft high). And the trees are only one feature of the estate. In reality, Bicton holds several gardens in one – the Italian Garden, Pinetum, American, Oriental and Hermitage gardens and the conservatories.

The old manor of Bicton, near Budleigh Salterton, dates from the reign of Henry I. The estate passed in time to the Rolle family, who held it for over 300 years before the Clinton family, the present owners, acquired it through inheritance.

The Italian Garden is the formal centrepiece. It seems to have been laid out about 1735 from designs by André Le Nôtre, gardener to Louis XIV. It is now flanked by two long herbaceous borders. A handsome Neoclassical temple, flanked by an orangery and the conservatories, looks down over a terraced lawn to a sunken garden with an ornamental pool and fountain. Bronze figures are grouped around, and from the

▼ Sun King's gardener
André Le Nôtre, garden designer to Louis XIV, exerted a tremendous influence on 17th-century garden planning. Bicton is said to be laid out to his designs, but he could have made little personal contribution, since he died in 1700, 35 years before the gardens were created.

fountain the eye travels on up a broad avenue cut through trees to a stone obelisk on a distant hilltop.

Many of the magnificent trees were planted during Victorian times; a Chinese juniper on the upper terrace is especially prominent. And adjoining the garden is the Pinetum, renowned for its lofty conifers, many of which were lost during the storms of the 1980s. There are rare specimens: Mexican juniper (*Juniperus flaccida*) and Tasmanian cedar (*Athrotaxis* sp.) among them. The Pinetum was established in 1840, extended in 1910 and is now in the process of being replanted.

Beyond the shade of the woodland garden is a charming 19th-century garden with a summerhouse known as the Hermitage, set among rhododendrons and overlooking a small lake.

The Victorians delighted in such unusual effects and the Hermitage is not the only curiosity at Bicton. There is also a little building constructed of flints and overlooking a picturesque rock garden. Known as the Shell House, after its collection of shells, it is situated at the northern end of the American Garden, an area laid out in the last century to display trees and shrubs from North America. The specimens include a particularly good Monterey cypress (*Cupressus macrocarpa*).

The mild Devonshire climate has assisted the growth of plants at Bicton. And, in the conservatories beside the temple flourish real exotica. One is devoted to bromeliads and dracaenas, another to fuchsias and a third to geraniums. The most arresting structure is the early 19th-century Palm House, half-domed and elegantly contoured with glass panes on a cast-iron framework. Within it grow tropical and subtropical plants, among them Kentia palms and New Zealand tree ferns.

Blenheim Palace Oxfordshire

It is like driving into a much-publicised masterpiece: the grouping of palace, lake and bridge is familiar through countless reproductions. And yet their reality is more impressive than a printed image could hope to express. Blenheim's grandeur is out of scale with the present century. In visiting the park you seem to trespass against the laws of time.

Queen Anne gave the royal domain of Woodstock to her victorious general, John the 1st Duke of Marlborough, in 1705. And she promised to build for him a palace worthy of his glorious achievements. It was to be called Blenheim after the German village where the duke had won a famous victory over the French in 1704.

Some 9 miles of drystone walling enclose the park today. And if you approach by the Triumphal Gate in Woodstock, its classic

▲ **Man of parts** Sir John Vanbrugh (1664-1726), soldier, actor and playwright, seems to have turned to architecture and garden design more or less for the fun of it. Yet he had a tremendous effect on both in his day, and made the baroque style his own, his two greatest works being Castle Howard and Blenheim Palace. The Treasury donated almost a quarter of a million pounds towards Blenheim Palace, yet even this fortune proved insufficient to meet the needs of Vanbrugh's vision.

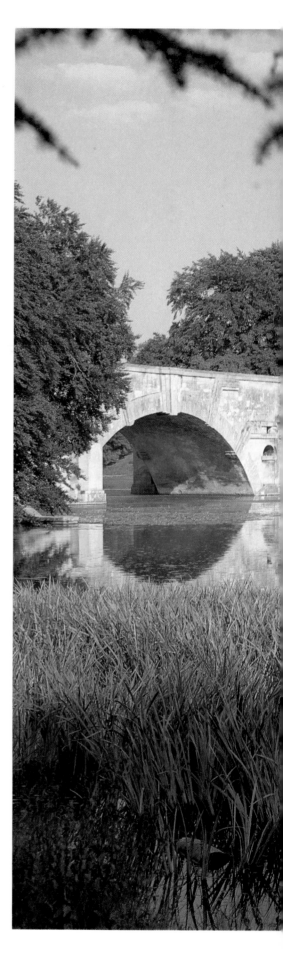

▲ **Blenheim Palace** Designed at huge expense, Vanbrugh's grand bridge spans the valley of the little River Glyme, which flows across the park. The main arch alone is more than 30m (98ft) in width, and within the structure of the bridge are 30-odd rooms, though most of them are flooded since 'Capability' Brown more than half a century later dammed the stream and created the lake that is now the glory of the park.

▲ **Fruits of victory** Blenheim Palace was Queen Anne's gift to her most successful general, the 1st Duke of Marlborough, in 1705. The original formal gardens were swept away by 18th-century landscaping; the present water terraces, with parterres of clipped box, were laid out early in this century by the French garden designer Achille Duchêne in the formal tradition of André le Nôtre.

vista bursts on the eye. There in the foreground is Vanbrugh's Grand Bridge, balancing with its mighty proportions the more distant mass of the palace itself.

What made the project so fantastic was the trifling nature of the river that it crossed. In 1708, when work on the bridge started, the Glyme was no more than a marshy stream. It was Lancelot 'Capability' Brown who justified its proportions by creating the great sweep of water seen today.

Brown was commissioned in 1764, long after duke, duchess and architect were dead. And he transformed Blenheim's appearance by damming the Glyme near Bladon to engulf the whole valley with water. He left only one small strip of rising ground marooned in the flooded basin. It was an inspired act. The moated knoll is known as Queen Elizabeth's Island, and survives as one of the park's most enchanting effects.

As for the lake, it is widely considered Brown's supreme achievement. Sir Sacheverell Sitwell called it 'the one great argument of the landscape gardener. There is nothing finer in Europe'. At the western end, Brown created a Grand Cascade which still roars with some fury today. But it is the great curved sheet, backed by hanging woodlands of beech, which gives Blenheim its spacious harmonies.

Blenheim's perspectives change with the sinuous course of the water. But one landmark which constantly recurs is the Column of Victory, topped by its lead statue of the 1st Duke. Standing 41m (134ft) high, it was completed in 1730 and holds the eye as firmly as palace and bridge.

Alchemy of autumn

The central vista of the park runs dead straight from the palace, across Vanbrugh's bridge and up to the Column of Victory. Beyond, an avenue of elms lost in the 1970s has been replanted in limes. The woods remain hauntingly beautiful and autumn brings its natural alchemy to their foliage.

Back from the main park, entirely different effects have been achieved. At the East Front is a sheltered Italian garden carpeted with scrolls and arabesques in dwarf box, with pink roses and topiary grouped around a mermaid fountain. The garden was laid out in the early years of the 20th century by the 9th Duke of Marlborough.

There is so much at Blenheim to delight the eye. The oldest feature is a never-failing spring known as Rosamond's Well, which was frequented by Rosamond Clifford, the lover of Henry II. An 8-acre kitchen garden holds considerable fascination, laid out for the 1st Duke in military style with walls bastioned like those of a fort.

And yet that first vision from the Triumphal Gate may remain as the most powerful memory. To describe it as fit for a king does it scant justice; it caused George III to exclaim: 'We have nothing to equal this!'

Blickling Hall Norfolk

A certain mystery surrounds the beautiful crescent lake at Blickling Hall. The mile-long curve of water which lies to the north of the hall is backed by woodlands of beech and oak. It is landscaped in the manner of Humphry Repton, who is thought to have been responsible for it. The lake is just one of the enigmas of Blickling, whose 46-acre gardens were laid out over many centuries and remain imprinted with the tastes of several epochs.

The house itself is Jacobean, a red-brick building rising with pinnacled symmetry from a foreground of green lawn and flanking yew hedge. It was reconstructed from a 14th-century fortified house between 1619 and 1625 for Sir Henry Hobart, Lord Chief Justice to James I. The moat, which surrounded the original medieval building, has been dry for three centuries; an account book of 1676-7 refers to it as a haven for summer bedding plants. Today it is a sheltered garden where fine old roses, camellias, hydrangeas and fuchsias are grown.

The park in which Repton's hand has been detected extends to the north and west of the hall. It was clearly laid out in the

▲ **Blickling Hall** The 16th-century fountain was set up at Blickling Hall as an eyecatcher in the midst of a formal garden created by Lady Lothian in 1872. It commands the view down a long vista of flower beds and clipped yew, and up flights of steps to the landscaped parkland beyond.

early 18th century, for an estate map dated 1729, which hangs in the house, shows the splendid artificial lake marked as the 'New Pond'. It was later extended.

Some features of the grounds can be dated with confidence. Not far from the water, for example, is a massive pyramidal mausoleum, rising to 12m (40ft) and built in 1794 by the Neo-classical architect Joseph Bonomi. Inside, contained in three marble sarcophagi, lie the remains of the 2nd Earl of Buckinghamshire (died 1793) and his two wives. A tower in the 'Gothick' style, built about 1773, was used by the 2nd Earl as a grandstand for the racecourse he laid out in the park to the north. It may also have been built to finish a vista from the house. But other features are as uncertain in origin as the lake. To the south of the hall, for example, is an elegant orangery known to have been in existence in 1793 and sometimes attributed to William Ivory and sometimes to Samuel Wyatt. A statue of Hercules, sculpted in 1632 by Nicholas Stone, stands inside, among tubs of plantain lily (*Hosta sieboldiana* 'Elegans').

The garden's main vista looks east from the hall to a fine Doric temple of the early 18th century. A parterre and raised terrace extend between the two, and this is probably the oldest part of the garden. Certainly it is the most complex in its history. It is thought that a great Jacobean parterre originally occupied the area. What is seen today is an array of beds first laid out in 1872 for Constance, Marchioness of Lothian. She had it planted in the somewhat fussy mid-Victorian manner, however, and it was again redesigned in the 1930s by Mrs Norah Lindsay, a well-known garden designer and a pupil of Gertrude Jekyll.

Sentinel yews
In place of the elaborate beds which had to be stocked annually with flowers in season, Mrs Lindsay simplified the design, retaining only four large rectangles in the parterre adjacent to the house. The corners of each are marked by sentinel yews clipped in formal topiary shapes. The two beds near the house are pastel toned with pink, blue and white flowers including phloxes, campanulas and delphiniums. The two further beds are more boldly massed with yellows and oranges: orange sunflowers, golden rods and creamy Nankeen lilies (*Lilium* x *testaceum*) among them. The spiky *Yucca filamentosa* are focal points in all the beds, providing them with a unifying element.

Near the temple, a lime avenue leads north-west to the Secret Garden, also known as Lady Buckinghamshire's Garden, a clearing with an 18th-century summer-house and a sundial dated 1697, all enclosed by high beech hedges. The original design is thought to be by Repton. An adjoining small shrub garden on one side was laid out in 1936, also by Mrs Lindsay.

▲ **Mellowed walls** Rose-red, Jacobean Blickling Hall and its lovely gardens look as though they have existed since time's beginning. But their positions were determined by the moat of a house, owned by the father of Anne Boleyn. Father and daughter are said to still haunt the drive lined by massive yew hedges. Now a National Trust property, Blickling Hall is surrounded by landscaped parkland around the curving lake.

▲ **Green lawn, blue distance** One of the great terraces at Bodnant, with its
formal pool aswim with water lilies, reaches out to embrace the Conwy Valley and
the far-off peaks of Snowdonia. This majestic platform was part of a gardening
concept that took 50 years to realise. Originally, a vast grassy slope descended
from the house, and establishing the five-tiered apron for Bodnant was a major
undertaking. It was begun in 1905 and took nine years to complete.

Bodnant Gwynedd

No garden in Britain commands finer long views. Looking south-west from the terraces at Bodnant, the eye ranges across the Conwy Valley to the mountains of Snowdonia beyond: Carnedd Llewelyn, Foel Fras, the Drum and Tal-y-fan are clearly discernible. And the foreground frame is exceptional. Level green lawns and formal rose gardens, the glimmer of lily pools and the deep shade of great trees all drop away to paradisiacal woodlands.

Bodnant has been called the greatest garden created in Britain during the last 100 years. The claim is a bold one, but amply justified by the splendour of Bodnant's effects.

Come to the garden in May and June and you are greeted almost immediately by the shock of sheer colour, for situated near the entrance is the astonishing Laburnum Arch overhung by shimmering cascades of bright yellow. The long, curved walk extends for 55m (180ft), between trees pleached over an arched framework. A bedazzling tunnel, the arch assaults not only the eyes but the nostrils too with its fragrance.

Family creation

Bodnant is the creation of the Aberconway family, who have been associated with the house and its grounds since 1875. The Laburnum Arch was established by Henry Pochin, great-grandfather to the present Lord Aberconway. Though some of the large native trees date from the 18th century, the tremendous old conifers rising from the lower garden were planted in the late 19th century by Henry Pochin, who, with the help of a landscape architect named Milner, laid out several of the first formal beds and shrubberies.

Bodnant, at the time of Pochin and Milner, lacked the impressive set-piece of today. This is a series of grand Italianate terraces which lead down from the West Front of the house towards the course of the Hiraethlyn, a tributary of the Conwy. The great stepped garden is the work of Henry Duncan, the 2nd Lord Aberconway, who from the turn of the century until his death in 1953, shaped the development of the whole. Skilfully assisted by his head gardener, F. C. Puddle, and, after, by the son C. E. Puddle, the 2nd Baron worked on the garden for more than half a century.

Five magnificent terraces run down from the west front, each with its own distinct character. The highest is the stone-flagged Rose Garden, and from it are glorious views down the four other steps, flanked by trees so that they channel the eye to the skyline of mountains beyond. Steps lead down to a lower level, where there is a French baroque fountain and pool overgrown with two white wisterias (*W. venusta* and *W. floribunda* 'Alba'). Below, you come to the wide Croquet

▲ **Under the terrace** Dropping down from Bodnant's five terraces, the grand views are lost, but the compensation is the half-secret dells, among rocks and rushing water. There, the garden's famed collections of exotic trees and shrubs have been established. Supreme among them are Bodnant-raised rhododendron hybrids and a wonderful gathering of rare species rhododendrons and azaleas which have been sent from many parts of the world to flourish in Bodnant's lime-free soil.

Terrace backed by fine shrubs which shelter against the terrace wall: eucryphias, magnolias and dwarf lilacs among them.

The third level is the beautiful Lily Terrace, its rectangular design broken by a semi-circular bay to the west. The pool is stocked with a wonderful diversity of water lilies, flowering from June to September in tones from snow white to wine red.

The fourth terrace is the Lower Rose Garden. It is reached by a pergola clustered with climbing roses and the blue-flowering, climbing *Solanum crispum* 'Glasnevin', a delight from early summer until autumn. Planted against the curved walls of the steps are *Magnolia grandiflora* 'Goliath', valued for its giant blooms and handsome evergreen foliage, and the Chilean lantern tree (*Crinodendron hookerianum*), distinguished by crimson flowers which hang like lanterns from long pedicels.

At the lowest level is the Canal Terrace, named after a long and narrow rectangle of water which is the centrepiece. Though planted with water lilies at either end, the central stretch is kept mirror-clear for reflections. A fine green lawn surrounds it.

Looking down the canal from the north you can see a charming 18th-century garden house at the other end, with its reflection caught in the water.

When you leave the terraces, the mountain vistas are lost. But there is rich compensation in the profusion of exotic trees and shrubs. The North Garden, for example, may be reached by either of the two upper terraces and is more secluded in mood. A sloping lawn here is enclosed by beeches, cedars and yews, and banked with magnolias, azaleas and eucryphias. Above all there are the rhododendrons: the bright blue *R. augustinii*, and the 'Penjerrick Cream', a creamy-yellow, fragrant rhododendron hybrid.

Remarkable rhododendrons

Stripped of all other features, Bodnant would remain remarkable for its rhododendron collection, which is among the finest in the country. The plants root readily in the garden's lime-free soil, and many were grown from seeds sent back to England by such intrepid collectors as E. H. Wilson, George Forrest, Frank Kingdon-Ward and Dr J. F. Lock.

The rhododendrons are in flower from December to the end of June: white, yellow, orange, red, pink and purple. Plant breeding has flourished for years at Bodnant, and the hybrid rhododendrons raised in the garden include the cherry-pink 'Winsome' and the scarlet 'Elizabeth'.

In 1949, the 2nd Lord Aberconway gave the garden to the National Trust, and it is now looked after on their behalf by the present Lord Aberconway, with the help of Martin Puddle, general manager and head gardener, and the third generation of his family to tend the garden.

Borde Hill Garden
West Sussex

When Colonel Stephenson Clarke bought the stone-built Sussex mansion of Borde Hill in 1893 he acquired an unremarkable garden. The property stood on a saddle of ground rising from the valley of the upper River Ouse, and the garden had been landscaped in conventional style. There were a few good trees and, to the south of the house, a large lawn extending to a ha-ha, which gave fine views towards the South Downs. There were equally pleasant vistas to the north, over wooded farmland towards the High Weald.

Yet this unexceptional domain was to provide the framework for one of the most luxuriant gardens in England. Within the half century before his death in 1948, the colonel had filled every dull space of the 40-acre garden with a vivid mass of colour: the blooms of rhododendrons, azaleas, camellias and magnolias.

The great transformation did not begin immediately. The colonel started by levelling the large south lawn to open up views beyond. But his plantings at first were fairly orthodox. In 1895, for example, he had a venerable *Magnolia* x *soulangiana* brought to Borde Hill by horse and cart from its original site near London. It may be seen today, growing near the Old House, a cottage in the garden.

What revolutionised Borde Hill – and other gardens across the face of the nation – was the great era of Far Eastern plant collecting. It began with E. H. Wilson's first expedition to China in 1899, and brought an especially rich harvest in the years 1912-30. The colonel, a keen naturalist and big-game

◀ **Borde Hill Garden** The astonishing array of exotic trees and shrubs at Borde Hill was the work of Colonel Stephenson Clarke, a well-known amateur plant collector. He began his plantings of rare rhododendrons, camellias, viburnums and others with seeds obtained from China, the Andes and outposts still further outflung. The greeny-yellow exotic-looking *Euphorbia characias*, however, is of less romantic European origin.

► **Joy of spring** Colour grouping was and is a major preoccupation at Borde Hill Garden. Here, a flowering cherry – the hybrid *Prunus* 'Accolade' – presides over a brilliant late-spring assembly of bloom-laden camellias.

hunter, helped to finance expeditions to the Himalayas, Tasmania and the Andes.

Borde Hill burgeoned as a result. From the Buddhists' sacred mountain of Omei-shan in Western China, for example, E. H. Wilson brought the seed of the fine ever-green *Viburnum cinnamomifolium,* which grows just outside the South Walled Garden; it has become one of the largest specimens in the British Isles. The garden boasts an award-winning *Rhododendron principis* (syn. *R. vellereum*) from the Tibetan Himalayas; this was an introduc-tion of the collector Frank Kingdon-Ward. And the great tradition of specimen hunting did not end with the pioneers. One of Borde Hill's most remarkable evergreens is a red-flowering *Mitraria coccinea* from the remote forest slopes of the Andes; it was raised from a cutting brought to Kew by air, sealed in a polythene bag.

The gardens at Borde Hill are laid out in largely informal style, with paths that meander through woods and glades. The open vistas to north and south are edged with trees, and two large dells have been incorporated into the design.

The rhododendrons, especially, are every-where, lining paths and crowding beds with profuse displays which last through spring and summer. You could almost complete an alphabet of exotica from the collection, beginning with the rose-coloured *Rhodo-dendron adenophorum* from Yunnan, to the dainty Burmese *R. zaleucum*, a real beauty with lilac funnel-shaped flowers.

Come to Borde Hill in late May and you are greeted by an exceptional display of deciduous azaleas which extend in vivid drifts to the east of the house. The area, known as the Azalea Ring, is planted chiefly

with the Knap Hill hybrids, selected for colour and scent.

Not far away, near the walled garden, are several examples of the free-flowering *Camellia* 'Donation'. This greatly loved shrub, with its large, deeply veined, orchid-pink double flowers, was raised at Borde Hill by Colonel Stephenson Clarke from a cross between *C. japonica* 'Donckelarii' and *C.* x *williamsii*. Raised before the Second World War, 'Donation' has remained one of the most popular camellias.

There are few formal features at Borde Hill. The Old House has a little garden of its own, with shrubs and bright borders. Not far away, you come across The Bride's Pool, filled with herbaceous perennials in pastel shades of blue, pink and white. The pool is named after the nearby statue of a veiled lady, known as The Bride, by Antonio Tantardini of Milan. She has a vacant air, as if overcome by the beauty of her surround-ings. During high summer, the herbaceous border, with its brick paths, comes into its own, as does the Round Dell with its exotic palms and bog plants.

At Borde Hill you are always aware of the trees. Their erect growth provides a stabilis-ing element in the profusion of exotic shrubs. They include an oriental plane, and a handkerchief tree (*Davidia involucrata*) from China. To the north, beyond the gar-den proper, are woods with rare conifers.

Bowood House Wiltshire

They called it the Picturesque Style. In the late 18th century, English gentlemen of taste were familiar with the natural land-scape pioneered by 'Capability' Brown. But

▲ **Wilderness to order** Bowood House is in Wiltshire, a county not often remarked upon for its waterfalls. This one is the offshoot of a landscape created in the mid 18th century by 'Capability' Brown, who, as was his custom, dammed a stream to make a lake as a major feature of the park. The cascade, though not created by Brown, is the lake's outfall, though the picturesque arrangement of the rocks was added some years later.

▲ Economical pruning
Impressive though it is, Bowood House is not as grand as it was in its 18th-century heyday. The larger wing, known as The Big House, was demolished in 1955 for reasons of economy. What remains is The Little House attached to the palatial orangery, designed by Robert Adam, and now a picture gallery. In the 18th century, too, 'Capability' Brown's landscape swept up to the windows; during Queen Victoria's reign, in the area adjacent to the house, the landscape effect was replaced by the present formality of rose beds, gravel paths and clipped yew.

they wanted to take the informal look further by introducing such 'awful' elements as crags and caverns and raging torrents into their private domains.

Bowood House, home of the Earl of Shelburne, beautifully illustrates those mixed aspirations towards serenity and dramatic interest. Here, in one of Brown's noblest landscapes, you also discover a rocky Cascade and mysterious Hermit's Cave. Both were entirely artificial creations included, like gargoyles in a cathedral, to tease little thrills of terror out of the complacent observer.

The great park at Bowood was designed by Brown between 1762 and 1768 for the 1st Marquess of Lansdowne. The landscapist brought all his skills to bear in creating suave perspectives across fields and beechwoods to the Wiltshire downland beyond. There had to be a lake, of course. At Bowood, Brown dammed two streams across the north end of a valley to the east of the house to create a long, serpentine water.

Brown required that the sweep should appear continuous. But his commission did not extend to flooding the neighbouring landowner's property. So he fitted the dam in at the northern boundary of the estate and concealed it in a clump of trees.

A small Doric temple, situated on a promontory by the dam, looks out across the water. Though fitting exquisitely into the setting, it was not in fact placed there by Brown but moved to its present position in 1864 from elsewhere in the grounds.

Nor is the Cascade Brown's creation. It was probably designed in 1785 by the Hon. Charles Hamilton, an inventive amateur known for his work at Painshill in Surrey.

Situated in a shaded valley just beyond Brown's dam, the Cascade roars splendidly amid the trees, the water falling in misty skeins over successive ledges of rock.

The Bowood House seen today is a building of warm golden stonework erected by Henry Keene in 1755. On the sunny South Front is a fine orangery, designed by Robert Adam in 1769 and now serving as a picture gallery. It looks down over formal terraces boldly massed with colour, among which the main level dates from the Victorian era. Ranks of clipped yews stand sentinel here amid rose beds whose dominant reds vie for brightness with the geraniums disposed in urns around.

The whole 82-acre area north and east of the house is known as the Pleasure Grounds, and though Brown provided the frame for the picture seen today, it has been filled since his time with a magnificent collection of trees and shrubs. A few of Brown's original trees survive; one tremendous cedar of Lebanon was sadly lost in the 1990 gales.

Separate from the Pleasure Grounds is a 50-acre woodland garden, part of Brown's original shelterbelt. Here walks wind amid oak, beech, chestnut and pine and stupendous displays of rhododendrons. This area is only open during the flowering season from mid May to the end of June.

Bramham Park
West Yorkshire

Here is a garden not landscaped by 'Capability' Brown. The boast may seem a curious one, but it remains a key to the garden's fascination. Bramham Park is 'One That Got Away'.

Throughout Britain from the late 17th century many important gardens were laid out in the French style pioneered by Louis XIV's gardener, André le Nôtre. They were characterised by formal symmetries: long vistas cut ruler-straight through woodland; hedged walks and geometrically aligned statuary, fountains and pools. When Brown and his followers introduced the natural look, a host of such gardens were swept from the face of the nation. Bramham Park is a rare survival – a little Versailles in West Yorkshire.

Robert Benson, 1st Lord Bingley and Lord Chamberlain to Queen Anne, built the house between 1698 and 1710. The 66-acre garden dates from the first decades of the 18th century, and miraculously came through the landscaping vogue with its formal features intact. Later owners also resisted the blandishments of the Victorian improvers. In fact, the only serious damage was done to the original as recently as 1990, when fierce gales brought down many trees. The woodlands, though, have been replanted to the original concept. The official handbook's claim is a fair one: John Wood's plan of 1725 would serve as a guide today.

'Curious gardens laid out with great judgment' was how one early visitor described them. The main vista in the whole design is a mile-long way, known as the Broadwalk, which separates the house from the garden. At one extremity is a Neo-classical temple, built by James Paine as an orangery and later consecrated as a chapel. The walk leads to a series of elaborate pools, water basins and stepped cascades.

The whole garden is a network of similar vistas, intersecting at focal points. Here ranks of tree trunks conduct the eye; there it travels through corridors of clipped beech. One series of ways converges on a pool and canal; another on an Ionic temple. At yet another intersection, five pathways come together at a magnificent decorated urn known as the Four Faces.

The effect is not drily austere. Daffodils have been widely underplanted in the woodlands and make spring a delight at Bramham. In summer there is a formal rose garden to enjoy, situated in a walled parterre in front of the house. And in the Black Fen Pleasure Grounds, where the obelisk is sited, plant growth is even more luxuriant. Thickets of wild rhododendrons abound among the trunks of venerable beeches, cedars, chestnuts and limes.

The Black Fen, too, is patterned with intersecting rides and vistas. The eye rarely roams freely for long, being tugged back incessantly to the designer's straight lines, an English garden where nature is entirely disciplined by intellect.

Branklyn Tayside

Small, they say, is beautiful – and in the case of Branklyn this is certainly true. Situated on a rocky west-facing slope above the River Tay, the garden today covers barely 2 acres. And when John and Dorothy Renton built the house in 1922, the area was still more limited. To achieve the present acreage they had to colonise part of a neighbouring orchard.

Later, Branklyn was to be called the 'finest 2 acres of private garden in the country', and to the amateur the story of its evolution is particularly pleasing. Branklyn was from the outset a very personal creation shaped by a husband-and-wife team who started with little or no knowledge of gardening science. They made mistakes, and it was only with time that the Rentons discovered what would prosper in Branklyn's good but rather acid loam, and survive its damaging late spring frosts.

One plant which 'took' readily to the garden was the acid-loving, poppy-like meconopsis. It was an early speciality of Branklyn and, towards the end of her life, Dorothy Renton was to receive a First-class Certificate from the Royal Horticultural Society for the azure-blue cultivar *Meconopsis grandis* 'Branklyn' raised by her.

But there is very much more to admire. The informal design grew around a wealth of rare and unusual plants garnered from all over the world. Branklyn was to be, in Dorothy Renton's words, a 'home from home' for any plant which the Rentons enjoyed growing and which itself favoured the habitat. Among the trees, for example, is a beautiful specimen of the orange-barked birch *Betula albo-sinensis septentriolaris* from China; this was grown from seed sown in 1926. There are many fine conifer specimens, and a fine array of choice maples for autumn colour. Small-leaved rhododendrons profit by the shelter of the trees, while viburnums, magnolias and hydrangeas contribute their own displays.

From the beginning, alpines and rock plants were a particular interest of the Rentons, and to accommodate them two large scree beds were laid out with advice from the great rock gardener Reginald Farrer. The screes are spangled with exquisites: starry-petalled pulsatillas, pink-and-white oxalis and daisy-like celmisias from New Zealand are just a few of the conspicuous items. There are dwarf rhododendrons in abundance, while the green and golden plumes of dwarf conifers provide stabilising verticals. Here, as elsewhere at Branklyn, the maximum use has been made of a limited area, and every corner is embroidered with interest.

Brighton - Preston Park
East Sussex

The beach is the magnet at Brighton, as at coastal resorts throughout the country. Yet back from the seafront, Brighton retains a dignified aura, with much fine Regency architecture and over 3,000 acres of parks and gardens. Come in by the main London road and you pass the largest of the town's open spaces. This is Preston Park, covering some 65 acres and a delight entirely in its own right.

It caters, certainly, for the athletic: there is a cycle track, cricket and football pitches, bowling greens and tennis courts. But from spring to autumn the park is also a blaze of colour. The formal Rose Garden contains more than 15,000 roses. No less emphatic in their exuberance are the Gardens of Greeting beds.

Quite different in mood is the walled garden of Preston Manor, half hidden among the trees in the north-west corner of the park. The Queen Anne house was bequeathed to the Borough in the 1930s, and its plot has the intimacy of a cottage garden, with crowded box-edged beds of old-fashioned flowers and an arch of trained laburnums. Adjoining the enclosed garden is a scented garden for the blind, equipped with guide rails and notices in Braille.

But Preston Park's most notable feature is its huge rock and water garden, known as the Rookery. Situated across the road from the main park, it was laid out in the 1930s on sloping ground with a rushing stream which tumbles down to a lily pool. The rocks are massed with aubrietas, dwarf pinks and candelabra primulas, while flowering cherries and many dwarf trees and shrubs vary the forms, textures and tones.

▼ **Plantman's paradise**
The creators of Branklyn were a husband and wife who over 40 years created an exquisite tapestry of plants, notably the scree beds of Sino-Himalayan alpines. John and Dorothy Renton became two of the finest plantsmen in the country. Since their deaths in the late 1960s, the garden has been managed by the National Trust for Scotland.

▲ **South coast splash** The rockery at Preston Park, owned and maintained by Brighton Borough Council, is one of the largest in Europe. It was built just before the Second World War at a cost of £4,500, a price considered scandalous at the time, though every penny of it has been blessed by Brightonians since. It is a year-round visual delight of rocky outcrops, tumbling waterfalls and still pools, with plantings to echo the seasons.

Brodick Castle Isle of Arran

The landscape is stern. Above Brodick Castle the ridge of the Arran mountains soars to 874m (2,866ft) at Goat Fell. The castellated mansion is situated 45m (150ft) up, and commands sweeping vistas across the Firth of Clyde to the Ayrshire coast beyond. The Vikings first fortified the site, and there is much in the setting that evokes Wagnerian images of the wild north.

And yet the gardens of Brodick are lush. Occupying a wooded valley under the massif, their 65 acres are sheltered from Arran's howling south-westerlies by the very ridge which confers its drama on them. The climate, moreover, is moderated by the warm Atlantic Drift and the loamy soil is enriched by quantities of leaf-mould shed by the enfolding forests.

The sandstone mansion, built at different stages from the 14th to 19th centuries, was a seat of the Dukes of Hamilton until 1895. It subsequently became the home of Mary Louise, Duchess of Montrose, daughter of the 12th Duke of Hamilton, and it was she who shaped the present garden. Rhododendrons were her passion, and her plantings still form the heart of the collection.

The rhododendrons were planted in the 1920s, that fertile period of Far Eastern plant collecting which transformed so many British gardens. The Duchess of Montrose financed several expeditions, and Frank Kingdon-Ward, one noted collector, was to name his discovery of *Rhododendron montroseanum* after her. But Brodick is particularly associated with George Forrest, himself a Scotsman, who contributed many of the large-leaved rhododendron species.

Monster blooms

The magnificent showpieces are grouped chiefly in the Lower Rhododendron Walk, an area which is largely free from frost. It is here that you come upon the huge *R. sinogrande*, largest-leaved of all, and the crimson *R. protistum* var. *giganteum*. Both were Forrest discoveries and have grown tree-tall at Brodick – beautiful monsters which bear blooms the size of men's heads.

Forrest also contributed the immaculate white, sweet-scented *R. maddenii* ssp. *crassum*, one of the loveliest and most tender rhododendrons, which is often grown under glass elsewhere. At Brodick it thrives in the open in a wonderful collection close to the house. The woodland garden has more than rhododendrons; it is known, too, for its lilies and primulas and its many rare trees and shrubs introduced by the Duchess.

East of the house, a walled garden of 18th-century origin offers a change in mood. Its formal flower beds are planted with rambler roses, carnations, fuchsias and begonias.

After the death of the Duchess of Montrose, the house and garden were given to the National Trust for Scotland.

▲ **Gift of the Gulf Stream** On the Isle of Arran, between Brodick Castle and the sea, is an opulent garden totally at odds with the wild Highland hills that surround it. The variety of its planting is the result of the labours of the late Duchess of Montrose, but its existence is due to the warm Gulf Stream, or rather to a quirky offshoot called the Atlantic Drift that sweeps up to these northerly latitudes. Fine formal gardens run down to the sea.

▲ Ragged reflections
Great clumps of *Rheum palmatum* cast palm-leaved reflections among the stream gardens of Burford House. The nearby River Teme feeds the streams, where moisture-loving plants crowd together in lavish variety of form and colour. Well-groomed lawns curve past island beds, stemming the exuberant tide of plants, shrubs and clematis.

Burford House
Hereford and Worcester

From 1954 and until his death in 1993, John Treasure transformed the grounds of this austere red-brick Georgian house from a scattering of a few good trees and an elegant summerhouse into an eloquently defined 20th-century garden. Contrasting its spare symmetry on the north front with curving vistas and beds on its south side, he elegantly described the setting of the house in the fertile alluvial loam of the River Teme. An architect by training, he had that rare combination of discipline of design and passion for plants, and the result is a garden of quiet serenity and constant fascination.

John Treasure's high standards of discipline are revealed in the crisply edged and well-groomed beds in the extensive green lawns. This is a plantsman's garden, laid out to display a myriad of forms and species in ordered frameworks. There are special combinations and ideas which gardeners will be inspired to study and copy.

Harmonising combinations of colour have been brilliantly achieved throughout the garden, and special use has been made of clematis – a favourite of John Treasure. The garden boasts more than 150 varieties

and is home to the National Collection. The small-flowered *viticella* and *texensis* varieties are richly represented and are shown at their best trailing through shrubs and heathers and over roses and conifers.

Pleasing associations of colour have been created among shrubs and perennials, especially those that thrive on neutral to limy soils, and among the moisture-loving plants that grow along the stream gardens. Their banks have been massed with marginals, the broad-spreading clumps of gunnera and ornamental rhubarb (*Rheum palmatum*) diversified with the beautiful foliage of hostas, the upthrust wands and pokers of *Primula vialii*, astilbes and exotic irises.

Burnby Hall Humberside

Looking across the lakes of Burnby Hall, at Pocklington, you could be forgiven for thinking them entirely natural creations. Reed-edged and informally contoured, they are famed for their water lilies, which form multi-coloured drifts in high summer. But the two lakes are in fact artificial, extending where there was once nothing more than bare fields. Major P. H. Stewart, who bought the property in 1904, had their 2-acre extent excavated and lined with concrete.

The lakes were constructed for trout fishing, a passion of the much-travelled owner. His collection of hunting and angling trophies from around the world may be seen in a small museum in the gardens. But during the 1930s, Major Stewart's interests turned more and more to gardening, and brick-walled soil beds were built on the lake floors to hold hardy water lilies, now part of the National Collection.

A wide variety of trees and shrubs flourish in the 7 acres of garden around the lakes, and there are rare specimens among the trees: some 20 varieties of holly, for example, Japanese maples and other delights. The two lakes are on different levels and linked by a stream flowing down through a well-established rock garden.

More recent additions include a rose garden and – a particularly thoughtful inclusion – a scented herb garden for the blind. It consists of two large raised beds, stocked with fragrant plants.

The water lilies, though, remain the chief attraction. Over 80 varieties are represented, and comprise one of the finest collections in Europe. They are at their best from June to September and beneath the glimmering pads you may glimpse the flash of ornamental fish.

Castle Howard
North Yorkshire

When Granada Television chose Castle Howard as the chief location for their much

▲ **Castle Howard** A grand parterre of manicured lawns, symmetrical yew hedges and central pool and fountain stretches out in front of Vanbrugh's masterpiece in Yorkshire, with lakes to the north and south of the house. The soldier, playwright, architect and landscapist died in 1726, long before the magnificent building and the grounds were completed, but his designs were faithfully followed through, and the layout remains much as in Vanbrugh's days.

▲ **Poetic vision** Level lawns spread out before the palatial grandeur of Castle Howard. The 18th-century soldier and playwright John Vanbrugh turned his creative talents to architecture, and conjured up this vision of formal harmony. Such elegant restraint gives way to 30 acres of informal woodland east of the house, where rhododendrons spread their glowing colours beneath the trees.

acclaimed filming of *Brideshead Revisited*, they brought a sublime private palace into living rooms throughout the nation. Yorkshire's finest historic house, set in more than 1,000 acres of parkland, astonishes today through its grandiose conception. And it was scarcely less impressive to 18th-century visitors. Horace Walpole, for example, likened Castle Howard to a fortified city, with outlying hilltop temples, woodlands and 'the noblest lawn in the world fenced by half the horizon'.

The building was designed in 1699 as a private residence for Charles Howard, 3rd Earl of Carlisle. His architect was the soldier-playwright Sir John Vanbrugh, who, remarkably, had never designed a building before. Yet, assisted by the experienced Nicholas Hawksmoor, Vanbrugh plunged with gusto into the world of bricks, mortar and measuring rods – and created a masterpiece at his first attempt.

You enter the estate today by a 5-mile avenue of beeches, and of limes which have survived from the original plantings. Two superb archways embellished with mock fortifications give notice that this is no ordinary estate, while immense perspectives across the rolling parkland unfold. A cross avenue marks the turning to the house, at an intersection graced by a tall obelisk, erected to honour Charles, 3rd Earl of Carlisle.

South from the house the eye travels from

watery sheet and noble bridge to two of the finest garden buildings in Europe – Vanbrugh's Temple of the Four Winds, and Hawksmoor's Mausoleum beyond. The former is a splendid domed building with Ionic porticoes designed by Vanbrugh and completed by Hawksmoor, while the hilltop Mausoleum has been likened to a small cathedral. Walpole, a connoisseur, wrote that the rotunda would 'tempt one to be buried alive'.

Closer to the house is a grassed parterre, designed by W. A. Nesfield in the 1850s. It beautifully matches the character and proportions of the house, having as its centrepiece a baroque-style fountain showing Atlas supporting a globe from which glittering waters cascade. Formal hedges of clipped yew lend distinction to the baize-like lawns.

Although the wide views and architectural features set the tone of Castle Howard, colour is not lacking. There are fine rose gardens, including one laid out in 18th-century style and filled with old shrub varieties: moss, damask and musk among them. It lies within an original walled garden of 11 acres which is famed for its Satyr Gate, flanked by colossal grinning heads.

Above all, honest daffodils confer a special radiance on Castle Howard. In spring they are everywhere, trumpeting stately fanfares of exuberance which recall the outrageous confidence of Vanbrugh himself, creator of this Yorkshire paradise.

▲ **Churchill's haven** The strains of political life were eased among the gently terraced gardens of Chartwell (left), the home of Sir Winston Churchill. Here the great statesman spent his leisure hours painting and building pools, rockeries and walls. The fish pond, stocked with golden orfes, was his special delight, and here fish still glide through untroubled waters.

Chartwell Kent

Its name is inseparable from that of Sir Winston Churchill. The great statesman bought Chartwell and its 80 acres in 1922, moving in with his family two years later. And through the decades of triumph and disappointment which followed, it remained a haven of tranquillity. 'You could rest comfortably here,' he once wrote to an ailing friend, inviting him to the house. 'Just vegetate as I do.'

In reality, Churchill scarcely idled in his retreat. When not preoccupied with affairs of state he wrote, he painted and, besides spending £18,000 on improving the gabled Victorian house, he threw himself into garden-making with gusto. Bricklaying was a particular passion; Churchill was such a keen amateur that in 1928 he took out a card as an adult apprentice of the Amalgamated Union of Building Trade Workers.

Early on, three railway truckloads of Westmorland stone were brought to Chartwell to furnish his projects for the garden. During ten years out of office, from 1929 to 1939, Churchill 'built with my own hands a large part of the cottages and the extensive kitchen-garden walls, and made all kinds of rockeries and waterworks and a large swimming pool which was filtered to limpidity and could be heated to supplement the fickle sunshine of an English summer'.

The house lies some 168m (550ft) above sea level, near the head of a wooded valley sloping steeply to the south. Its green, terraced lawns command lovely views across to the Weald of Kent, while a clear spring – the Chart Well – feeds the pools and lakes. The fish pond was a particularly favoured spot, where the statesman loved to watch the gliding of his golden orfes. It has been said that the lakes below are a little obtrusive if measured against the highest standards of formal landscaping. Certainly, during the Second World War, they made Chartwell so easy to identify from the air that they had to be covered with brushwood as protection against enemy pilots.

Some of the plantings were Sir Winston's choice. He ordered the trees for the orchard, for example, where quinces, damsons and Kent cobnuts – long since disappeared – were among his favourites. But Lady Churchill contributed as much to the garden as her husband. Her taste was essentially for country simplicities; she created a rose garden and widely planted such 'cottage garden' shrubs as lavenders, fuchsias and potentillas. Buddleias were also established to attract butterflies, which her husband adored.

In addition, it was Lady Churchill who had the Marlborough Pavilion commissioned. This is a summerhouse, approached by a vine-covered loggia, which is one of

▲ Golden procession
Yellow roses parade down the slopes of the Golden Rose Garden, introducing a formal note at Chartwell.

▼ Engineering magic
Chatsworth found in Joseph Paxton (below) its own grand master of special effects. His illuminations kept Queen Victoria spellbound, and his conservatories were forerunners of his masterpiece – the Crystal Palace.

Chartwell's most attractive features. Plaques and bas relief friezes commemorate the soldiering achievements of the 1st Duke of Marlborough – Sir Winston's illustrious ancestor whose great estate at Blenheim presents such a marked contrast to Churchill's unobtrusive country retreat.

There is no Column of Victory at Chartwell. On the contrary, its associations are intimate, recalling above all the hobbies and pastimes of Britain's wartime leader. A white-flowering *Magnolia grandiflora*, for example, still grows by Sir Winston's bedroom window; he used to delight in its blooms, which featured in his canvases. At Chartwell you come upon the gravestones of two favourite brown poodles and, nearby, a croquet lawn where Churchill used to play with a casual single-handed style.

The most striking formal feature at Chartwell is the Golden Rose Garden, created to commemorate not a battle but a marriage. The garden was a present to Sir Winston and Lady Churchill from their children, and laid out in 1958 to celebrate their golden wedding anniversary. It lies in the original walled kitchen garden where much of the statesman's bricklaying can be seen. Yellow and gold rose varieties line a sloping walk with a sundial at its centre. 'Peace' and 'Arthur Bell' are among the plantings, while the long beds are edged with drifts of blue catmint.

It was a gift appropriate to Chartwell. For the house was always a home, and the garden a union of tastes. Churchill himself once sketched his life story in the briefest of terms: 'I married and lived happily ever afterwards.' Today, Chartwell is a National Trust property, the house and garden open to the public from April to October.

Chatsworth Derbyshire

When Queen Victoria and Prince Albert visited Chatsworth House in 1843 they were treated to a fantastic display of illumina-

tions. At night the garden's fountains and waterfalls, its great conservatories, and the River Derwent itself sparkled with multi-coloured lights, so that the whole domain appeared a fairyland. The Duke of Wellington, accompanying the royal couple, was so dazzled by the display that he determined to find out how it had been achieved. Rising at dawn he scoured the garden to find the abandoned lanterns, charred grass where the fires had been, and the debris left by the hundreds who had come to attend the entertainment.

He found nothing. The garden was as immaculate as if the display had never been. Joseph Paxton, engineer of the entertainment, was ahead of him. He had arranged for gangs of workmen to toil all night to remove every trace of his efforts. Wellington was amazed: 'I should have liked that man of yours,' he told his host, the Duke of Devonshire, 'for one of my generals.'

The names of Chatsworth and Joseph Paxton will always be intimately associated. Remembered today chiefly for his design of the Crystal Palace, built in London to house the Great Exhibition of 1851, Paxton learned his architectural skills at Chatsworth. He was head gardener there from the age of 23, and it was from his work on the conservatories – more particularly his construction of a Lily House in 1850 – that he conceived his revolutionary plan for the Crystal Palace.

The Lily House and Great Conservatory (so spacious that a horse and carriage could be driven through) were sadly demolished after the First World War. But there is much else at Chatsworth that recalls Paxton's hand. Charged with one of England's noblest country seats, he contributed a whole chapter in its history.

Well-groomed parkland

Chatsworth House lies on the banks of the River Derwent, in an area of well-groomed parkland once backed by what Daniel Defoe called the 'houling wilderness' of Derbyshire moorland. The dark moors have retreated from the vistas today, forced back by two centuries of landscaping. But they still formed a sombre frame for the estate when the first house was built in 1552, by Sir William Cavendish and his wife Elizabeth Hardwick.

Little remains of the Elizabethan gardens. A high, balustraded stone wall retaining the South Lawn is a vestige, and there is a Bower house and hilltop Hunting Tower. The 1st Duke of Devonshire (1641-1707) built the main block of the great house seen today, and it is from his time that the garden's main features date. There is, for example, a lovely fountain on the South Lawn, with sea-horses carved by Caius Cibber. A more sensational survival, though, is the great Cascade executed by the Frenchman M. Grillet.

▲ **Grand cascade** Three great periods of garden design – 17th-century formal, 18th-century landscape, and mid-Victorian – are illustrated at Chatsworth. The main features were laid out in the late 17th century, in formal French style, executed by George London. The few parts that survive include the Grand Cascade; this streams in a never-ceasing flow down a ladder of steps from a temple designed by Thomas Archer in 1696.

▲ **Serpentine hedge** The great living gardening traditions continue at Chatsworth.
With the 20th century came the introduction of fine herbaceous borders, terraces
and an outstanding rose garden. The serpentine hedge of beech was planted in
1953, a pleached lime avenue ten years later. In 1970, a new display
greenhouse was erected to hold the Amazon water lilies and the bananas first
introduced by Paxton.

The Cascade forms a glittering display against the hillside to the east of the house. Water streams over the dome of a temple at the top, gushing from ornate fountains to flow down a long, stepped ladder of falls. Daniel Defoe, who visited Chatsworth in 1724, provided a description which holds good today: 'out of the mouth of beasts, pipes, urns etc, a whole river descends the slope of a hill a quarter of a mile in length, over steps, with a terrible noise, and broken in appearance, till it is lost underground'.

Water – spouting, tumbling or flowing in the serene sweep of the river – supplies Chatsworth with many of its finest effects. The 4th Duke of Devonshire (1720-64) brought in 'Capability' Brown to landscape the park in natural style. Several fountains installed by M. Grillet were obliterated, and the landscapist wrought his own tricks with water. Brown altered the bends on the river to improve the views, and selected a new site for a bridge to span its course (this was to be executed by the architect James Paine).

Many of the trees seen today on the south-west slopes of the park are original plantings by Brown. He brought the grassy parkland right up to the walls of the house, so that many formal features were lost. The Chatsworth gardens of today are chiefly the creation of the 6th Duke of Devonshire (1790-1858). It was he who discovered Paxton while the young man was working in the gardens of the Horticultural Society at Chiswick. Impressed by the youth's intelligence, the duke brought him back to Chatsworth to take charge of his Derbyshire seat, then in a state of neglect.

Paxton's ingenuity is evident everywhere.

Though the Great Conservatory and Lily House have vanished, a range of botanical glass cases positioned against the so-called Conservative Wall survive in testament to his architectural skill. Built by Paxton in 1848, they ride up the sloping ground as if on an elegant escalator. The large central case contains two rare *Camellia reticulata*, planted by Paxton, which have grown to a great size and provide a beautiful display in March and April.

At Chatsworth, Paxton had vast boulders moved to create romantic arrangements of rockwork; they include the Wellington Rock with its waterfall leading down to the Strid (an imitation of the famous narrows of Wharfedale). He established the fine pinetum and arboretum, sending expeditions to India and America to seek out new seeds and specimens. The seedling of an early Douglas pine came from Derby fully grown and with so much soil round its roots that, it is said, turnpikes had to be removed along the route. It was in Paxton's Great Conservatory that the giant water lily of the Amazon (*Victoria amazonica*) first flowered in Britain and its size caused him to build the Lily House for it.

But among all Paxton's works, one sensational feature surpasses all. This is the Emperor Fountain, capable of playing its jet 84m (276ft) from the long Canal Pool in the South Lawn. It was installed by Paxton in honour of a planned visit by Tsar Nicholas of Russia in 1844; a visit which ironically never took place. To provide the necessary water pressure, Paxton had to dig a lake 8 acres in area on the hills above. The miles of conduits, pipes and valves are Paxton's design and are still in excellent working order.

◀ **Landscaped moors** The River Derwent wends its way through verdant parkland – those Derbyshire moors now tamed by two centuries of landscaping. Even the bends in the river were redefined, by 'Capability' Brown in the 18th century. The man-made waters of Chatsworth's Canal Pool stand out in formal contrast, and Joseph Paxton's Emperor Fountain sends its pillar of white spray soaring 84m (276ft) into the air. To the right, glimpsed through the trees, are the bronze-leaved curves of the serpentine beech walk, and the maze established on the site of Paxton's former conservatory.

▲ Chenies Manor Spring comes to this ancient Tudor house with massed displays of bedding tulips that fill the beds in a formal layout dissected by flagstone paths. Formal yew topiary and clipped box roundels break the velvety green of the grass sward.

The Victoria lily still blooms at Chatsworth – in a new greenhouse which was completed in 1970. Other recent features include a yew maze planted on the site of the Great Conservatory, a serpentine beech walk, and a living ground-plan of Chiswick Villa (the Devonshires' London residence) planted in clipped box at the West Front of the house. Chatsworth's splendours stretch back over four centuries, and the garden is not the creation of a single individual. Yet it remains the case, as the 7th Duke noted in his diary on Paxton's death in 1865, that 'there is no one whose name will be so permanently associated with Chatsworth as Paxton'.

Chenies Manor
Buckinghamshire

Just beyond the edge of hearing there is the tinkling of virginals or the pleasing sound of a lute. Or, if not, there should be. Elizabeth I, like her father Henry VIII, stayed at the manor, sat beneath one of its oaks to watch the hunt go by and walked in its gardens. Sometimes, on early summer mornings, it would not seem impossible to see the short turf spring back from her step.

Neither 'Capability' Brown nor any other improver ever laid hands upon the gardens at Chenies, which are purely Tudor and quite charming. The lawns have taken 400 years to achieve their velvet quality, and the stone flags that form many of the paths are worn by generations of pensive strollers. Here are yew walks and pleasances, a sun-

dial, an ancient well and a sunken garden bordered by beds of old-fashioned flowers with sweet perfumes. It is approached by wide, shallow steps and its stone paths are guarded by low drums and mounds of box, with reinforcements of yew pompoms in the background. In the first days of the year there are snowdrops in the grass, in the spring some 6,000 tulips in bloom, and in the summer beds of roses.

Chenies' most famous feature, however, is its Physic Garden, which embraces one of the most comprehensive collections of herbs in the country. There are plants from which perfumes are made, plants that yield dyes, herbs for cooking and herbs medicinal, many still used in modern drugs.

But perhaps the most appealing plants – and the ones best fitted to their background – are the ones that had the greatest attraction for our ancestors. There is angelica, for example, that was 'contrarie to all poysons', including the bite of mad dogs and serpents. Bluebells whose glue was used to set flighting feathers upon arrows and to make starch. Borage to dispel melancholy, comfrey to aid 'such as are bursten and that have broken the bone of the legge', and larkspur that could paralyse a snake in mid-strike.

Claremont Landscape Garden Surrey

It is amazing what neglect can do to a garden. The 50-acre landscaped estate at Claremont in Surrey was described in 1727 as 'the noblest of any in Europe'. Four great names in English gardening history – Vanbrugh, Bridgeman, Kent and Brown – contributed to its evolution. Claremont's illustrious owners included Lord Clive of India, and its visitors young Princess Victoria.

But from the 1920s the estate suffered decades of neglect. Garden architecture fell to ruin, and the landscaped lake silted up. Some trees succumbed to disease while others, unchecked, grew rampant. Even in 1949, when the National Trust took on the property, no funds were available to meet the scale of Claremont's needs. It was not until 1975, when the Slater Foundation presented a grant of £70,000, that thorough restoration could begin. Further grants and donations provided the sum in excess of £120,000 needed for the task.

Claremont was first laid out in 1715-26 for Thomas Pelham-Holles, Duke of Newcastle and twice prime minister. He commissioned Sir John Vanbrugh and his collaborator Charles Bridgeman to shape the estate, and their works are the oldest relics in the garden. Topping a knoll close to the house, for example, is Vanbrugh's fine Belvedere Tower. It stands proud at the head of an avenue leading from a bowling green – dense overgrowth in 1975.

▲ **Tudor relics** The red-brick manor house at Chenies was a favourite retreat for the young Queen Elizabeth I. The Royal Oak under which she rested still stands, as do the massive walls around the sunken garden. Planted with swathes of cottage-garden flowers and sweetly scented old-fashioned roses, the ancient gardens also contain an historic turf maze and an extensive physic garden of medicinal and culinary herbs.

▲ **Landscape restoration** During two decades the National Trust has restored the 50 acres of Claremont Landscape Garden to its historic reputation. The great English designers Vanbrugh, Bridgeman and Kent in turn laid out the gardens early in the 18th century. The lake is the work of William Kent, who also created the small island with its flintstone pavilion for picnics and fishing parties. Later, Queen Victoria and her family were frequent visitors.

◄ **Archaeological find**
The turf amphitheatre at Claremont – a strange conceit of early 18th-century garden design – is the sole survivor of its kind in Europe. Shrouded in trees as part of a later landscaping scheme, it lay hidden for more than 200 years, only to be unearthed again during recent restoration work. Its curving lines followed those of a circular pool below, transformed years later into a lake by the great landscapist William Kent.

A much more surprising discovery was a 3-acre turf amphitheatre, designed by Bridgeman and situated above the lake. Stripped of its vegetation, it has survived as the sole example in Europe of this curious 18th-century fad. The amphitheatre was never intended to stage plays, but was gouged from the hillside for visual effect.

The curved amphitheatre was originally designed to echo the shape of a formal round pool below. But the lake seen today is an informal water, naturalised by the pioneer landscapist William Kent. He was commissioned in the 1730s when neat symmetries were going out of fashion. In the lake he made a little island on which a flint-work pavilion was set up for picnics. By 1975 it was merely an unroofed shell, and it proved the single most costly item to restore. It is now fully refurbished, the lake has been dredged and its margin strengthened with elm planking.

Winding woodland groves of beech, chestnut and yew survive from Kent's day, with a ha-ha which the landscapist created as a sunken barrier between the garden and the countryside beyond. Kent's Cascade, shaped as a stone bridge, has vanished however – it was replaced in the late 18th century with a naturalistic grotto. This was included, as in so many gardens of the period, to inspire a sense of mystery in the viewer.

Vanbrugh, Bridgeman and Kent all worked for the Duke of Newcastle. When he died in 1768, Claremont was bought by Lord Clive of India. The great soldier and administrator commissioned 'Capability' Brown to demolish Vanbrugh's original house and replace it with the Palladian building seen today, which is now a school. Brown did not much change the garden, though, for Kent was his respected mentor. His chief alteration was to move the route of the old Portsmouth Road so that coaches and wagons no longer rumbled along the lake's edge.

In essence, Claremont remains a testament to 18th-century taste in garden making. A few new features, including the Camellia Terrace, were introduced from 1816, however, when the house served as a country residence for Prince Leopold of Saxe-Coburg, the uncle of the future Queen Victoria. As a young princess she would often visit Claremont and after her accession she returned frequently with Prince Albert and her family. 'It brings back recollections of the happiest days of my otherwise dull childhood,' she once wrote.

Cliveden Buckinghamshire

There are gardens which delight through diversity, and others in which one feature surpasses all. Cliveden belongs to the second category. Though its Buckinghamshire acres contain many attractions – temples, statuary and a water garden, for example – the famous view down to the Cliveden Reach of the Thames is a breathtaking centrepiece. It is, quite simply, one of the finest prospects in England.

The great terrace was the work of William Winde, who built the first house at Cliveden in 1666. His patron was George Villiers, 2nd Duke of Buckingham. The house itself underwent many later changes; it was twice destroyed by fire, and the present mansion dates from 1851. It was built by Sir Charles Barry, architect of the House of Commons. A famous political centre in the 1930s, Cliveden is now a National Trust property, and the house a luxury hotel.

Cliveden today is associated chiefly with the Astor family, who acquired the property in 1893. William Waldorf, the 1st Lord Astor, did much to develop the gardens and had a particular fondness for the Italian manner. He positioned much classically styled statuary around the grounds and one colossal item greets you at the outset of a visit, where the entrance drive winds through a rhododendron valley. It is a Fountain of Love, executed in gleaming marble, with lifesize female figures attended by cupids grouped around a vast scallop shell of Verona marble. From the monumental sculpture, a wide avenue of limes extends to the yew-hedged forecourt; the approach is from the north and the Thames views come as a wonderful surprise when you reach the south front of the house.

Aged climbing plants bask in the sunshine of the terrace's retaining wall and immediately below is a second balustrade, equally handsome, which was brought by Lord Astor from the Villa Borghese in Rome. Beyond, spreads the great parterre lawn with its geometry of wedge-shaped beds of santolina, senecio and catmint delineated with box; it ends at a statue of Pluto and Proserpine, also brought from the Villa Borghese.

Down below there are woodland walks leading to the river, and paths which rise and fall among the tree-clad cliffs. One of these is of special interest. It leads by an Octagon Temple and War Memorial Garden to the celebrated Canning Oak. The tree is said to have been planted long before the Duke of Buckingham's time, and takes its name from the great statesman George Canning (1770-1827). He loved to loiter in the shade of the old oak, delighting in the views of the Thames framed by its boughs. And he was not alone in admiring them. Garibaldi, the Italian patriot, a guest at Cliveden in 1864, compared the views to

▲ **Patterned perspectives** Like some vast ceremonial carpet spread out to greet the Thames, the great terrace at Cliveden stretches in lawns and geometric patterns of box-edged beds to the river. The diarist John Evelyn, who visited Cliveden in 1679, paid tribute to the terrace vistas, noting that they extended 'to the utmost verge of the horizon, which with the serpentining of the Thames is admirably surprising'.

▲ Terrace borders The wide herbaceous borders at Cliveden are planted for continued seasonal interest. In high summer, dense clumps of yarrows, heleniums, salvias and phlox, backed by dark blue monkshoods, frame venerable walls and grassy parterres.

'some of the mightiest river prospects of South America'.

The path leads on to a grass-tiered open-air theatre where in 1740 the aria *Rule Britannia* was first performed. You pass by an 18th-century temple in Palladian style to another creation by Lord Astor. This is the Long Garden, whose central mown walk is flanked by statuary, box hedging and topiary. The mood is set by the pale stonework against green foliage, but a south-facing wall shelters a host of choice shrubs which enlivens the area with colour. In spring, for example, the tender *Azara microphylla* from Chile scents the air with its clusters of yellow flowers; *Ribes speciosum*, the flowering currant, later contributes bright scarlet, fuchsia-like blooms.

There are many pockets of colour at Cliveden, including a rose garden laid out in 1956 by Sir Geoffrey Jellicoe. It is in the process of being restored to its original abstract design. Perhaps the most surprising feature is a complex water garden complete with a pagoda. Primulas and irises edge the winding lakeside, with azaleas, rhododendrons, magnolias, bamboos and weeping birches massed around. Tucked away in the north-east corner of the grounds, the watery area offers a delicate complement to the majesty of the Thames, flowing serene to the south.

Compton Acres Dorset

This is a wilderness transfigured. Heather, bracken, gorse and pines – the rough mantle of Dorset heathland – clothed Compton

Acres in Edwardian times. The house was built in 1914 to exploit the clifftop views over Poole Harbour. But it was not until after the First World War, when the late Thomas William Simpson bought the property, that a garden was made from the rugged bluff.

When the conversion came, though, it came on a grand scale. Heather slopes were gouged and terraced, vast tonnages of stone and soil imported. As the planning proceeded, fine bronzes, marbles and lead figures were brought in to adorn the garden; fountains began to spurt and subtropical plants to take root where the bracken and briars had been. The cost amounted to £220,000 (more that £2 million by present-day reckoning).

Mr Simpson's gardens are in essence those seen today. But there has been an irony in their evolution. No sooner did the extravagant estate start to take on an air of maturity than the Second Word War intruded. The head gardener died, and his assistants were called up for service. Soon after the war the owner himself died. Compton Acres deteriorated to the condition of a shadowy jungle. It was left to Mr J. S. Beard, who bought the property in 1950, to reclaim the wilderness.

Compton Acres was conceived as a living museum of garden styles. There are no fewer than eight separate gardens, each planned as a self-contained unit: Roman Garden, Italian Garden, Palm Court, Rock and Water Garden, Woodland and Subtropical Glen, Heather Dell, Garden of Memory and Japanese Garden. They are separated by high banks and sunken paths, so that the transitions come suddenly upon you.

Following (as is wisest) the prescribed circuit, you first enter the Roman garden. This is laid out as a shady, circular retreat with a miniature pool, old Italian carved stone seats and delightful lead statuettes. It is only a prelude, though, to a more spacious elegance. Fine wrought-iron gates and herbaceous borders backed by Purbeck stone give access to the Italian Garden, a grand formal set piece of colour and ornament combined. It bursts in full glory on the eye as you come through the stone entrance archway: a central lake in the shape of a cross embellished with carved stone fountains and water lilies.

At one end of the water is a Temple of Bacchus, at the other bronze figures of the famous Wrestlers of Herculaneum. Beds are massed with seasonal colour – spring tulips and forget-me-nots give way to the blooms of summer annuals and roses. The 32 flanking columns of weathered Bath stone echo the seasonal transitions, garlanded in spring with *Clematis montana*, and in summer with *C. x jackmanii*.

Terraces at the head of the pool lead to a long and narrow Palm Court, where more fine statuary may be seen. The centrepiece

▲ **Japanese garden** The man-made water garden at Cliveden makes no attempt to compete with the sweep of the River Thames where it marks the southern borders of the grounds. A Japanese pagoda, reflected in the still water, encapsulates the contemplative atmosphere, with water lilies gliding on the glassy surface, ringed in spring with native primulas.

▲ **Lofty detachment** The Japanese garden at Compton Acres in Dorset is one of eight different garden styles developed in the latter half of this century. Unique in Europe, it was assembled stone by stone from authentic materials and includes a sunken lake with a splashing cascade, mythical stone-carved animals and an inscrutable bronze crane. Azaleas and Japanese acers clothe the rocks, and Japanese arrowheads grow at the water's edge.

is a magnificent Venetian wishing well carved four-square from a solid block of stone. The palms and the paved setting confer a hot Mediterranean aura on the court, and you come at the end to a bronze, the Dying Spartan Soldier.

From the Palm Court a sloping path leads you into an entirely different habitat. Romantic views open up of a distant fern-edged waterfall, and as you approach the Rock and Water Garden the sound of running water is everywhere, gurgling and splashing from cascades to still pools. King carp of purplish hue glide beneath rustic bridges and among water lilies; the largest of them are more than 30 years old and at least 60cm (2ft) long.

Chain of lakes

The waters eventually descend to a chain of lakes in the Woodland and Subtropical Glen. This narrow ravine (or 'chine' as it is called in Dorset) once offered a secret pathway for stocking-capped smugglers from Poole. Today, instead of contraband, it shelters a host of subtropical plants: bamboos, palms, mimosas, jacarandas, eucalyptuses and rhododendrons.

There are breathtaking vistas from the south-west front of the house; it looks out across the glittering sheet of Poole Harbour, flecked with the bobbing sails of yachts. Brownsea Island and its castle are beautifully delineated and, beyond, the eye travels to the ridge of the Purbeck Hills. It is a huge and exhilarating prospect, and the garden makes no attempt to compete. The well-groomed lawns extend, as it were, a green carpet of welcome to this one feature which no garden maker could import.

From this sweeping panorama you come to the charming Heather Dell, where the harbour is seen only in tantalising glimpses. Here, in the acid soil, grows the native ling, *Calluna vulgaris*, in numerous forms and varieties, and several species of *Erica*, including *E. arborea*. This Mediterranean import thrives in the sheltered climate and easily reaches tree-like proportions, decked in spring with scented, pure white bell flowers. *E. carnea*, with its white, pink and purple flowers and green, russet and golden foliage, covers the winter ground with sheets of colour. The local Dorset heath (*E. ciliaris*), robust and free-flowering, spans the bridge between the spring-flowering tree heather and the winter-flowering types, blooming unceasingly from July through to winter.

Near the Heather Dell is a small, circular Garden of Memory, laid out in 1956-7 to commemorate Mr Beard's son, killed in action during the Second World War, and his two daughters, both tragic victims of polio. From the Garden of Memory, a winding path leads to the gate of Compton Acres' last great surprise: a complete Japanese Garden.

It is reputed to be unique in Europe for its authenticity. Designed by a Japanese architect, it was also assembled stone by stone entirely from articles brought from Japan. Granite pagodas, a stepped temple and an imperial tea-house framed by wisterias are among the most eye-catching garden ornaments. Near a summerhouse are a figure of the goddess who protects small children, and an ironstone Buddha believed to be 3,000 years old. A bronze gate is ornamented with two dragons trying to reach two doves that symbolise the struggle between good and evil. The plants include acers and flowering cherries, azaleas and hydrangeas, lilies and aralias, most of them Japanese varieties.

The centrepiece of the whole fantasy is a sunken lake with cascades, stepping-stones and bridges. Here and there, sacred red-crested cranes cast in bronze, and little carved animals peer out amid the flowers and shrubs. Each has its own mythological significance. There is, for example, a 'broken bridge' designed to trap evil spirits; a carved toad laughs at the deception.

▲ **Italian bias** Of the eight distinct garden styles explored at Compton Acres, the Italian Garden demonstrates the most formal elegance of them all. Bold geometric shapes are defined in colour – the blue of the cruciform pool with carved stone fountains and water lilies, the green of the grass, and the ever-changing hues of the bedding plants. In the foreground, the Wrestlers of Herculaneum are frozen in bronze, and in the distance the Temple of Bacchus completes this interpretation of Italian sophistication.

Cotehele Cornwall

The house at Cotehele, which is approached through a maze of high-banked Cornish lanes, is a beautiful example of a late medieval knightly dwelling. Though built in the reign of Henry VIII, its grey granite walls and lancet windows recall the Gothic era. Cornwall under the Tudors was a backward region whose frequently ruffian gentry kept alive the building styles – and the feuding ways – of the years of the sword.

The house stands above the River Tamar, and its 7-acre gardens slope deep into the wooded valley. You enter by ancient sycamores grown to a great height in the sea-cleansed air, while the spruces and larches rising from the valley slopes are so tall that their tops reach the same level as the house. These trees provide protection against that great scourge of West Country gardens – the sledgehammer gales that come raging in from the Atlantic.

Screened from the wind, Cotehele is favoured with a warm climate, high rainfall and a good, lime-free soil. The garden's most attractive area extends from the front of the house, where a series of terraces descend towards the valley below. They were laid out in the 19th century in simple strips of lawn and flower beds; two splendid magnolias (*M.* x *soulangiana* and *M.* x *s.* 'Rustica Rubra') that were blown down have been replaced with young trees.

The formal upper garden terraces have a splendid lily pool, walled rose garden and

▲ **Exotic banks** A spring-fed stream threads its way down a steep-sided glen in a series of pools and cascades. A medieval dovecote takes a beleaguered stand among giant conifers, rhododendrons, azaleas and hydrangeas, and Japanese acers for vivid autumn colour.

▲ **Invasion forces** The grey granite walls of Cotehele manor house, now a National Trust property, have stood unconquered since Tudor times, threatened only in the 20th century by an advancing army of glorious narcissi and daffodils. Roses and other climbers now clothe the walls around formal courtyards and fine terrace gardens. These, like the steep valley gardens, are open to the public throughout the year.

wide herbaceous borders, as well as a cutting garden for the house. A bulb meadow, where a collection of old Cornish narcissus varieties is being established, is pure joy in early spring.

Below the formal gardens, the ground slopes sharply to reveal panoramic views over the valley.

Coton Manor Northamptonshire

Colour plays tricks in this 7-acre garden. You may glance at a planting of shell-pink azaleas, for example, and see a blur of the same hue detach itself from the mass to strut on delicate stilts across the lawn. Coton Manor's flamingoes seem to enjoy the deception, often lingering by the pink shrubs. And they are only a few of the feathered exquisites which roam freely around the lake and lawns.

The present house, near Ravensthorpe, was built in 1926 by Mr and Mrs Harold Bryant, incorporating a 17th-century farmhouse. For all the mellow Northamptonshire stonework, this was a working farm at the time, and Mrs Bryant had a job on her hands to shape a garden from it. Haystacks, for example, had to be removed from the old kitchen garden to make the rose garden seen today. An existing farm pond was reshaped to make the formal rectangular lake, and trees were established both for shelter and ornament. A large, flowering cherry (*Prunus* 'Kanzan') by the lake is one springtime eyecatcher which dates from the initial planting. There is also an especially fine tulip tree (*Liriodendron tulipifera*) and an unusual black walnut (*Juglans nigra*), planted in 1926.

Like so many gardens in Britain, Coton Manor suffered inevitable deterioration during the Second World War, and needed much restoration afterwards. Commander and Mrs Pasley-Tyler (daughter of the garden's creators) took up residence in 1950. And, almost immediately, the manor acquired the first of its winged ornaments. Ownership has now passed to the third generation of the same family.

Birds were originally introduced purely for practical reasons. In summer, the main pond used to become choked with algae, and a brace of black East Indies ducks was brought in as a remedy. It worked: the waters cleared and the feeders proved attractive features in themselves. Thereafter, the owners introduced more unusual fowl: grey West African cranes, for example, and Caribbean and Chilean flamingoes. Today, black swans and blue macaws are among other exotics on display.

The birds, however, are only a small feature of a garden which delights entirely for itself. The overall design includes the rose garden, terraces, herbaceous borders, herb garden, conservatory and wild-flower mea-

dow. All are maintained at a high standard which bears tribute to the energy of the owners. There is also a 5-acre woodland area carpeted with bluebells in late spring.

Particular attention has been devoted to offering interest in late summer and autumn. Grey and silver-leaved plants abound, while bright splashes are provided by late-flowering varieties: mauve-coloured asters, the scarlet Cape figwort (*Phygelius capensis*) and Chinese monkshood (*Aconitum carmichaelii*). Among the rarer plantings are yellow waxbells (*Kirengeshoma* species).

Cragside Northumberland

You can create a micro-climate with trees, planting them for shelter against cold winds or as shade against burning summer sunshine. The trick is worked in countless small gardens throughout the country. And Lord Armstrong, the 19th-century industrial magnate, achieved the same effect when he planted out his estate at Cragside in Northumberland. The scale, though, was hardly modest: in a property of 1,700 acres he had over 7 million trees planted to make woods where bare moorlands had been.

Lord Armstrong was a giant in his day: inventor, engineer and the leading arms manufacturer in England. Yet he was also a lover of nature who had walked the rugged hills and loitered by the clear brooks of Upper Coquetdale as a boy. Untamed, the landscape has a sullen beauty, wooded only sparsely in the dips in the moorland and whipped by winds which seem to blow in straight from the Russian steppes. Armstrong bought the land at Cragside in 1863, to make himself a retreat; the architect Richard Norman Shaw designed the vast gabled house which presents such a striking silhouette today, perched on its craggy slope above the Debdon Burn.

Almost 1,000 acres of the original estate have survived as a country park today, under the management of the National Trust. The formal gardens are some distance from the house and reached via a path that gives views over the magnificent 3-acre rock garden densely planted with heathers, azaleas and other shrubs. The path descends steeply, crossing the Debdon Burn by a rustic bridge and climbs through gigantic conifers to the Clock Tower.

The tower overlooks the formal walled garden consisting of three large terraces, the upper one of which holds ferneries, grottoes and a large man-made pool. On the middle terrace is the Victorian Orchard House, where trained fruit trees were grown in huge earthenware pots, each set on a rotating turntable. The lower terrace is laid out in the Italian style, its centrepiece a cast-iron rose loggia built at Lord Armstrong's works on Tyneside.

▲ **Climate control** A colossal screen, made up of 7 million trees, was erected at Cragside against the searing destruction of the east winds. Lord Armstrong, arms manufacturer and inventor, devised this protected micro-climate for his Northumberland retreat in the 19th century.

▲ **Moorland retreat** Red-gabled Cragside House is perched above the Coquet Valley and looks out over millions of trees and shrubs. Close to the house is the huge natural rock garden, flaming with yellow-flowered deciduous azaleas in spring and blazing in autumn with rich leaf colours. The grounds descend to a magnificent pinetum at the bottom of the valley, with self-sown foxgloves clinging precariously to the rocky slopes.

▲ **Chalkland in bloom** King John once had a hunting lodge at Cranborne, but since 1603 the estate has belonged to the family of the 1st Earl of Salisbury. Now his descendants coax luxurious bloom from the hard chalk. The walled garden, entered through an archway between Jacobean gatehouses, includes long borders imaginatively planted with shrubs and herbaceous perennials, old-fashioned roses and summer bedding along wide grassy paths.

Cranborne Manor Dorset

A firm rule is observed in the wilder garden areas of Cranborne Manor: no mowing before the last week of July. Beneath the old beeches and fruit trees, wild flowers are allowed to multiply in their thousands: narcissi, cowslips, primroses, anemones, fritillaries and orchids. All contribute a springtime exuberance in this 12-acre chalkland garden.

The original stone manor at Cranborne was built in 1207 as a hunting lodge for King John. Renovated in Tudor times, the house passed in 1612 to Robert Cecil, 1st Earl of Salisbury. The Cecil family have held the manor ever since. And though it suffered damage during the Civil War and neglect in the 18th century, the house and its garden were restored in Victorian times, when a road was even re-routed so as to avoid the brick-built gatehouses.

You enter today into a cobbled court overlooked by Jacobean towers. Though the flower beds and cobbling are recent introductions, this and other formal courts around the house derive from designs made by John Tradescant the Elder in the early 17th century. Some ancient beeches and limes also survive from his original avenues, while there is a particularly interesting relic in the Jacobean Mount Garden to the west. Such points of elevation were common features of 17th-century gardens, and included to provide views over the owner's estate.

The garden is watered by the little River Crane, from which Cranborne takes its name. Carving its course to the north of the house, it is a winterbourne, and dries out in summer. For about seven months of the year it runs through a stone channel broken with pools and cascades. The present Marquis and Marchioness of Salisbury were responsible for this and many other improvements. In the flower beds, for example, they had the hard chalk foundation broken to a depth of 90cm (3ft) so that plants can root more easily. The result has been seen in more luxuriant growth; a walled White Garden in the North Court, for instance, has flourished particularly well. Conspicuous among its pale delights are large examples of *Daphne blagayana*, a spring-flowering dwarf with great cream clusters of fragrant blooms.

Other attractions include a herb garden enclosed by high yew hedges. In this aromatic plot, roses and other scented flowers grow among the herbs to provide delicate miscellanies of fragrance.

A rose pergola and avenues of beeches and pleached limes are among the other attractions of this very English garden. Until recently, Cranborne also contained an avenue of Cornish elms, which featured in the film *Tom Jones*. They were lost, sadly, to Dutch elm disease, and have been replaced with stripling London planes. But Cranborne survives with its charm intact.

Crathes Castle Grampian

It would be difficult to find a more romantic background to a garden. The pale walls of Crathes Castle simply soar against the skyline to a miraculous crown of corbelled stonework and overhung turrets. This is one of Scotland's most beautiful fairytale castles – and it is authentic, too. Alexander Burnett, 9th Laird of Leys, began the building in 1553 and it was completed by 1594.

Titanic yew hedges planted in 1702 set the tone of the gardens seen today. Up to 2.7m (9ft) high and as much in width, they are kept trimmed with surgical precision. Though little is known of the 18th-century garden, the yews indicate that it was formally laid out. And it seems to have been well tended.

The north-east is known as Scotland's 'cold shoulder', and is exposed to cruel easterlies and vicious frosts. They can make gardening as much an act of defiance as of creation. But if Crathes' climate is not favourable, the soil is a good loam and a screen of trees offers a degree of protection. Some potential for gardening was there when Major-General Sir James and Lady Burnett of Leys took up residence in 1926.

Each had a special interest: he was an enthusiast for rare trees and shrubs, while she had an artist's instinct for design and colour associations. Though their mixed aspirations sometimes led to friendly skirmishing, a great harmony resulted.

The garden at Crathes extends down a broad south-east slope beginning under the castle walls. The Burnetts laid it out as a series of rectangular plots, which incorporate the great yew hedges as dividers.

Undoubtedly Lady Burnett's most famous conception is the White Border situated in the Lower Garden below the yews and entered along an avenue of limes. The backdrop is a clipped hedge of purple plum (*Prunus cerasifera* 'Atropurpurea'), and

▲ Summer fairytale
Taken straight from the pages of some tale of enchantment, the pale walls of Crathes Castle rise behind the flower-spangled dream world of the June Border. This has a summery exuberance, flecked with the colours of lupins, poppies and bearded irises. The gardens of Crathes Castle, now a property of the National Trust for Scotland, are open daily.

▶ **Rural ride** Deep in his book, the Travelling Chinese Philosopher rides for ever past the south front of Dyffryn House. If he and his ox could move, it would take them more than two hours to make a full tour of the many beautiful gardens on the 50-acre estate. The philosopher is one of four fine oriental bronzes presented to Dyffryn by the Hon. Grenville Morgan.

grouped in the long mixed border is a host of showy exquisites including white roses, white phloxes, white delphiniums, fragrant *Philadelphus* 'Sybille' and feathery *Cimicifuga racemosa*. The border includes grey-leaved hostas, silver-leaved *Salix lanata* and blue globe thistle (*Echinops humilis*).

A fine old Portugal laurel (*Prunus lusitanica*), clipped to toadstool shape, stands at the centre of the Lower Garden and from it the borders radiate.

The compartments divided by the borders and paths each have a character of their own. There is a Camel Garden, for example (named after two raised island beds in the middle), and a Trough Garden whose central stone trough is overhung by a shapely *Prunus serrula*. The Golden Garden was also conceived by Lady Burnett but not begun until 1970, after her death.

Lady Burnett's themes and designs might be thought ample reason to visit Crathes. But for the connoisseur of rarities, Sir James's contribution adds an extra dimension. As a soldier he had travelled widely in the Far East and brought a taste for exotic specimens to the garden. The official guide gives pride of place to a rare *Staphylea colchica* 'Rosea' in the Double Shrub Border

in the Lower Garden. This is an exceptionally lovely shrub which blooms with deep pink flowers in May.

On the higher level is an elegant Pool Garden laid out by Lady Burnett in 1932. While the pond itself is framed by L-shaped hedges and beds, a broad border is picked out in, for example, red *Papaver commutatum*, deep purple *Cotinus coggygria* 'Atropurpureus' and the golden marjoram (*Origanum vulgare* 'Aureum'). Two exceptional honeysuckles lend their yellows, *Lonicera tragophylla* from Western China and *L. splendida* from Spain.

Dyffryn South Glamorgan

It was once described as being among Wales's 'best kept secrets'. Barely 3 miles west of Cardiff, Dyffryn House, which wears a sober, ambassadorial air, is maintained as a conference centre. It also has some 50 acres of garden in almost every style imaginable and its many attractions are being extended and improved all the time.

The present house was begun in 1893 by John Cory, a prominent South Wales businessman and philanthropist. His son

Reginald was chiefly responsible for the garden's design, in which he was assisted by the landscape architect Thomas Mawson. The essential features were established between 1900 and 1915, when many fine trees and shrubs were introduced. Reginald Cory was a keen horticulturalist, who not only helped to finance several plant-collecting expeditions but also took part in some of them himself. In 1937 Dyffryn was bought by Sir Cenydd Treherne, who later presented it to Glamorgan County Council. It is now administered by the counties of Mid Glamorgan and South Glamorgan.

To appreciate the diversity of Dyffryn's attractions you have only to explore the gardens to the west of the house. Here you come upon a whole complex of gardens within a garden, each 'room' enclosed behind yew hedges. There is, for example, a double-sided herbaceous border 85m (93yd) long and massed with 130 groups of perennials. The rose garden relays the history of the rose from antiquity until the present time. Add 76m (250ft) of glasshouses where cacti, orchids, begonias, coleus and other display plants flourish, and you have a bewildering jigsaw of plots in this area alone. To the eastern side is Reginald Cory's arboretum, which houses many fine specimens of plants sent back from those early expeditions.

Dyffryn Gardens are currently being developed using Cory's and Mawson's original plans, and at the same time reflecting Reginald Cory's great interest in plants from around the world. Drawing over 50,000 visitors a year, Dyffryn's 'secret' is out.

Elvaston Castle Derbyshire

South Derbyshire does not possess the rugged skylines for which the Peak District to the north is renowned. Watered by the rivers Dove, Trent and Derwent in their lazier moods, the terrain is remarkably level in places – and Elvaston is one of them. The grounds of Elvaston Castle quite defeated 'Capability' Brown when he was asked to landscape them; he refused the commission because 'the place is so flat, and there is such a want of capability in it'.

The neo-Gothic castle was styled on an existing manor house for the 3rd Earl of Harrington. It was his invitation that 'Capability' Brown turned down. But though the landscapist baulked at the proposition, he did present the earl with six cedars of Lebanon by way of compensation. They were planted to the east of the house, where they still grow today.

It was Charles Stanhope, the 4th Earl of Harrington, who supervised the creation of a landscape. He brought in a talented young Edinburgh gardener named William Barron to shape his 200 flat acres. The work began in 1830, and the two men laboured in partnership until the earl's death in 1851.

Throughout that period, the gardens were closed to visitors. The earl's instructions were, 'if the Queen comes, Barron, show her round but admit no one else'.

If the flat horizon does not intrude today it is a tribute to Barron's energy and ingenuity. To create interest in the level terrain he employed a variety of devices. North of the house, for example, he created a lake backed by masses of artificial rockwork. To the south he laid out long formal vistas leading to the stately Golden Gate (brought from Versailles by the 3rd Earl). Barron introduced topiaries, informal lawns and small gardens bounded by tall hedges. Above all he brought the trees which form such a feature of what is seen today.

Like so many of his Victorian contemporaries, Barron especially favoured conifers and evergreens: pines, yews, cedars and monkey puzzles abound, and there is an especially varied selection of hollies. Many of the trees were transplanted fully grown, using tree-lifting vehicles of his own devising. Some were real rarities brought from far afield. It was at Elvaston, for example, that the first Caucasian fir (*Abies nordmanniana*) was planted in England.

The grounds suffered serious neglect during the present century, but they have been well managed as a country park since 1969. Careful tree surgery has saved many an imperilled specimen, while new features include the Rhododendron Dell and an Old English Garden with herbaceous borders, rose garden and herb garden. Elvaston, in short, is entering a second age of magnificence – not bad for a garden without 'capability'.

Exbury Hampshire

To the general public the Rothschild name means wealth; to connoisseurs of rhododendrons it has a more specific significance. Rothschild means Exbury – and a wealth of

▲ Dwarfs and giants
Swelling topiaries, like giant mushrooms, mark the boundary of the formal parterre which spreads out before Elvaston Castle like a great patterned carpet. Established in 1970, the design of the parterre is drawn with closely clipped dwarf box.

▲ **Exbury azaleas** Lionel de Rothschild devoted his share of the family genius to creating a different kind of wealth. On 250 acres of acid loam overlooking the Solent, he fashioned one of the most sumptuous gardens in Britain, much of it stocked with new hybrids of rhododendrons and azaleas that he developed himself.

rhododendron hybrids and species without parallel in Britain.

In 20 years of gardening at his Hampshire estate, Lionel de Rothschild created over 1,200 rhododendron and azalea hybrids. The Exbury strain of azaleas in particular is famed the world over, and for specialists a visit to the garden is akin to an act of pilgrimage. To those with no more than a casual interest it is equally rewarding. In springtime, Exbury's 250 acres are upholstered with unimaginable beauty.

Lionel de Rothschild acquired the Hampshire estate in 1919. Situated by the Beaulieu River among woodlands of oak, beech and pine, Exbury enjoys the temperate climate of the Channel coast. Its soil is a very acid loam in which lime-loving plants perish all too easily. Even roses take some coaxing to produce a decent display. But the rhododendron and its relation the azalea root with glee, and these were Lionel de Rothschild's passion.

Over a period of ten years an army of 150 men laboured to create a woodland paradise. Some 20 miles of piping were laid down to conduct water to every nook in the garden, so that the soil remained cool and moist. A railway was even constructed to bring sandstone blocks for a rock garden in which, it is said, each stone was individually sited by the owner.

As for the rhododendrons, Lionel de Rothschild co-sponsored expeditions to the remotest Himalayas to extend the stock of known species. And at Exbury he had 3 acres of greenhouses built together with laboratories for hybridisation. When 'Mr Lionel' died in 1942, his eldest son Edmund continued to experiment and to develop the garden.

Pageant of colour

The pageant of colour unfolds at Exbury between spring and early summer. And despite the vast range of specimens their arrangement is informal. A maze of paths winds among woods and glades, which divide into three general areas.

Yardwood to the north has an abundance of yews (which were even mentioned in the Domesday Book). The focus of interest here is the great rock garden, planted with dwarf rhododendrons and other rock-hugging plants. Witcher's Wood, the central area, has a long, curving path lined by the lovely 'Lady Chamberlain' rhododendron. The hybrid was raised at Exbury and blooms in late May in shades of apricot-pink.

Exbury's hybrids are especially concentrated in the third area, Home Wood to the south. It centres on a chain of pools and a magnificent display of the deciduous azaleas for which the garden is also famed. Complex in parentage, Exbury hybrids make up a gaudy clan. Often deliciously scented, they bloom in a wide range of colours: the orange 'Sunte Nectarine', white 'Oxydol', salmon-red 'Eddy', rich golden-yellow 'Edwina

▲ **High season at Exbury** Renowned throughout the world for its magnificent collections of rhododendrons and azaleas, the Home Wood at Exbury reaches one of its several peaks in April and May. Then the massed banks of rhododendrons beneath a venerable tree canopy come into their full glory, their brilliant colours reflected in a series of glistening pools and ponds. Much later, the autumn spectacle is almost as stunning.

▶ **Royal shelter** No longer needed to protect the kings of Scotland, the palace walls at Falkland now shelter fine herbaceous borders. At the same time they support roses, ivies and other climbers, while cracks between the massive stones provide precarious footholds for pinks, thymes and other trailing perennials.

Mountbatten' and salmon-pink 'Cecile' are just a few.

The largest of the pools is edged with candelabra primulas and hung with the white *Wisteria venusta*, while bamboos, pieris and the feathery swamp cypress (*Taxodium distichum*) provide a diversity of foliage and form. The main crossroads of paths in Home Wood is marked by a planting of one of the best-known Rothschild rhododendrons: the magnificent 'Crest' with its May-flowering trusses of luminous yellow.

The plant has an interesting history. Lionel de Rothschild made several crosses between its parents, *R. wardii* and *R.* 'Lady Bessborough'; they are known as the Hawk Group, and shortly before the war he offered a pan of seedlings to his friends. Naturally enough, they took the largest and healthiest-looking ones. Of the few that were left over, only the very smallest was planted out at Exbury. It did not, in fact, flower until after the war, by which time its creator had died; but it caused a sensation as one of the best yellows available.

Exbury also boasts magnificent examples of the ancestral species gathered from China and the Himalayas: the giant *R. sinogrande*, the blue *R. augustinii*, the lucent yellow *R. campylocarpum* and *R. concatenans,* whose leaves have the fragrance of incense.

There is more to enjoy at Exbury than the rhododendrons. Camellias and magnolias – also lovers of acid soil – are beautifully represented, and down by the river are daffodil meadows which contribute an exuberance all of their own. Autumn's muted tones are enlivened by the scarlet glow of Japanese maples and the vivid pearls of many berried shrubs.

Falkland Palace Fife

Falkland Palace has always been a place of recreation – principally as a hunting lodge of the royal Stuarts. But it also offered other relaxations – its royal tennis court, built for James V in 1539, is the oldest in Britain, and it seems that there was always a garden to enjoy too. A plot was certainly established in 1456, when the records note that a gardener's wages were paid, then withdrawn as undeserved. Did the palace gardeners idle as much as their royal patrons, or were the Stuarts especially hard taskmasters? One or the other seems to have been the case, for in 1484 it was stated that no more wages would be paid unless the king's table was kept supplied with fruit.

The garden clearly underwent changes over the years. Great stone walls were built n 1513, and a note on work in progress for 1628 included 'planting and contriving the garden anew'. But what visitors see today is something contrived much more recently than that. During the Second World War – for all its pedigree – the garden was farmed for potatoes as part of the Dig for Victory campaign. Afterwards, when the noted landscape architect Percy Cane was brought in, he had the barest of canvases to work with.

Cane achieved a harmony of new and traditional features, using an old engraving of the garden only for general guidance. A great lawn, for example, still occupies the central area as in the days when James V used to practise archery at the 'lang butts' on it. But where clumps of trees had been, Cane laid out a series of half-moon island beds. Massed with shrubs and perennials, they define a perimeter walk and offer vivid foreground frames for the East Range of the palace. Here and there, carefully placed trees lead the eye up to the dramatic stonework: columnar cypresses provide the main vertical accents, while Japanese cherries, maples and laburnums offer colour.

Around the main lawn there are in addition three particularly good herbaceous borders. One is devoted largely to lupins and irises; another to the pastel blues, pinks and whites of delphiniums, erigerons and salvias. The third or Great Border runs along the east wall for 183m (200yd).

Red and yellow are the colours of the Stuart livery. They are formally massed in the floribundas of a rose garden to the west of the main lawn area. Woods and orchards stretch away beyond, while north of the lawn is a hedged water garden. This is a fairly recent feature, laid out by the National Trust for Scotland with two rectangular lily pools as its centrepiece. The royal tennis court nearby is, of course, much more ancient: older still are the Lomond hills, looming overall.

Felbrigg Hall Norfolk

The North Sea is little more than 2 miles away from this Jacobean house, but a great wood of 600 acres screens it from coastal winds. The trees were first planted in the late 17th century, and many oaks and sweet chestnuts have survived from that time. By the hall is an orangery of 1705, and the large old camellias inside still give fine displays from April to June. In short, much at Felbrigg speaks of a settled peace, recalling the hall's slow evolution over hundreds of years in the hands of the Windham family.

In 1969 the property was bequeathed to the National Trust, which has preserved its tranquil aura. An 18th-century walled garden of 2½ acres is an especially interesting feature. It has been restored as a 'potager', or formal kitchen garden, which once served the hall with fruit, vegetables, herbs and cut

flowers. Divided by high walls into three sections, it originally required a vast garden staff to meet its needs. For example, there is a large octagonal dovecote of the 1750s which alone must have presented problems of maintenance.

Today, extensive box hedging lines the paths in the walled garden. Many fruit trees are grown against the walls in traditional fashion: figs, peaches, plums and nectarines. Grapes flourish in a greenhouse, and even a grapefruit tree crops.

But the great vegetable beds have largely disappeared. Instead, the walled garden contains a wealth of flowers and shrubs chosen for colour and fragrance. In spring, cool blues, mauves and whites are conspicuous: there are chionodoxas, ceanothuses and a fine selection of lilacs. Two large rectangular plots contain 20 different species of hawthorn, while roses, paeonies, phloxes, buddleias, carpenterias and romneyas flower in their appropriate seasons. Autumn holds a special attraction – and not only for its ripening fruits. The margins of the shrub borders are adrift with *Colchicum tenorii,* a rare autumn crocus which blooms in thousands.

▼ **Modern potager** A cluster of bell jars for forcing rhubarb is a reminder of the great days of the kitchen garden at Felbrigg Hall. Then, tended by a small army of gardeners, it supplied the hall with vegetables, herbs, fruit and cut flowers – not to mention provisions from the octagonal dovecote. The high warm walls still shelter espalier-trained fruit trees, but most of the 2½ acres is now given over to shrubs and flowers.

▲ **New Forest glade** A stepping stone path which leads through billowing heathers to a low thatched cottage belies the scale of Furzey Gardens. There are 8 acres in all, including a water garden, a fernery and fine borders of flowering and foliage shrubs, many of which delight with blazing autumn colours.

Furzey Gardens Hampshire

The name holds promise of rustic charm, enhanced by the Tudor thatched cottage in the garden. Not that the main house is old, it dates from only 1922 when three brothers Dalrymple acquired the property. But they built low and roofed their new house with thatch in keeping with the character of the cottage. And the grounds were 'furzey' indeed at the time, comprising 8 acres of rough gorse pastureland.

Today, Furzey Gardens remain pleasingly informal in layout. Grassy paths meander among trees and rough-mown glades; no pesticides are used, and wild flowers are allowed to seed themselves in abundance. In spring, bluebells spread in dappled sheets under the New Forest oaks, while wood anemones and naturalised narcissi colonise beneath silvery birches.

The gorse waste has gone though. Two of the brothers were skilled gardeners: while Hew Dalrymple was chiefly responsible for Furzey itself, Bay Dalrymple founded the well-known Bartley Nurseries near by. Hybrids developed there may be seen not only at Furzey Gardens, but in gardens throughout the country. The lilac-flushed broom *Cytisus* 'Minstead' is one example; another is the pink candelabra primula *P. pulverulenta* 'Bartley Strain'.

At Furzey, tonnes of good peaty soil were brought in to leaven the New Forest clay and permit a wide range of choice plants to take root. From April to June, massed banks of azaleas provide vivid drifts of colour. Come in late May and you find the gardens lowing with the scarlet of the Chilean fire bush (*Embothrium coccineum*), more widely planted here than anywhere else in the country. In late summer there are four different varieties of eucryphia to admire; two examples of the evergreen hybrid *E. x nymansensis* are about 15m (50ft) high, fragrant white-flowering giants which bear their blooms into early autumn. Then, when the leaves turn under October skies, a host of fiery shrubs come into their own: amelanchiers, enkianthuses, liquidambars, disanthuses and others.

Even in winter there is much to fascinate the eye. Furzey contains one of the largest heather gardens in the country; the variety *Erica x darleyensis* 'Furzey' was developed here and is among the winter-flowering varieties on display. In the cold doom-days of February the lovely little *Rhododendron moupinense* may be seen blooming among the jasmines and snowdrops, a rarity far from its Szechwan home.

A fernery and water garden are more recent features, and the abundance of primulas renews the colour cycle from early spring. Despite its impression of informality, Furzey is a place that captivates all the year round.

Great Dixter East Sussex

A roofscape of tile-hung gables, tall brick chimneys and oasthouse cowls overlooks these five Sussex acres. The 15th-century house and its outbuildings are famous for their restoration by the architect Sir Edwin Lutyens, who worked at Great Dixter from 1910 to 1912. He also designed the surrounding gardens, laying them out in different compartments and so helping to establish a now much emulated style.

But though Lutyens structured the spaces, he did not furnish them. The plantings were undertaken by the owner, Nathaniel Lloyd, who had his own ideas about gardening. Lutyens, for example, envisaged that the compartments should be walled with brick; the owner preferred yew hedging. In the end, a happy compromise evolved: both materials were used as dividers, while the old barns, sheds and oasthouses provided further screening.

Great Dixter today remains a tribute to the Lloyd family's gardening talents. When the owner died, his wife continued his work and remained active with her trowel until her 91st year. She died in 1972, and it is to their son Christopher Lloyd, an eminent writer on gardening, that Great Dixter owes its present standard of excellence.

'Excellence' might not seem the appropriate word when you first arrive at the entrance. The house stands on the High Weald, about 55m (180ft) above sea level, and there is no smooth baize carpet of welcome. You approach, on the contrary, by the roughest of lawns which looks frankly

unkempt at first glance. Look again and you notice a haze of colours; this is a wild meadow garden, studded in spring with fritillaries, narcissi and native orchids. Clovers and moon daisies succeed before the first mowing and, by September, autumn crocus and colchicums have taken their place.

The essay in wild gardening was begun by Mrs Lloyd and has been continued by her son. It is not to every visitor's taste, as Christopher Lloyd has readily conceded, though conservationists acclaim it. But there is nothing controversial about the garden 'rooms' you enter next – their decor is maintained to an exceptional standard.

Within the sound formal design, the plantings are informally luxuriant. Mr Lloyd is as interested in colour contrasts as in plant harmonies. There is much experimentation, and colour combinations change from year to year. The great showpiece is the Long Border, its main section 64m (70yd) in length and 4.5m (5yd) deep, backed by yew hedging. It is a truly mixed border, with many shrubs and even small trees mingling with the herbaceous subjects. Here, for example, a white-flowering escallonia catches the eye amid purple salvias and glowing mats of ruby sedums. There, golden clouds of Mount Etna broom billow

▲ **Joint effort** The architect Sir Edwin Lutyens (below) was responsible for the restoration of the house and for most of the garden design at Great Dixter. But the sunken garden, with its octagonal pool, was designed by the owner of the house, Nathaniel Lloyd.

▲ **A well-chosen garden** The Long Border at Great Dixter is pure delight from
spring until late autumn. In a glorious mixture of trees, shrubs, climbers and
perennials, colour is never absent. The lower corner is a riot in high summer, with
feathery Mount Etna broom shielding red roses and blue campanulas while clouds
of sweet-scented, white-flowered herbaceous *Clematis recta* billow against a
scrambling honeysuckle.

ver a red pillar rose. Tamarisks and gleditsias, hostas, phloxes and asters, ornamental grasses, silver-leaved plants, wands of colour, spangled drifts – all surge and lap in brimming promontories down to the York stone path. Though the climax of the display comes in mid summer, choice plantings extend it from April to November.

This richness and variety is characteristic of the plantings throughout Great Dixter's compartments. There is, for example, a large sunken pool garden whose formal design is softened by a wealth of unusual plants spilling from raised borders and growing against the walls. The strange climber scrambling up the tiled roof of a barn is the rarely seen, crimson-flowered and red-berried *Schisandra rubriflora*.

There are 18 garden 'rooms' at Great Dixter, each with its own character. The tropical garden is a recent introduction: enclosed by scalloped yew hedges it is planted for summer effect with large-leaved cannas, hardy bananas, castor-oil plants, dahlias and other exotic plants. The topiary enclosure has 18 birds sculpted from yew and linked by hedging of Michaelmas daisies. They make a curious flock, perched on their green cones, and have grown plump since Nathaniel Lloyd first shaped them. The old kitchen gardens are now given over largely to ornamental plants, though espaliered pears still line the paths. They are entwined by many varieties of clematis, a favourite plant of the owner.

Hydrangeas are another speciality of the garden: they seem to relish its fairly heavy clay. Great Dixter is remarkable, too, for the number of annuals which feature in its thickly planted borders. Besides generous plantings of stocks, mignonettes and nasturtiums the garden is graced by such delicate subjects as pale cleomes and bright Mexican sunflowers (*Tithonia*). Biennial foxgloves and sweet Williams also take their place in the borders.

Of course, it takes effort – which is why so many modern gardens lean heavily on labour-saving shrubs and perennials. But as Christopher Lloyd has written: 'Effort is only troublesome when you are bored.'

Haddon Hall Derbyshire

If any garden distils the romance of the rose it must be Haddon Hall's. The house is one of the finest to survive from the Middle Ages, and in high summer England's favourite flower bursts on the eye in dreamy profusions of blooms. The garden offers more than a visual experience. Those cloudy fantasies of colour drifting against the mellow stonework also tug deep at the inner emotions, as if emblematic of time and beauty combined.

'A good old house, all built of stone', was how one 17th-century visitor described the

hall. It stands on a slope above a curve of the Derbyshire Wye and, dating from the time of the Tudors and earlier, it is built of the same dove-grey limestone as its escarpment. If Haddon is wedded to the landscape, it is also wedded to romance. The Manners family have held Haddon Hall since 1567, the Vernons occupying it before them. And a fittingly picturesque legend surrounds the transference of the property. It is said that around 1563 Dorothy Vernon, heiress of Sir George Vernon, owner of the hall, eloped with John Manners, son of the Earl of Rutland. She escaped, so tradition alleges, by an old packhorse bridge which still graces the Haddon estate.

The gardens slope chiefly southwards to a loop in the Wye by a series of old stone-walled terraces. Their handsome balustrading, stairways and paving all date from the early 17th century. The overall design has changed little since that time, but Haddon acquired an abandoned aura during the 18th and 19th centuries, becoming a place of Gothic fascination. 'A gloomy and solemn silence pervades its neglected apartments, and the bat and the owl are alone the inmates of its remaining splendour', noted

▲ Roses all the way
Haddon Hall is the kingdom of the rose. Wherever you go in the gardens there are roses – climbers and ramblers scramble up the walls, around the doors and over the arches, while hybrid teas, floribundas and shrub roses fill the beds on the south- and west-facing terraces in front of the hall.

Rhodes's *Peak Scenery* in 1819. It was the 9th Duke of Rutland, father of the present owner, who from 1912 restored the property.

Masses of foliage were cleared: walls were freed from the python grip of ivy, and threatening limes and sycamores felled from the upper terrace. On the second level, ancient yews grown to giants were replaced with young specimens which have since been kept neatly trimmed.

Then came the roses. They were a special love of Kathleen, the 9th Duke's Duchess, and though the impression they create is of ancient enchantment, the varieties are mostly new. In particular, floribundas produce dazzling displays in the upper garden. These free-flowering roses, so familiar throughout the country today, were only developed in the 1920s by the Danish hybridist Svend Poulsen. At Haddon today a fantastic abundance garlands the formal beds, shading from white through the palest of pastels to tones of the richest blood-red.

For fragrance and perfection of form the hybrid teas hold pride of place, while for sheer magic nothing could compete with Haddon's climbers and ramblers. They burst among balustrades, festoon mullioned windows and overhang ancient portals. The varieties are too many to list, but mention might be made of two conspicuous pink roses: 'Albertine', that vigorous old favourite whose coral flush comes in June, a brief but incomparable vision; and 'New Dawn', a more recent introduction, which blooms throughout the summer.

Rampant clematis also clothe the ancient stonework, and noble delphiniums here and there contribute the pure blues which no rose has yet learnt to emulate. There is a rectangular fountain pool and, below, a steep drop to a lower garden of different character. In the creviced masonry of its retaining walls, aubrieta has rooted in vivid mounds, and choice shrubs flourish in the beds beneath. Yet it is above all for its roses that Haddon is visited; theirs is the motif of the garden as it was of the Yorkists and Lancastrians whose wars the ancient hall survived.

Hampton Court
Greater London

Almost everyone has heard of the Maze at Hampton Court; it is the garden feature which has entered the folklore of a nation. And the palace itself is equally renowned, as a focus of pomp and pageant since Tudor times. Thomas Wolsey, a future cardinal and the most powerful of Henry VIII's subjects, acquired the site by the Thames in 1514 and built a palace there worthy of his status. Later, when the cardinal fell into disgrace, he presented the building to the king in an attempt to regain royal favour. The gesture was in vain. Henry enlarged the great residence as a monument to his own extrava-

gant sovereignty – and Wolsey died on his way to the Tower.

Hampton Court lies on the north bank of the Thames some 7 miles upstream from Westminster. Today, the palace gardens and neighbouring parkland form a green, historic space in the suburban sprawl of Greater London. Yet the palace was conceived as a country retreat in a place where the air was of an 'extraordinary salubrity' after the squalor of London, and to which luxurious royal barges would come decked out for glittering entertainments. Tudor, Stuart and later kings and queens all contributed to its evolution.

It is known, for example, that Henry VIII's grounds included a pond, knot and herb gardens, with bowers and shady walks and a splendid Mount Garden topped by an arbour bristling with heraldic beasts borne high on painted poles. Little physical evidence, however, remains of the Tudor gardens. The Mount Garden was levelled in the 17th century, and a tiltyard where knights once jousted is now stocked with roses and shrubs. Only one small knot garden today illustrates the Tudor style; this is a modern reconstruction of interlacing beds hedged with dwarf box and lavender and filled with plants of the period.

More has survived from the Stuart era. Radiating from the east front, for example, are three avenues of lime trees originally laid out in the time of Charles II. One avenue has been replaced, and a second, in the Home Park, is in the process of restoration. These are two of the network of avenues that form the historic *patte d'oie* (goose-foot) pattern.

Black pyramids of yew
By the palace, the 'heel' of the foot is a semicircular Great Fountain Garden designed by Henry Wise for William and Mary. Here huge conical yews cast dagger-edged shadows across the lawns. The trees were originally intended as slender obelisks, but 300 years of growth has turned them into the 'black pyramids' which Virginia Woolf once described.

In this historic jigsaw of a garden, some pieces were retained as the years passed; others replaced or obliterated. Queen Anne added a red-brick orangery, and George III brought in 'Capability' Brown. Happily, though, the landscapist did not sweep all away with his customary enthusiasm for naturalism. In fact, he made only two significant contributions. One was characteristic: a formal terrace Privy or Private Garden laid out for King William III by Wise in 1702 was smoothed out to make grassed banks – the restoration in the 1990s of King William's unique *parterre à l'anglaise* has been a major undertaking.

'Capability' Brown's second contribution is the Great Vine. In 1768, as head gardener at Hampton Court under George III, he

▲ **Wolsey's folly** When Thomas Wolsey, Archbishop of York, bought the manor of Hampton in 1514, he set about building a house. It ended up as the largest in England – the building itself covered nearly 4 acres – and to frame it, he enclosed a park of 2,000 acres. In 1525 he gave the estate to Henry VIII and it has remained in royal hands ever since.

▲ **Royal bedding** Hampton Court is famous for its bedding displays in the Pond Garden. In spring it brims with swathes of tulips, hyacinths and narcissi, and in summer with the vibrant colours of summer bedding plants, a tradition that goes back to Victorian times and is faithfully maintained. The so-called Wilderness Garden is pure joy in spring – golden carpets of naturalised narcissi beneath flowering cherry and crab apple trees.

▲ **Palatial grounds** The huge semi-circle of lawn, segmented by avenues of clipped trees and with a great fountain at its centre, gives some idea of the size of Hampton Court's gardens. Each of the three avenues is 183m (200yd) long. The tree-lined canal, stretching away at the top, runs for more than half a mile through the Home Park. The Pond Garden, with its dazzling bedding displays, is to the left of the white-roofed building, the Banqueting House, on the river bank near the boats.

planted a cutting of a 'Black Hamburgh' vine. That vine is still growing and is probably the oldest in the world. You can taste Brown's fruit, too – the grapes are on sale to the public in late August and September.

Queen Victoria's great contribution was to open Hampton Court to the public in 1838. There was an immediate and sensational interest evidenced by an influx of 120,000 visitors in the first year alone. Since her time there have been several additions: the new knot garden, for example, and two fine herbaceous borders. The Twentieth Century Garden was opened in the late 1980s; it is laid out in modern style and planted with new cultivars and varieties.

But it is the Maze above all which has captured the public imagination. Labyrinths are as old as the tale of the Minotaur, but the craze for hedge mazes as intriguing garden features seems only to have developed in the 17th century. The example at Hampton Court is the oldest planted hedge maze in Britain and was laid out by George London and Henry Wise during the reign of Queen Anne. Almost 300 years later, the green corridors of the Maze, maintained at 1.8m (6ft) high by 60cm (2ft) wide, continue to baffle and perplex.

Harewood House
West Yorkshire

It might be likened to some great open-air opera house. The royal box, as it were, is a huge balustraded terrace laid out in florid and opulent style by the Victorian architect Sir Charles Barry. But the stage beyond was set by an earlier master who worked with woodland, water and rolling hills. This was the incomparable 'Capability' Brown, and Harewood's is one of his finest backdrops.

Harewood House was built in 1759, and its 300 acres have been owned by the Lascelles family for more than two centuries. Three great arbiters of 18th-century taste contributed to the building's air of distinction. While Robert Adam and Thomas Chippendale furnished much of the interior, Lancelot Brown was commissioned in 1772 to model the parkland.

The landscapist worked at Harewood for nine years, for a fee of £6,000. And the 1st Earl of Harewood was rewarded with what Dorothy Stroud, Brown's biographer, called 'one of the most delectable landscapes'. Where rough gritstone farmland had been, smooth lawns emerged, sloping to a 30-acre lake, designed by one of Brown's students, urving around scenic tree groupings and stretching through encircling woodlands to far distant horizons. Today, the overall impression remains much as Brown planned it. Disaster occurred in 1962, when 20,000 trees were destroyed in a storm. But though many beeches and oaks grown to a huge maturity were lost in the calamity, they have since been replaced.

In Brown's scheme, suave lawns were brought right up to the walls of the house. Today, the great terraces extend from the front, providing a platform from which to take in the long views. Sir Charles Barry, architect of the House of Commons, built them in the 1840s in the grand Italianate manner. In 1994, the intricate patterns of box hedges and bedding plants of the parterre originally designed by Barry were restored to their former glory after decades under grass.

You can spend a lot of time on the elaborate platform, admiring both foreground and landscape. But to fully appreciate Harewood's attractions it is worth coming down from the terraces. A wealth of interesting trees and shrubs have been planted in gardens and parkland. Immediately below, for example, you come upon a tall *Eucryphia* x *nymansensis*, palely petalled and nectar-rich with creamy blossom in August; there is also a maidenhair tree (*Ginkgo biloba*).

Down towards the lake, paths lined with azaleas lead to a waterfall, and a rocky dell where ferns, primulas and similar plants thrive in the moist soil. Here, too, the weird and massive *Gunnera manicata* unfurls its great umbrella leaves. Rhododendrons flourish in abundance: *R. racemosum* of Yunan is among the most widely planted, flowering in spring in shades of pink. A rustic bridge leads to an old-fashioned rose garden and the entrance to the walled garden which houses part of the National Hosta Collection.

Harlow Carr North Yorkshire

In choosing an ideal site for a garden you might well look first for good soil, mild climate and a sheltered position. When, after much consideration, the Northern Horticultural Society selected Harlow Carr as a plot they plumped for the reverse of each attribute.

Lying some 152m (500ft) above sea level and prone to whipping south-westerly winds, the site is both cold and exposed. The soil, moreover, is a very heavy and acid loam overlying beds of dour millstone grit – the rock of the neighbouring moorlands which is impermeable to water and so offers no natural drainage.

Harlow Carr Botanical Gardens were founded in 1948, precisely for its challenge. The aim of the society was to study the problems of gardening in the north of England; to discover what could endure and give value in a typically uncompromising setting. If a plant could be coaxed to bloom in these Yorkshire acres the chances were that it would survive almost anywhere in the north.

From the outset, certain plants were favourites to succeed. Rhododendrons, for example, enjoy an acid soil and, growing naturally among the snows of the Himalayas, are no strangers to extremes of cold. Today, some 450 species and hybrids enrich the garden with their opulent colours, and they have been widely planted in the woodlands. One of the first to appear is the large-leaved *R. calophytum* of Western China. It blooms through the mad March days, bearing speckled trusses of pink-and-white flowers with a deep red blotch at the base. Month by month, other luxuriants follow in crimsons, yellows, creams and mauves. The season ends only in July with, among others, the very late flowering 'Polar Bear' hybrid, a white rhododendron.

Heathers also prosper at Harlow Carr.

▼ **Harewood House** The Parterre on the Terrace Gardens faithfully recreates Sir Charles Barry's original designs of the 1840s. Impressive spring bedding displays are followed by eye-catching summer shows. Beneath the terrace is a well-stocked herbaceous border, 137m (150yd) long and embellished with urns and statuary.

▲ **Successful challenge** Lush foliage runs riot in the Stream Garden at Harlow Carr. Ferns, hostas and other moisture-loving marginals flourish in the dappled shade and damp soil along the stream banks. They are living proofs of how successfully the Northern Horticultural Society has met the challenge of coaxing an outstanding garden from a cold and exposed site with near-barren soil in North Yorkshire.

They, too, are acid lovers, though much peat has been required to provide a truly acceptable habitat for them. The main heather collections are in the Tarn Meadows, the Trials Area and South Fields, where the National Calluna Collection (over 300 cultivars) is maintained. Over 600 heather species and cultivars are represented – tree heaths as well as low, spreading shrubs.

Although plants are labelled and studied for garden value, Harlow Carr has also been laid out for ornamental effect. And it has been fascinating to see what has flourished. A wide variety of Japanese maples provide splendid colour in both spring and autumn, and the Chilean fire bush (*Embothrium coccineum* var. *lanceolatum* 'Norquinco Valley') has been an outstanding success, bearing sensational orange-and-scarlet blooms in May and early June.

A formal trials and demonstrations area has been laid out, in which horticulturists are invited to test their wares. You can judge for yourself the comparative performances of new and established varieties: for example, of dahlias, chrysanthemums, delphiniums, and a range of summer bedding plants. The failures are as interesting as the successes. In 1978, for example, the International Camellia Society tried out 140 species and cultivars of this lovely shrub. Almost every one died in the hard winter which followed. All had been one-year-old plants, and the lesson for northern camellia growers was that, for safety, only more mature specimens should be planted.

In this garden for gardeners, many different habitats have been created. There is the Peat Garden, for example, whose abundant primulas include Harlow Carr's own popular hybrids. To make raised beds for alpines, the soil has been lightened with leaf-mould and gravel; a Limestone Rock Garden provides a fascinating contrast. Here the alkaline soil permits saxifrages, campanulas, dianthuses and helianthemums to flourish. Elsewhere there are Bulb and Foliage Gardens, a youthful arboretum and a display house for alpines. Harlow Carr also contains one of Britain's four vegetable sanctuaries, where old and endangered cultivars are nurtured. Four other National Collections are held: hypericum, polypodium, dryopteris and rhubarb.

Heale House Wiltshire

For six nights in October 1651, the future King Charles II took refuge from his Roundhead pursuers at Heale House, before taking ship to France. At the time of his secret visit, a house had already stood beside the Avon for a hundred years or so, and a 16th-century part remains today. Most of the present house dates from early this century, when it was enlarged by the Hon. Louis Greville, in whose family it remains.

Eight acres of immensely varied gardens stretch away from Heale House. The focus of the tunnel garden is formed by round box bushes, from which three avenues of apple trees radiate, their arching branches trained across the paths. The borders are stocked with plants that will tolerate patchy shade, such as pinks and hostas.

On the top terrace to the west of the house, dark yew hedges form a backdrop against which the brilliant red, gold and purple of sumach, prunus, weigela and mock orange leap to life in early summer. Below, the beds of the fish pond terrace are planted for continued seasonal interest, with iris, cyclamen, fritillarias, pulsatillas, autumn crocus, and a tangle of roses and clematis.

The balustrade of the river walk at the eastern end of the house is lined with rambler roses, Japanese quince and polyanthus. On the lower terrace to the south of the house is a close-set hedge of musk roses – 'Penelope', 'Cornelia', 'Buff Beauty', 'Moonlight' and 'Felicia'. The lower lawn is bordered by an old tiled cob wall, made of mud and chalk and now a rarity because of the difficulty of maintaining them.

No element contributes more to the endearing diversity of Heale House gardens than the Japanese water garden to the south of the river. Louis Greville brought home from diplomatic service in the East a complete Japanese tea-house, a miniature Nikko bridge, and four Japanese garden designers. The thatched tea-house and bright red bridge still stand, but the original, strictly formal and alien layout of the garden has given way to something more native and relaxed. It is a wild water garden, where ponds have been narrowed to form streams winding between trees of the original planting – maple, liquidambar, cercidiphyllum, magnolia, cherry – and where very un-Japanese splashes of colour are provided by primulas, scillas, bog arums, anemones, bluebells, and golden lysichitums.

▲ **A queen's home** When Anne Boleyn, queen to Henry VIII, died in 1536 by the executioner's sword, her family's fortunes declined – and Hever Castle, her childhood home, entered its Dark Age. Rescue came centuries later, in 1903, when William Waldorf Astor bought the castle and its 640 acres and embarked upon a massive restoration programme employing an army of workmen over four years.

Hever Castle Kent

Two different traditions rub shoulders at Hever. One is the romance of English history embodied in the moated castle; and the other is the American spirit of enterprise which inspired the present-day gardens.

Rising four square from a lily-strewn moat, Hever Castle dates from the 13th century. It was acquired by the famous Bullen family and is renowned as the childhood home of a daughter of the house – Anne Bullen (or Boleyn). After her execution, the little castle declined, so much so that by the turn of this century it was being leased out as a farmhouse. Bacons and hams hung from noble beams and potatoes lay heaped in the chambers when, in 1903, Mr William Waldorf Astor acquired the castle.

▲ **Roses in remembrance** The 'new' rose garden at Hever Castle is planted with
20th-century hybrid tea and floribunda roses. They soothe away the memories of
a bitter past and lend soft colours and delicate scents to porphyry columns and
ancient statues from other, more troubled and long vanished civilisations.
Elsewhere are grottoes, pools and falls, and the Anne Boleyn Orchard and Walk,
splendid in rich autumn colours.

▲ **Architect's groundplan** Clipped hedges of box and yew define the structured spaces of Lawrence Johnston's garden. An ordered framework underlies the informal planting schemes, echoing the principles of his architectural training. Hidcote is a garden of many compartments, each with its own planting style. There are plots agleam with water, for example, or, as here, heady with old-fashioned roses and enlivened with topiary sculptures.

Born into a fabulously wealthy family, William Astor had served as American Ambassador to Rome. And there he acquired a life-long love of European culture. He became a naturalised British subject and brought to Hever both wealth and energy. For four years over 1,000 workmen laboured to transform the grounds. A whole mock medieval village was erected near the castle to house his staff and friends. Acres of flood-prone meadowlands were drained, and a new outer moat was dug for the castle. Additionally, Astor had a 35-acre lake excavated to the east, into which the River Eden was diverted, and towering Scots pines were transplanted from Ashdown Forest, in Sussex.

As for the gardens proper, they were laid out in varied styles. Close to the castle, a Tudor atmosphere was recreated with formal courts, rose gardens and a croquet lawn. Also within the outer moat, Astor established a maze, and a topiary feature unique to Hever: this is the Chess Garden, in which golden yews have been clipped to form a set of giant pieces. Castle walls and pergolas in this area are hung with wisterias, clematis, honeysuckles and jasmines.

Very different in mood is the vast Italian Garden which William Astor had laid out some distance from his castle. The great walled plot lies beyond the outer moat, and was built to accommodate an enormous collection of antique statues and sculptures – Greek, Etruscan, Roman and Asiatic – which he had amassed in Italy. They stand today like weatherworn exhibits in some extraordinary roofless gallery: altars, sarcophagi, marbled busts and porphyry columns. The high south-facing wall of yellow sandstone stretches for more than 183m (200yd), and besides the sculptures in its niches, it shelters a wealth of shrubs and perennials: ceanothus, magnolias and purple-leaved vines, fragrant lavenders and verbenas. At the eastern end, an immense loggia, hung with wisterias, looks across a magnificent bay-fronted piazza which swells into the lake like the prow of a ship.

South of this great walled domain is a rose garden and a rock garden shaped from mighty slabs brought from Chiddingstone Causeway. Blue-flowering shrubs – rhododendrons and hydrangea varieties, for example – have given the area the name of Blue Corner.

Hidcote Manor Gloucestershire

Glance through any modern plant catalogue and you come upon products of this garden. There are popular 'Hidcote' varieties of lavenders and hypericums, for example. But the name is known equally through a whole approach to modern gardening which has become a byword of 20th-century taste. Uniting formal planning with informal

▲ **Cottage harmonies** Smooth thatch and immaculate topiary overlook the cloudy
profusion of a cottage garden enclosure. Designed as a collection of open-air
rooms, each with its own theme of colour or mood, Hidcote has been likened to a
series of cottage gardens. The airy exuberance of form and hue in informal
groups defied the rigid garden codes of the Victorians, and helped to establish the
more natural gardening style of the 20th century.

planting, it is known to gardeners everywhere as the Hidcote style.

The garden lies on the scarp of the Cotswolds some 4 miles from Chipping Campden. It covers, in reality, no more than 11 acres, but its fame – and complexity – are such that the physical scale means little. Hidcote is, above all, one of the most influential gardens ever laid out.

Hidcote was bought for Lawrence Johnston by his mother in 1907. At that time there was no garden at all; only one fine old cedar by the house and a clump of good beeches a little way off. Johnston terraced his undulating domain, which stands fairly high on the Cotswolds. The now-famous hedges were planted partly as shelter against chill winds and partly to provide open-air rooms for different effects, firm verticals to hold the eye, and pure ornament in themselves. Apart from conventional yews, Johnston made hedges of euonymus – the spindle tree – and others of combined evergreens. The most inspired creation was a 'tapestry' hedge composed of hornbeam, yew, holly and beech, which offers varied blendings of colour and texture throughout the year.

It was a time of turmoil in gardening style. A wealth of new plant material was pouring into Britain, and the Victorian habit of organising brigades of plants in severe bedding schemes was being challenged by gardeners such as William Robinson and Gertrude Jekyll. They wanted to see the exotics blend into the English scene; effects should recall the chance harmonies of natural woodlands and cottage gardens.

Lawrence Johnston absorbed their enthusiasm. In fact, Hidcote has been likened to a whole series of cottage gardens, and it proved an inspiration to contemporaries. Vita Sackville-West (creator of Sissinghurst), for example, noted how 'flowering shrubs mingled with roses, herbaceous plants with bulbous subjects, climbers scrambling over hedges, seedlings coming up wherever they have chosen to plant themselves'.

The central vista at Hidcote extends from the old cedar, through a cottage-style garden to a circle of lilacs and hellebores. It then enters a corridor of red-foliaged and red-flowered plants and leads on up steps to a pair of gazebos. Above is a walk flanked by hornbeams grown like hedges on stilts. The squared masses of foliage are borne on bare trunks in the formal French manner – a memorable and much photographed effect. The walk leads eventually to great wrought-iron gates and views across Shakespeare country.

This, though, is only the main axis. Among the diversity of small gardens leading off, you come upon repeated surprises. There is a paved fuchsia parterre enclosed by tapestry hedges. From it you enter a circular pool garden whose raised waters almost fill their enclosure, reflecting both sky and surrounding vegetation.

One enclosure, Mrs Winthrop's Garden, is named after Lawrence Johnston's mother and is planted in shades of blue and yellow. Another, the Pillar Garden, is dominated by solemn columnar yews; tree paeonies and rare old double tulips contribute to its miscellanies of colour.

For spare elegance, nothing could compete with the Theatre Lawn, a vast expanse of immaculate greensward which rises at one end to a turfed stage. From the platform rise two huge beeches, acting out their own silent drama.

The Hidcote style has been copied since Johnston's day, in plots both large and small. But like all great works of art, the garden survives as a masterpiece outside its context in time. You can come simply to admire the roses, for example, planted in abundance to bring colour and fragrance to the borders. Johnston favoured especially the old French varieties.

Modern hybrids were also included, blending into the colour schemes. There is, for example, a little area under the old cedar devoted to white-flowering and silvery plants; here the hybrid rose 'Grüss an Aachen' contributes its creamy blooms. Additionally, two yellow hybrids are especially associated with Hidcote. One is the climber 'Lawrence Johnston', named after the owner by a French hybridist. The other is 'Hidcote Gold', a robust bush rose with fern-like leaves, which was raised in the garden itself in 1948.

The garden's own creations hold special interest. There is the 'Hidcote' hypericum, a popular evergreen shrub bearing bright yellow, saucer-shaped blooms. And there is the 'Hidcote' lavender, widely valued for its compact form and rich purple flowers. Additional delights include 'Hidcote' varieties of fuchsia, verbena, campanula and penstemon – all much prized and internationally known.

The garden has been managed by the National Trust since 1948, and its hybrids date chiefly from the period since Lawrence Johnston's death. But the Hidcote style, the tradition of aesthetic excellence which he established, these have remained enduring legacies of a garden-maker whose gifts amounted to genius.

Hodnet Hall Shropshire

Water is the theme of these 60 Shropshire acres, water tumbling in flights through informal woodlands and water dammed at different levels to form chains of pools and lakes on which glide stately and mysterious black swans. Yet, when the garden was started in 1922, Hodnet had no more than a muddy stream and marshy hollow. It was Brigadier A. G. W. Heber-Percy who, with

▲ **Hodnet Hall** Formal terraced gardens run down to a chain of lakes inhabited by black swans and carpets of water lilies. Majestic trees and plantings on the grand scale of acid-loving shrubs are the very essence of English country-garden style, magnificent in concept and less than a century old.

modern earth-moving equipment, contoured the lush, liquid vistas seen today.

A scenic Broad Walk runs along the south front of the Victorian house, and looks down to the main lake below. Beyond you can see a red-brick dovecote of 1656, and the views extend as far as the distant Long Mynd, Shropshire's strange lump of wild moorland. The panorama, like the pools, was brought into the garden by clearing many trees to open up the far horizon.

Hodnet's soil is lime-free, a stiff clay overlying red sandstone, and it favours acid-loving plants. Rhododendrons, azaleas, camellias and magnolias shock with colour in season. Thirsty hydrangeas have also been planted in masses, and enjoy fairly high rainfall and moist conditions. It is thought that the abundance of water has moderated the garden's temperature: the pools rarely freeze over, and mists rising from them tend to keep off severe frosts. The tender *Phygelius capensis*, or Cape figwort, of South Africa, is just one among many unusual shrubs which have profited, bearing its scarlet-lobed, yellow-throated blooms in late summer.

As might be expected, the margins of pools and streams abound with primulas, irises, astilbes and gunneras – moisture-loving denizens of damp places which have been planted in great drifts at Hodnet. The

white-petalled wake robin (*Trillium grandiflorum*) is conspicuous in many a shady nook, blooming in spring among the bluebells and kingcups which lend native enchantment to the scene.

Flowering cherries, lilacs and laburnums splash their colours in season, and for autumn warmth there are Japanese maples and berrying shrubs.

Inverewe Highlands

The headland lies at a latitude further north than Moscow's, in terrain strewn with peat hag and eroded rock. *Am Ploc Ard* – the old Gaelic name for the Inverewe peninsula – captures something of its former brutish austerity. It means the 'High Lump', aptly describing the mass of red Torridonian sandstone which forms the core. In this corner of Wester Ross the soil is acid and shallow, and for much of the year the area is exposed to the salt lash of vicious southwesterlies. Until 130 years ago, practically nothing grew there at all.

Yet today Inverewe is a paradise where Chusan palms and the tree ferns of Australia grow tall in the company of silvery eucalyptus, Moroccan broom and the giant Himalayan lily. In all, its 60 acres contain some 8,000 species of tree, flower and shrub drawn from both hemispheres of the globe. Inverewe is a man-made wonder, the invention of Osgood Mackenzie, who bought the property in 1862. But a compassionate Mother Nature has played her part too, contributing one asset without which the enterprise would have been impossible. This is the warm flow of the Gulf Stream, that kindly North Atlantic Drift which caresses Cornish headlands as well as the *Ploc Ard*.

Gale-torn, rock-strewn and thinly soiled, Inverewe may have been, but Mackenzie realised that it was relatively free from frost, the plant killer that destroys more readily in Kent than on Mackenzie's northern headland. In fact, in his book *A Hundred Years in the Highlands* (1922), the Scot was to claim that he could grow in the open air at Inverewe as many plants, and as good, as was possible at Kew under glass. And though the north-western climate may have worsened somewhat since his day, that claim remains largely true.

The first problem was to counter the gales and driving rain, and against them he planted an outer windbreak of Corsican and Scots pines. Within, thick hedges of *Rhododendron ponticum* were established, while many foreign and native trees contributed to the screen: a few *Sequoiadendron giganteum* from California, for example, and many common silver birches.

Additionally, soil was brought to the site in creels, the large wicker baskets used by Scottish fishermen, to improve the soggy carpet of black peat.

The official guide to Inverewe acknowledges that the garden does not lend itself to a formal conducted tour. Overall, the impression is of some luxuriant woodland jungle through which paths wind according to their own secret logic. Inverewe has been likened to 'some wild corner in Burma or northern China', an impression which owes much to the profusion of rhododendrons.

The garden profited by the 20th-century discovery of many larger-leaved varieties and one tremendous specimen of *Rhododendron protistum* was raised from seeds sent home by the Scotsman George Forrest. But they bloom in all shapes and sizes and the collection has been expanded over the years to include, for example, Exbury hybrid azaleas and plantings of the tender Maddenia group of rhododendrons, which are more usually grown under glass. There are remarkable camellias too, and the climate has proved ideal for the cultivation of New Zealand plants. Inverewe holds the National Collection of *Olearia*, *Brachyglottis*, and *Ourisia*. There is also a large collection of plants from the southern Alps.

Among the many richly lined pockets of interest, one is especially rewarding. This is an enclosure to the north-east of the garden, and some distance from the windswept shore. It is pleasingly known as Bambooselem after its sheltering plantations of bamboos, and

the centrepiece holds pride of place among all of Inverewe's denizens. This is a magnificent 12m (40ft) *Magnolia campbellii*, a plant of Himalayan origin whose flowers, borne on leafless branches, are always susceptible to frost. Inverewe's specimen, though, flowers safely almost every year in early April, bearing hundreds of great pink chalices 20cm (8in) across.

Grouped around in Bambooselem are scarcities culled from far and wide. There are hoherias from New Zealand, for example, and the climbing *Hydrangea petiolaris* from Japan. Chile's exotics are well represented here as elsewhere at Inverewe, and among them a rare *Gevuina avellana*, or Chilean hazel, is conspicuous for its lustrous green leaves and white flowers. In spring, Bambooselem is remarkable for its widespreading carpets of American trout lilies (*Etrythronium revolutum*).

Kew Royal Botanic Gardens
Greater London

It is Britain's great plant zoo, a 300-acre giant of a garden containing over 40,000

▲ **Tropical paradise** The barren hills on the far side of Loch Ewe are the measure of Osgood Mackenzie's achievement at Inverewe. Palms flourish and all manner of exotic flowering plants luxuriate in the garden he created by bringing soil and shelter to a spot that was once as barren as the hills across the water.

▲ **Exotic plunder** Sir Joseph Banks went round the world with Captain Cook, returning with thousands of plants then unknown in Britain. Later, as director of Kew, he sent more plant collectors to scour the Tropics. The treasures that they and their successors brought back were displayed at Kew.

species and varieties. At Kew you can see cacti and carnivorous plants, rare orchids and primeval trees, flowers in every shape and size, from the tiniest star-like alpine to the giant aquatics of the Amazon. Famed internationally as one of the finest botanic gardens in the world, Kew even requires its own station on the London Underground to accommodate the floods of visitors who come, like the plants, from the four corners of the earth.

Yet the Royal Botanic Gardens offer more than a collection of exhibits. In a complex history spanning more than two centuries, Kew has acquired temples and pagoda, woodland gardens and formal bedding schemes, tree-lined vistas and landscaped lake. This great national institution is also, more simply, a very beautiful garden.

Sir Joseph Banks, the botanist who accompanied Captain Cook on his first famous voyage of exploration in 1768-71, was one of the early directors. And he brought back from his travels many thousands of exotic specimens, notably from the Australian coast, where Botany Bay was named after its wealth of plants. 'Capability' Brown was among the head gardeners, ruling with such authority that even George III dared not quibble with his plans.

Kew Gardens were handed to the nation in 1841, and continued to expand both plant collections and acreage thereafter. And today some splendid landmarks testify to the expense that has been lavished upon them. There is the ten-storey, 49m (163ft) high Pagoda, for example, erected in 1761-2. This was designed for Princess Augusta by Sir William Chambers, a pioneer of Chinese taste. The magnificent Palm House is in part the work of Decimus Burton, who also designed the Temperate House. These and innumerable smaller monuments and plant houses make Kew fascinating for its garden architecture alone.

One of Kew's oldest inhabitants is a towering 23m (75ft) tall maidenhair tree (*Ginkgo biloba*), planted in 1762. Ginkgos are miraculous survivors from the primeval forests. Identified through fossil imprints, they are the sole representatives of a family of trees which flourished over 180 million years ago. The curious fan-shaped leaves have earned the tree its other name of maidenhair tree (after the maidenhair fern which the leaves resemble).

But this is a garden of remarkable specimens, descended from seeds culled from the Congo and Antarctica, from desert basin and high Himalayas. And many a tale is told of their discovery. The explorer Archibald Menzies, for example, was attending a banquet in Chile in 1794. He was handed some nuts for dessert and pocketed some odd-looking items. Menzies grew the nuts into seedlings which he presented to Kew – they became the first monkey puzzles ever seen in England.

▲ **Princess of Wales Conservatory** Opened in 1987, this tropical house is computer-controlled, with micro-climates to suit plants from different parts of the Southern Hemisphere. In the vast open grounds is Kew Palace itself, galleries with botanical paintings and a lake with an abundance of wildfowl. Numerous other attractions include formal rose gardens, a huge grass garden and the charming 17th century-style Queen's Garden with its pleached laburnum walk.

For specialist interest, Kew has extensive gardens devoted to azaleas, bamboos, heaths and many other groups of plants. There is a superb rock garden and even a walled cottage garden. But for the first-time visitor what fascinates above all are the great glasshouses – cool, tropical, humid or dry.

In the great Palm House, reopened in 1989 after much refurbishment, you discover a lost world of mysterious vegetation. The air in this glass-roofed jungle is loaded with warm, luxurious scents, and strange fleshy forms as well as more common types of palms greet the eye.

The Princess of Wales Conservatory, opened in 1987, is a tropical glasshouse in a wholly modern mould. Huge in capacity, to avoid overwhelming its Victorian surroundings it takes the form of a 'glazed hill' – low ridges of glass covering sunken displays. Photo-electric cells close blinds automatically when the sun becomes too bright, and heating, ventilation and humidity are computer-controlled. The plants of ten climatic zones flourish here, from the mangroves of tropical swamps to the weird *Welwitschia mirabilis*, which sucks moisture from deep within the arid Namib desert of south-west Africa.

Some of the most intriguing exhibits in the new conservatory are probably the carnivorous pitcher plants and Venus flytrap, and the giant water lily *Victoria amazonica*. In their two days of life its flowers turn from white to pink to purple, and its leaves, up to 1.8m (6ft) in diameter, float on the water like vast green trays.

In the Temperate House you come upon such oddities as the sausage tree (*Kigelia africana*) from East Africa.

The new Evolution House, opened in 1995, traces the evolution of plant life from the earliest algae to the multitude of present-day flowering plants. The fascinating story of plant evolution and its impact on the environment is illustrated in numerous exhibits of fossil remains and living plant materials found in a diversity of habitats.

▲ Preserved under glass Climates other than our own are recreated under airy structures of iron and glass. The Temperate House holds plants from countries only slightly warmer than Britain. Despite extensive repairs, it remains true to the original designs by Victorian architect Decimus Burton (below).

▲ Snow-bound at Kew Caught in a frozen web, the majestic Palm House at Kew was built in the 1840s, when it was the largest glasshouse in the world. In the 1980s it was extensively replanted and refurbished and now houses unfamiliar plants as well as bananas, pawpaws, cocoa and coffee trees.

▲ **Queen Victoria's water lily** Named in honour of Queen Victoria, the gigantic *Victoria amazonica* 'Longwood' needs hot-house treatment – and plenty of space. At Kew, it is housed in the Princess of Wales Conservatory, where the floating leaves can reach 1.8m (6ft) in diameter and with their upturned edges resemble enormous platters. The huge scented flowers open at dusk and change colour from creamy white through pink and rose to purple.

▲ **Victorian serenity** The gardens at Knightshayes Court, a large Gothic-style
Victorian house, have been developed during the second half of the 20th century.
The terraces near the house include a paved garden surrounded by a
battlemented hedge of dark green yews; within its shelters are planting schemes
of white, silver and pink to complement antique statuary and cisterns. On the
terrace below, topiary hounds race in full cry across the greensward.

Knightshayes Gardens Devon

As with old music-hall artistes, high-Victorian architecture has now been around long enough to achieve a place in the English heart, and even examples like Knightshayes Court, with its gargoyles, heavily mullioned windows and pious, carved inscriptions, now inspire more affection than astonishment. The house was built in the 1870s on a lovely site above the River Exe for Sir John Heathcoat-Amory. It now belongs to the National Trust.

As far as horticulture was concerned, Sir John seems to have been content with the conventions of his day. For much of the house's history, its gardens depended for effect upon labour-intensive Victorian formality – bowling green, terraces, a programme of bedding-out and seasonal colour. There were also some magnificent trees, left over from the garden of a Georgian house that had stood on the same site.

Many of the trees remain, including the largest Turkey oak in Britain, some huge beeches, Scots and Monterey pines, a handsomely shaped Wellingtonia and much fine topiary. So do the terraces, though their intricately patterned beds have been replaced by grassy walks. But for the most part the garden was revolutionised by the grandson of the builder – another Sir John – and his wife.

It was a lengthy and loving revolution that began shortly after the Second World War with the planting of shrubs, perennials and climbers about the terrace and the house. Later, among the yew battlements, an old paved garden was recreated, centred upon an ancient pair of stone benches acquired from the Bank of England's refurbishment and an 18th-century lead cistern from the Goldsmiths' Hall in London. The colour accent here is silvery or pale grey foliage with soft pink flowers to add a touch of warmth to the stone. Near by is what was once the bowling green. A lily pond was created in 1957 in which golden orfes now twitch an occasional fin. A weeping silver pear adds to the tranquillity of the scene, watched over by a Victorian sculpture of a bather.

This part of the garden is rounded off by an Alpine terrace, falling away to one of Knightshayes' most original concepts: the Garden in the Wood. Each year, from the late 1940s to the early 1970s, Sir John and Lady Amory brought a piece of woodland 'approximately the size of a tennis court' into the garden by thinning the trees and planting among them magnolias, azaleas, rhododendrons, paeonies, a host of flowering shrubs and masses of bulbs, as well as climbing roses that have been encouraged to clamber up among the branches. This enchantingly contrived wilderness now extends to over 30 acres with three outliers – Holly's Wood, Sir John's Wood and Michael's Wood, the last named after the head gardener, Michael Hickson.

Lanhydrock Cornwall

The best way to approach Lanhydrock House and Gardens is not by the obvious route from Bodmin, but by the road from Liskeard, which climbs up over the moors – and, suddenly, there it is, the entire 200-acre estate, laid out among the dark woods on the far bank of the Fowey, with the pale granite of the house peering round the shoulder of a hill. From this distance, some 2 miles off, the visitor can absorb the entire prospect: the twin wide ribbons of the famous sycamore and beech avenue, the smooth turf, the meticulously planned specimen trees and, in season, the glowing rhododendrons and magnolias. It is a scene of great peace, permanence and Englishness precisely reflecting the family that created it. They were the Robartes, beginning with Lord Robartes, a Parliamentarian general and statesman at the time of the Civil War.

The road plunges down the hill to an old bridge and then to a lodge gate and the avenue, whose sycamores were planted by the general in 1648, and are now coming to the end of their long lives. A line of beeches was added in the early 1800s and, as the sycamores succumbed, these, too, were replaced by beeches. Pricking the sky at the far end are the granite pinnacles of the delightful little gatehouse. The pinnacles are actually little stunted obelisks, each of which is topped by a ball. It is a motif that is repeated on the house, the garden walls and throughout the garden. Beyond the gatehouse, and in something of a contrast, is Lanhydrock itself, plain and perhaps severe.

The garden is unusually formal for Cornwall, a county that seems generally to prefer its great gardens to carry a hint of the wild moors. At Lanhydrock, 19th-century terraces are laid out around the house, and

▲ Pinnacles of fame
The formal gardens at Lanhydrock, now a National Trust property, are delineated by ball-topped obelisks and massive, close-trimmed Irish yew cones. A magnificent 17th-century bronze urn is the centrepiece in a spring bedding display edged with dwarf box.

▲ Colourwashed forest
The ancient forest of St Leonard glows with a foreign fire – the warm tints of flowering shrubs introduced from the Orient in the last century. Sir Edmund Loder built his woodland garden at Leonardslee around a chain of old hammer ponds. The rock garden (above), with its evergreen azaleas and dwarf conifers, is a photographer's paradise in May.

rose beds delineated by low box hedges in knot-garden style. Dotted about the smooth turf-like sentinels are 29 Irish yews which look as though they have been shaved with a freshly honed razor, so smooth are their lines. They are accompanied by some magnificent bronze urns, the work of Louis Ballin, goldsmith to Louis XIV. They once stood in the garden of the Château de Bagatelle, Queen Marie Antoinette's mansion in Paris.

Plant choice tends to be opulent, with a strong accent upon magnolias, whose varieties have been carefully chosen to extend the season for as long as possible. Some of these, like the *Magnolia grandiflora* that flowers in summer and autumn, stand by the house, but most are in the shrub and woodland garden that climbs up the slope behind the church. Some are of astonishing size, but are matched in their grandeur and glory of colour by rhododendrons, azaleas, camellias, hydrangeas and ornamental flowering fruit trees – crab apple, quince and cherry. Behind a curved yew hedge is a pretty little herbaceous garden of unusual combination, which features yuccas, green-flowering hellebores, paeonies, kniphofias and agapanthus. Over all is the backdrop of the Fowey Valley woods, through which a pair of beautiful walks have been carved.

Leonardslee West Sussex

The ancient Forest of St Leonard in Sussex owes its name to the saint who is said to have slain a dragon in the woods. And wherever blood fell from the dragon's wounds, lilies-of-the-valley are supposed to have sprung up; they grow wild in abundance among the native beeches and oaks.

But you could be excused for missing these traditional attractions at a first visit. Thick with exotica, the gardens burst in spring with the flamboyance of rhododendrons and azaleas, in autumn with the fires of countless rare trees. The kaleidoscope effects are magnified by reflections caught in the central chain of old hammer ponds.

The Georgian-style house at Leonardslee stands some 90m (300ft) above sea level, looking down on the woodland valley garden and out across rolling countryside to the South Downs beyond. Accumulations of leaf-mould have clothed the sandstone landscape around Leonardslee with a rich and fertile loam. Rhododendrons, azaleas, camellias and magnolias – all natural forest-dwellers – do exceptionally well in the lime-free soil.

The exotics came to Leonardslee after 1889, when Sir Edmund Loder first began planting the property. A keen naturalist and raveller, he personally dressed the native woodland over 30 years, employing no landscape designer. A wealth of flowering shrubs were just beginning to flood in from China, Japan and the Americas. They were, on the whole, creatures of the forests, where they found shade and moist leafy soil – their natural habitat; they tended to perish all too easily in an open English landscape.

Woodland gardening was the solution, and at his wife's family home, Leonardslee, he found the ideal location. He thinned the native trees while taking care not to destroy the valuable shelter they provided, or to mar the natural beauty of the setting.

Rhododendrons were Sir Edmund's passion, and they flourish today in infinite variety in the 100-acre gardens. In April and May especially, the woodlands glow with spectacular banks and furrows of luxuriance deriving from both wild Asiatic species and modern hybrids. Among them, pride of place is held by the crosses which commemorate the founder. Sir Edmund raised many hybrids in his garden, but none has won more acclaim than the 'Loderi'.

The 'Loderi' Rhododendrons were first raised at Leonardslee in 1901, by crossing *R. griffithianum* and *R. fortunei*. They have since proved invaluable to gardeners: vigorous, sweetly scented and with spectacular flowers in shades of pink and white. 'King George' is perhaps the most sumptuous of the strain. Other varieties include 'Pink Diamond', 'Sir Edmund' and 'Venus'.

The present owner, great-grandson of Sir Edmund Loder, maintains the property to the highest standard. The natural woodscape is enhanced with masses of colour and foliage, and you meet few artificial symmetries as you wander the winding paths.

Different areas have their own character. Camellias were a speciality of Sir Edmund, and of his grandson Sir Giles Loder. Many aged specimens grow in the sheltered parts of the valley, and one area was planted with hundreds of different varieties of *Camellia japonica*. Magnolias thrive, too, and *M. campbellii* is one of the largest in the country.

In the Dell, the snowdrop tree (*Halesia carolina*) is hung with delicate white bells, and gunneras flourish by the stream. At the bottom of the valley, paths follow and cross the seven lakes, where reflections of the azaleas provide breathtaking colour, particularly the views up Mossy Ghyll, a moist little ravine filled with fragrant yellow azaleas.

All around at Leonardslee are the great trees whose columnar trunks, leafy canopies and spires provide the essential architecture of the garden. Wallabies have been used for over 100 years to mow the grassy valley banks, and herds of fallow, sika and axis deer roam the parks.

The rhododendrons at Leonardslee are at their best from early April until June. Flowering trees and summer wildflowers provide interest until September. Then, as autumn arrives, the nyssas, amelanchiers, liquidambars and Japanese maples light up the dragon woods and burnish the pool chain with fire.

Levens Hall Cumbria

Some people feel uneasy about topiary, thinking, like Joseph Addison, that they 'would rather look upon a tree in all its luxuriancy and diffusion of boughs and branches than when it is thus cut into a mathematical figure'. Addison was writing, though, at the beginning of the 18th century, when the Landscape Movement was making its first stirrings, and topiary was consequently about to go through one of its periods of unpopularity. Nevertheless, the art has been around for a considerable time; the Romans clipped box and bay into geometrical shapes in their neat gardens, while *topiarius* was their term for 'gardener'.

The topiary at Levens Hall in maturity presents one of the most fantastical gardening collections in the country. There are cones and corkscrews, circles, pyramids and peacocks, a group called 'Queen Elizabeth and her Maids of Honour', another known as 'Coach and Horses', and all made of dark green or gold box or yews, some of which have grown to great size. These giants are

▼ **Clipped imagination**
Since the 17th century, succeeding generations of gardeners at Levens Hall have expressed their artistic visions in topiary – the trim and fanciful shapes of clipped box and yew. Waves of spring and summer bedding plants lap at the walls of their box-edged beds, isolated highlights of colour in a sea of green.

surrounded by little lawns and beds, each bordered by tiny box hedges that are as meticulously shorn as their 6m (20ft) high neighbours. The beds are filled with the traditional flowers of the English spring and summer garden, and the outside borders with swathes of pink and white roses. Looming benignly over all is the old stone house of Levens, whose youngest part dates from about 1580, and whose oldest is probably part of a medieval pele tower.

Though the topiary garden is the best-known feature of Levens, it is only part of a unified plan of park and formal garden that was unusual in its years of conception – the last and first decades of the 17th and 18th centuries – and is now a unique survival. As with most great survivals, it is the result of a happy blending of circumstances. It all began with the 'Glorious Revolution' of 1688, when James II was deposed and William of Orange was made king in his stead. At the same time, the ousted monarch's Keeper of the Privy Purse and close friend Colonel James Grahme (or Graham) came to the prudent conclusion that it was time to retire from public life and tend to his garden at far-off Levens Hall. He was accompanied by another casualty of the change of regime, the ex-royal gardener Guillaume Beaumont, one of the most brilliant horticulturists of his day. Together, they transformed the estate.

The results of their labours can still be seen, not only in the topiary garden but in the other formal plantings as well, including a kind of gigantic cartwheel of clipped beech. The spokes are paths, one of which runs out to the park, where it seemingly joins up with an avenue of trees. In fact the two are separated by a ha-ha, or sunken wall, a device that prevents livestock from straying into the garden, yet permits the impression, from the house at least, that park and garden are one.

A mile-long avenue of oaks has been planted along the valley of the Kent, leading the eye to a gorge that squeezes the lovely river almost to a torrent, and clumps of trees have been established to emphasise different features in the landscape. Such ideas were innovations in the 1690s and helped to make Levens a unique example not only of its period but of an important halfway house in garden design.

Lingholm Cumbria

Beatrix Potter and her family spent summer holidays at Lingholm in the late 1890s, where she wrote *Squirrel Nutkin*, and used the garden, woods and natural world around her as subjects for her many sketches.

However, at Lingholm it is gardening on the grand scale. The outlook is to the wide sweep of Derwent Water and to the bold hills beyond, while the acid, peaty soil and reasonable protection from the most savage of the east winds makes it the perfect setting for one of the most extensive rhododendron collections in Britain.

It all started over 60 years ago with plantings in the surrounding woods, and this casual arrangement continues still. Rhododendrons and azaleas have been permitted to climb and expand to their full height and girth, often at some distance from the paths. Visitors who see a gleam of colour through the trees should explore farther; some of the loveliest shrubs have been established quite deep in the woods.

Spring is a good time to come to Lingholm, when the grass in the old orchard can hardly be seen for daffodils, and the rhododendrons and azaleas are beginning their cycle of colour. Nevertheless, species and hybrids have been carefully selected to extend the flowering season as long as possible. Early blooming plants may be flowering in January in a good season, while the white *Rhododendron auriculatum* is still in bloom in August. Several species, such as the white-and-pink *R. fortunei discolor* and the yellow *R. brachyanthum* emerge in June and July. Meconopsis and primulas are other highlights of spring and early summer. New and increased planting schemes have ensured extended colour throughout the season, with herbaceous borders and hydrangeas, culminating with gentians and a riot of superb autumn colours. Happily, all plants are well labelled.

Logan Botanic Gardens
Dumfries and Galloway

Even if you are familiar with the Gulf Stream's benevolent effect on Scotland's west-coast gardens, Logan may come as something of a shock. Enter the walled enclosure and you immediately meet a number of towering cordylines – the cabbage palms of New Zealand – whose long trunks soar high overhead to burst like rockets in explosions of spiked foliage.

Logan lies about halfway down the Rhins of Galloway, a narrow peninsula joined to the mainland by a slender neck of land. It cuts like a ploughshare into the Irish Sea and is the southernmost part of Scotland, washed on three sides by the warm Atlantic Drift. Temperatures are kindly and frosts are unusual.

The McDoualls of Logan owned the land from the 12th to the 20th centuries. The ruins of their medieval castle overlook the gardens from the west, while many sheltering walls of brick and stone have long screened plots from the wind. But it was not until the late 19th century, when subtropical gardening 'took off' on the west coast of Scotland, that Logan's potential began to be exploited.

James and Agnes McDouall, and their

sons Kenneth and Douglas, assembled plants from the world over. And their work was continued by the late Mr R. Olaf Hambro, who owned the house and garden for ten years. In 1969, management of the gardens passed to the Royal Botanic Garden at Edinburgh.

The complex of old walled gardens forms the core of the design, with extensive woodlands to south and west. And you get an early indication of what is to come in approaching by a stepped avenue of Chusan palms (*Trachycarpus fortunei*). These are the hardiest of all the true palms grown in the British Isles.

Australasian tree ferns have also proved successful at Logan. Resembling triffids with their broad-spread sheaves of fronds, they are natives of tropical rainforests, and rarely seen in Britain outside heated glasshouses. Two species, though, flourish in the open at Logan: *Dicksonia fibrosa* and *D. antarctica*.

While ferns, palms and cordylines confer their surreal forms on the gardens, a wealth of tender shrubs and flowers lend their hues. For conspicuous colour, the scarlet Chilean fire bush (*Embothrium coccineum lanceolatum*) probably holds pride of place, burning so fiercely in May that you feel it could really set light to its neighbours. But there are other competitors: a climbing berberidopsis, also from Chile, hung with rich red in late summer; and a sensational rata from New Zealand which flares with colour through its crimson stamens.

If your taste is for cooler colour temperatures, you might explore the nearby Water and Tree Fern Garden. In May it is remarkable for its drifts of *Meconopsis grandis*, a majestic, poppy-like plant from the Himalayas whose lovely blue flowers are borne waist high on their stems; and the white lily of the Nile (*Zantedeschia aethiopica*) contributes its white arum spathes in early summer. At Logan, you can explore the whole colour spectrum; there is even an evergreen shrub from New Zealand, *Pseudopanax laetus*, whose nectar-rich flowers are near-black.

Logan is renowned for its 11 separate gardens, one maintained as a gunnera bog and crowded with these Brazilian giants. Another is outstanding for its historic interest. This is the Peat Garden, laid out by Kenneth and Douglas McDouall in terraced banks of local peat to provide beds for dwarf rhododendrons.

London, Chelsea Physic Garden

Almost next door to the Royal Hospital with its tall cupola and scarlet-coated Pensioners, in the statelier part of Chelsea, is the lovely but near-invisible Physic Garden. How a

4-acre garden manages to be so self-effacing in this busy part of the capital is something of a mystery, but there it is. It is shielded from the Embankment's traffic flow by tall iron railings close-backed by trees, and on the other sides by high walls.

The Chelsea Physic Garden was founded in 1673 by the Worshipful Society of Apothecaries, and in appearance and spirit it remains a 17th-century garden to this day. The 'Physic' in its title was, and is, used in the older sense, meaning the healing acts of plant-based medicine.

Consequently, a vast collection of plants was assembled at the garden, growing ever larger as new lands were discovered and new species were brought back by explorers. Then, in 1712, Dr (later Sir) Hans Sloane purchased the Manor of Chelsea, so becoming the garden's landlord. Ten years later he let the site to the society at a rent of £5 a year in perpetuity, and at the same time suggested the appointment of Philip Miller as head gardener. Miller held the post for half a century, during which time Chelsea became the finest botanic garden in Europe. Miller himself published his great *Dictionary of Gardening*, whose 8th edition employed, for the first time, the Linnaean

▲ **Hidden healing** Tucked away from London's traffic, behind high brick walls, the Chelsea Physic Garden guards its healing herbs and rare plants. A statue of Sir Hans Sloane presides over the garden he rented, from 1722 in perpetuity, to the Worshipful Society of Apothecaries. Plants gathered for their medicinal, agricultural or botanical interest have established a world of quiet dignity in the heart of a teeming city.

▲ Midsummer reverie
The air lies drugged and still over Queen Mary's Garden, intoxicating with the perfume of 40,000 roses. Rank upon rank of fragrant blooms parade through the summer months, massed around the lawns, avenue and lake. This lovely garden, large rockery and an open air theatre lie within the vast expanse of Regent's Park – among the attractive 19th-century villas of the Inner Circle.

greenhouse, quiet and cool, where fern sprout from mossy rocks. Embraced withir the lawns is a parade of dozens of beds, al extremely attractive at most times of th year. There are corners devoted to the plant of Australia, South Africa and parts of th United States, and beds ablaze with paeonies In the medicinal quarter, more soberly hue plants illustrate the history of medicine, an groups of the more familiar culinary herbs like rosemary, thyme, fennel and sage mingl their scents in one entrancing bouquet witl the perfumery plants, such as lemon verbe na, lily-of-the-valley, lavender, apothecary' rose (rose of Lancaster) and nutmeg-scente pelargonium.

Bringing the Physic Garden right up t date is a new and unique Garden of Worl Medicine displaying plants used medicinall in Chinese and Ayurvedic (Hindu) medicin and by many of the world's tribal an indigenous peoples.

London, Queen Mary's Garden

Kensington Gardens has its magic, mos especially on autumn evenings when mist haloed lights blackly silhouette the trees but for north Londoners at least there i nowhere at all like Regent's Park. Ken Woo and Hampstead Heath are impressive, 'Capability' Brown contrived landscap running into a real wilderness. But Regent' Park is all that a city park should be, an gives a glimpse too, in its surroundin architecture, of what all of London could b if the world had its time over again. To th south there is the incredible colonnade elegance of the Nash terraces, like giganti wedding cakes in white-and-blue icin sugar. Then, to the north, there is the Zoc with its browny-yellow concrete crags – th Mappin Terraces, built for mountain goats from behind which, in summer dawns, ther comes the thunderous roar of lions to shak the stucco of Primrose Hill and St John' Wood. In between, there is the Broad Wal and the Avenue Gardens, newly restored t Nesfield's designs of 1863, and at the hear of the park there lies the Inner Circle an Queen Mary's Garden.

The Inner Circle consists of pretty earl 19th-century villas, private residences anc in their midst, a vast pair of black-and-gil wrought-iron gates that were presented i 1935 by Sigismund Goetze, a German artis who lived in the area, to mark the Silve Jubilee of King George V and his consor Queen Mary. The exquisite little par beyond was also named in Queen Mary honour when it was taken over by the Roya Parks Department from the Royal Botanica Society, some three years earlier.

The garden has many attractive feature: but in high summer the ones that first gree

system of plant naming evolved by the Swedish botanist Count von Linné – still in international use today.

Botanical milestones mark the garden's annals. Chelsea sent the cotton seeds to found the staple crop of the American colony of Georgia, and built one of the first rock gardens in Britain, partly from old stones taken from the Tower of London. Dr Ward, Master of the Apothecaries in the 1850s, designed a plant travelling case – in effect, a small, sealed greenhouse – that transported bananas from China to Fiji, tea from Shanghai to India, and rubber from Brazil to Malaya, so altering the economies of nations. Nowhere on Earth can there be four more fruitful acres.

Such a record should make the Physic Garden awesome, but indeed it is not. Rather, it is a peaceful place to stroll in, and in which to enjoy its infinite variety. (This happy odyssey is available to the public, on Wednesday and Sunday afternoons from April to October, and during the duration of the Chelsea Flower Show.)

The first thing to strike the visitor will probably be the tender specimens which flourish in the almost Mediterranean micro-climate, including a 9m (30ft) tall olive tree. It manages to produce pounds of fruit and is the largest olive grown outdoors in Britain.

Formal gravel paths lead to such unex-pected corners as The Fernery, a small he senses are the blaze and near-visible perfume of 40,000 rose bushes. They are arranged in large beds down an avenue, about the lake and out into the lawns. As a general rule, each bed is devoted to a single variety and the plants crowded closely together to provide a showing of maximum grandeur. The roses are superbly tended, so that the beds blaze anew as each flowering peak is reached. Throughout the season, it is possible to walk each day through the garden and never see quite the same display twice. Many of the varieties shown are old friends, but the place is also a testing ground for new ones.

Roses are the garden's reasons for existence, but it has many other attractions, not least its sense of smallness and cosiness within the wide spaces of the surrounding park. There are winding paths, a rock garden of Far Eastern aspect and smothered with alpines, a couple of vaguely classical statues, a lily pond, fossilised tree trunks and wildfowl of remarkable tameness.

Lyme Park Cheshire

What a strange cold place it is,' complained a 17th-century gardener. The reason is easy enough to explain: set on the wild edge of the Peak District well above the fertile Cheshire plain, Lyme Park rises to an eleva-

tion of 372m (1,220ft) above sea level. The splendid mansion stands at a higher altitude than any other historic house in England and, with its classical façade, cultured lawns and parterres is deliciously improbable against the backdrop of rugged moorland.

The Leghs of Lyme occupied the site for exactly 600 years until 1946, when the estate was given to the National Trust. The property covers over 1,300 acres and was famed in Tudor times for its breed of mastiffs. Gardening seems to have flourished in the 17th century, when great efforts were made to get apples to prosper. It was clearly a struggle though; the same gardener who noted the cold also complained that 'he cannot have things soe early as his neighbours'. Fruiting and flowering were delayed, then as now, by the challenging climate and persistent cloud cover.

Yet the nurture of plants has succeeded at Lyme Hall, as a visit will amply illustrate. The 15-acre gardens seen today are chiefly the work of the first Lord Newton, who contoured the terraces in the late 19th century. One legacy of his time is a Dutch Garden laid out on a parterre surrounding a fountain pool. You can look down from above on the ornate beds where over 12,000 bulbs contribute to a dazzling springtime display. In summer, no fewer than 15,000 plants are bedded out; the display changes from year to year but it always includes *Penstemon*

◄ **Oasis of elegance** The Palladian mansion of Lyme Hall remains serenely indifferent to the encroaching scrub of Cheshire's moors. The formal gardens around the house are largely the work of the 1st Baron Newton (above), who countered the surrounding wilderness with acres of cool lawns and elaborate parterres. Behind the protective walls of the Dutch Garden, spring and summer patterns are drawn out with thousands of colourful bedding plants – demonstrating the abundance of artifice in defiance of the barren hills.

▲ **Masterpiece in iron**
Scrolls, leaves, fruit and crescent moons embellish the wrought-iron pergola in the gardens of Melbourne Hall. Known as 'The Birdcage', it spans a long walk lined with ancient yews and is the work of Robert Bakewell, the 18th-century artist in iron.

'Rubiconda', which was developed at Lyme in the early 1900s. Other regulars include begonias, golden fuchsias, verbenas, heliotropes and scarlet lances of *Lobelia cardinalis*.

Lord Newton also built the conservatory to the east of the house. It is fronted by panel beds as vivid as those in the Dutch Garden and today shelters two venerable camellias. A rose garden and herbaceous borders are other formal features, while a tumbling stream gushes down from the moors into a lake south of the house. It has carved a ravine, now informally planted with flowering shrubs and aquatics. In spring, primulas, rhododendrons and azaleas splash their colours amid the evergreens, while hydrangeas and hypericums follow in summer. The wild garden is scarcely 'wild' by the standards of the high moors, but provides a pleasing counterpoint to the sophistication of the Palladian mansion.

Melbourne Hall Derbyshire

This is a garden of light and shade. Melbourne's 16 acres form a lucid composition of broad sunny lawns and carefully aligned vistas executed in the manner of the early 18th century. But to one side there runs a sombre yew tunnel, 183m (200yd) long and enclosed by centuries-old trees.

And as if to demonstrate how light and shade may be united, there is an exquisite wrought-iron pergola, a masterpiece of repoussé work which frames both the sky and the view back to the house with the utmost delicacy and grace. It was designed by Robert Bakewell, a celebrated ironsmith of the early 18th century, who lived and worked at Melbourne for many years.

Melbourne Hall itself is a greystone building constructed during the 16th century and much enlarged in 1721 by Thomas Coke, Vice-Chamberlain to Queen Anne. It was Coke, too, who had the gardens laid out in the French style associated with André Le Nôtre, head gardener to Louis XIV. The designer was an Englishman, Henry Wise, who was much influenced by the French master's work. Melbourne, like Versailles, was to be graced with formal symmetries of fountains, lawns and tree-lined vistas – albeit on a smaller scale.

Remarkably few examples remain in Britain of this once very popular style. Most were swept away in the landscaping fervour of the 18th century, and Melbourne is perhaps the finest of the survivors. Only Bramham Park in Yorkshire competes as a period piece.

The central vista leads the eye from the east front of the house, between shelving, rectangular lawns and down to a formal lake known as the Great Basin. Side vistas

▲ **The Cheshire Plains** In the foothills of the Pennines nestles one of the National Trust's most spectacular gardens. Set in 1,300 acres of parkland, the 15-acre formal gardens at Lyme Park include a Dutch-style parterre where intricate geometric beds surround a large fountain pool. Picked out in green and golden dwarf box, the beds are infilled with summer bedding plants in a tapestry of vivid colours that are painted afresh each year.

▲ **Great Basin** The large lake at Melbourne Hall, known as the Great Basin, is part of the original design by Henry Wise, royal gardener under William III, Queen Anne and George I. The gardens are laid out in the style of Le Nôtre, landscapist of Versailles, with ruler-straight avenues of ancient trees and vistas of exquisite statuary. A series of terraces runs down from the house to the lake, at the far end of which is Robert Bakewell's 'birdcage' pergola.

Melbourne Hall Dating from the 16th century and much developed by Sir Thomas Coke early in the 18th century, Melbourne Hall was the birthplace of Lord Melbourne in 1779. As Home Secretary he was responsible for the deportation of the Tolpuddle Martyrs. The hall still looks much as it does in this view of 1875.

across the main axis, and there is a second area which stretches at right-angles away to the south. Here venerable avenues extend between flanking limes and walls of yew hedging, converging at radial points. The whole was composed with set-square and compass, and at key intersections fountain pools and statuary focus the eye. There are many delightful cherubs and mythological features executed by the 18th-century Dutch sculptor Jan van Ost (known in Britain as John Nost). Among his ornaments, the most imposing is a majestic lead urn representing *The Four Seasons*, which look out as boldly as ships' figureheads from their massive decorative vessel.

Running back down the south side of the garden there is the dark yew tunnel. It is older than the rest of the garden, and a path of mystery which is faintly disquieting to walk. No one knows quite when the yews were planted, though the records show that they were once supported by a wooden frame which had already decayed by 1726 and had to be removed. The trunks of the aged trees lean and bend, tangles of branches jut weirdly at awkward angles. You could not ask for a greater contrast to the sunlit composition whose refined symmetries extend to the north.

Ness Gardens Cheshire

If you think heather blooms only in shades of purple, then a visit to Ness will amaze you. Its heather garden is famous throughout Britain, and in high season becomes one vast rumpled patchwork of colour – whites, blush pinks and deep, fiery reds all mingling with dark green and burnished-gold foliage. The whole glorious display unfolds in late summer and early autumn – and derives from *Calluna vulgaris*, the common ling or moorland heather.

The Merseyside area, long a centre of transatlantic shipping, might at first seem to hold little interest for the gardener. Yet the region has strong horticultural traditions in which Liverpool University's Botanic Gardens at Ness hold pride of place. They are situated on the Wirral peninsula, above the estuary of the River Dee, which bounds the headland to the south.

Ness began as the private garden of a very remarkable man. Arthur Kilpin Bulley, who built the house in 1898, started out as a Liverpool cotton broker with an abiding passion for gardening. He founded the

famous seed and plant firm of Bees Ltd, and to obtain foreign specimens he corresponded with both businessmen and missionaries abroad. The initial experiments with imported seeds were disappointing. 'Ness', said his wife, 'could claim to possess the best international collection of dandelions.'

But Bulley persevered, eventually hiring a young Scotsman named George Forrest to seek seeds in western China. Bulley financed the great plant hunter's first two expeditions of 1904 and 1910; in 1911 he was to launch the equally renowned F. Kingdon Ward on his career. The Bees seed catalogue became ever more exotic as successive expeditions, which Bulley helped to fund, returned with their botanic treasures. And the whole gardening world profited.

At Ness, several of Bulley's original plantings may still be seen today. Shelterbelts of trees – poplars, holm oaks and Scots pines – screen the gardens from gales, while a fine azalea border, planted in 1900, is stocked with venerable specimens. In the extensive collection of rhododendrons is *R. roxieanum*, grown from seeds sent from China by George Forrest.

Among the older plantings, another Forrest original holds pride of place at Ness. This is a *Pieris formosa* 'Forrestii', an evergreen shrub whose name commemorates its discoverer. Ness's specimen stood 3.6m (12ft) high until the hard winter of 1962-3,

▲ **Heather tapestry** The gently sloping rock garden at Ness, part of University of Liverpool Botanic Gardens, becomes a brilliant patchwork of colour in late summer. Lings and heaths unfold a dazzling display of white, pink, crimson and purple blooms, offset by the greens, russets and golds of the foliage.

when it was cut right back to ground level. Undaunted, the shrub has returned almost to its previous proportions. It is spectacular for its youthful foliage of flaming scarlet and, in spring, while those fires are still flickering, it becomes quite astonishing. Hosts of drooping white panicles come into bloom, like snowfalls on a burning bush.

Arthur Bulley died in 1942, and his garden suffered neglect during the war years. Much that is seen today has been achieved since 1948, when his daughter generously presented the whole estate to Liverpool University for a botanic garden. A condition of her gift, though, was that a specified area of ornamental ground should be kept open to the public. Ness, then, is young for a botanic garden. Though much changed and expanded since Bulley's day, it retains the character of a private garden.

The new features at Ness include herb and terrace gardens, herbaceous borders and a good collection of roses laid out to show their development from European and Far Eastern ancestry. A young arboretum is interesting for its specimens of *Betula jacquemontii*, the purest of the white-stemmed birches in cultivation – the true albino of the family. Arthur Bulley's original rock garden has been almost entirely remade, but includes among its colourful attractions of early summer the *Primula bulleyana*. Orange-budded and opening to gold, it was collected by Forrest and named after the owner.

The more strictly scientific enterprises include a native plant garden, whose specimens have all been raised by seeds or cuttings from plants growing wild in Britain. Here you can see the purple *Primula scotica*, unique to Scotland in its wild state, the rare blue *Gentiana verna* of England and a white tufted saxifrage (*Saxifraga caespitosa*) culled from the slopes of Snowdonia. Seeds from these and many other scarcities are supplied to the Seed Bank at Kew – and also replanted in their native habitats.

Above all, the heather garden at Ness is outstanding, its plants quilting a slope above the Dee in their thousands. The tender tree heath (*Erica* x *veitchii*) is among the first to flower in spring, its white blooms borne freely in long racemes. Month by month the garden quickens with colour until the grand set-piece of late summer and early autumn. It is then that *Calluna vulgaris* reveals its rainbow hues. A vast range of cultivars is represented: the white 'Alba Plena', silvery-pink 'Elsie Purnell', the more deeply rouged 'Peter Sparkes' and the crimson 'Darkness' are among the most conspicuous. The tones of golden-leaved ericas contribute to the fantastic patchwork, and several of the callunas themselves have bright foliage. There is 'Robert Chapman', for example, which flowers in soft purple and whose leaves change with the seasons from gold in spring, through orange to the red of glowing embers in mid winter. Sprawling in tufted drifts down the slopes the whole tribe lights its setting with vivid, improbable radiance.

Newby Hall North Yorkshire

To view herbaceous borders conceived on the grand scale you could do no better than visit Newby Hall. The central axis of its gardens is a grass walk 320m (350yd) long extending from an Adam house to a landing stage by the River Ure. This broad green gangway is framed on either side by immense drifts and swells of flower and foliage, backed by clipped hedges of yew.

Newby Hall has been the home of the Compton family since 1748, when an ancestor, William Weddell, bought it through a legacy from his uncle. Robert Adam was commissioned to make extensive alterations to the building, which has survived as one of the finest in a county noted for its historic houses. The superb gardens, though, are almost entirely of this century. The late Major Edward Compton, father of the present owner, was responsible for their design. 'I found I had inherited an exceptionally beautiful home,' he said, 'but no garden to speak of – a lovely picture but no frame.'

Beginning in 1923, Major Compton spent over 50 years in developing his 25 acres to provide the required frame. Much skill and taste were needed to create a setting worthy of the elegance of the house. And these qualities the owner had in abundance. He was greatly influenced in his approach by Lawrence Johnston's innovations at Hidcote in the Cotswolds. Newby, too, was to be laid out with a sound formal structure, but planted informally to soften the lines of the design. The great walk with its double herbaceous borders was Major Compton's first creation, planned to connect the south front of the house with the river below, and to form a main axis for the garden. It begins and ends with stone balustraded terraces.

Off the main axis he planned a series of formal gardens, each to show a particular season's plants at their best. First came Sylvia's garden, named after his wife, a sunken garden with early flowering plants which are at their best in April and May. Then came the rose garden, converted from a grass tennis court. This he filled with June-flowering old-fashioned roses – Albas, Damasks, Gallicas and Mosses – the whole surrounded by a copper-beech hedge. An excellent foil for delicate rose colours.

Next came the July garden for high summer; then the famous double borders for late summer and, finally, the autumn garden filled with a host of rewarding plants for the tail end of the season. The gardens he designed are a major contribution to 20th-century gardening.

▲ **Golden tunnel** In early summer, golden chains of *Laburnum* x *watereri* 'Vossii' droop from a series of arches supported on mellow stone pillars. The walkway leads from a Victorian waterfall, splashing into peaceful pools, to the enchanting rose garden at Newby Hall. Filled with old-fashioned roses, it is underplanted in blue – baptisias, hebes and herbaceous clematis in profusion – an unforgettable sight in June.

When the present owners, Mr and Mrs Robin Compton, came to Newby in 1977 they found a large and magnificent garden in a sad state of neglect. Renovation and simplification were vitally required – a daunting task has been successfully tackled over the succeeding years.

To enable visitors to see the best of Newby, whenever they come, three separate leaflets have been written for spring, summer and autumn with an arrowed map. The suggested walks differ according to season, but their main features are the same – starting with Sylvia's garden, now completely replanted by Mrs Robin Compton with her favourite plants, many to be at their best in the spring. An old Byzantine corn grinder holds the eye at the centre, while many low-growing plants cushion its paving and beds. The lady tulip (*Tulipa clusiana*), white with pink streaks, is especially attractive in April. Other plants have been carefully sited for foliage effects throughout the year; they include artemisias, salvias and that silver gem *Chrysanthemum haradjanii*.

The walk continues to the rock garden planted by the famous Ellen Willmott at the turn of the century, enormous in scale and full of wild charm. It skirts a waterfall and winds beneath a curving laburnum pergola to the rose garden, one of the highlights of summer. From the rose garden, the walk continues to the great borders. Many old favourite herbaceous plants are to be found here, but roses, too, have been introduced to give variation in height and form.

Cross the great central vista of the herbaceous borders and you come to a garden of equal proportions to the rose garden. This is the autumn garden, laid out just before the Second World War on the site of an old croquet lawn. When the evenings begin to draw in, this is a riot of colour with buddleias, fuchsias, hydrangeas and many unusual and late flowering salvias – protected all round by a wattle fence over which climbers romp; clematis give colour and honeysuckles lay their scents on the air.

The walk ends with the orchard garden, a sun trap surrounding apple trees, and the tropical garden, so called because it is filled with plants whose leaves and habits resemble those thriving under tropical conditions. Last but not least is the white garden, which was planted in 1980 by Mrs Compton with her favourite white plants.

▲ **Poet's home** The ruined cloisters of Newstead Abbey, where the poet Byron played as a boy, may have helped inspire his love of the romantic.

Newstead Abbey
Nottinghamshire

Some time in the 12th century, a community of Augustinian friars set up a priory in a corner of Sherwood Forest called Newstead. They remained there for almost 400 years, until Henry VIII dissolved the monasteries in the 1530s. It was then rebuilt as a country mansion which served many generations of the Byron family. The last of these wa the romantic poet George Gordon, 6th Lor Byron – 'mad, bad and dangerous to know as he was once described.

He loved the ruined cloisters, especiall the battlements through which the 'hollov winds' whistled. Associations with th poet's life and work are to be found al around the 25-acre gardens and 300 acres c

▲ Newstead Abbey in the 19th century.

▲ **Eastern touch** Byron, with his taste for the exotic, would surely have approved of the Japanese Garden planted a century after his death.

surrounding parkland. The Upper Lake, for example, is one of several waters fed by the River Lean which contribute to Newstead's beauty. It is commemorated in the epic poem *Don Juan* as a place of lucid depth, a haunt of nestling wildfowl where:

The woods sloped downwards to its brink
And stood with their green faces fixed upon
The flood.

In the smooth lawns south from the house is the stump of an oak tree planted by Byron when he first inherited the estate (at

he age of ten) in 1798. It never prospered
much in the acid, sandy soil. East of the
building you can see the tomb of Boatswain,
Byron's beloved Newfoundland dog which
died of rabies and is commemorated in the
poet's inscription as the only true friend he
ever knew.

But there are much older echoes at
Newstead. You approach the priory gates by
the huge Pilgrim Oak, dating from the time
of the friars. A medieval fishpond bordered
by dark and ancient yews was used by the
brethren for breeding carp. From it, a
narrow tunnel leads to the Eagle Pond, so
named because the friars are said to have
thrown an eagle-shaped brass lectern into it
at the time of the Dissolution. It is a beautiful rectangle of water, edged by terraced
banks awash with ferns.

The poet Byron was not the only member
of his family to leave his mark on the
gardens. His uncle, from whom he inherited
the estate, had been known as the Wicked
Lord Byron after an assortment of infamies
which culminated in his trial for the murder
of a neighbour. Convicted only of man-
slaughter, he retired to Newstead, where he
continued in his depredations. He brutalised
his wife, let the house fall to ruin, and felled
trees all around it simply to spite his son.
But the Wicked Lord did not only destroy.
His enduring monuments include two little
mock forts on the Upper Lake where he
used to hold sham naval battles with his
brother (an admiral known as Foul Weather
Jack). He also set up statues of a male and
female satyr in a dark grove at Newstead,
which superstitious villagers named Devil's
Wood. The grove has gone, but the statues
still stand, looking rather less satanic on
green turf.

The poet was forced by debts to sell the
estate in 1817, and several notable features
date from later years. Most of the trees near
the house are of fairly recent origin; among
them you can see an especially fine example
of *Davidia involucrata*, the pocket handkerchief tree from China.

The great Garden Lake, sweeping south
of the house, also dates from a time after the
Byron connection was broken. The outflow
of water forms a cascade which flows down
to the Japanese Garden, complete with tea
house. Other Victorian and 20th-century
features include rock, heather and iris gardens. Among the most recent introductions
is a rose garden laid out in 1965 where the
old kitchen garden had been. Its southern
border is devoted to historical and shrub
roses where the holy rose (*Rosa sancta*) is a
conspicuous attraction. This is a plant of
immense antiquity, whose large, single pink
blooms delight the visitor as they did the
Egyptians some 8,000 years ago. The rose
makes a fitting flower for the old priory –
even if it is rather less appropriate to the
colourful family which for so long made
Newstead Abbey its home.

Nymans West Sussex

Drive from London to Brighton by the main
road and at Handcross, about 5 miles south
of Crawley, you will see Nymans signposted
to your left. It is not a promising introduction, but if you leave the tarmac lanes with
their hurtling capsules of humanity you
quickly enter a very different world where
the roar of traffic is muffled by trees grown
tall in the fertile soil of the Sussex Weald.
Nymans' 30 acres are tranquil and secluded.
Though lying at about 150m (500ft) above
sea level the gardens are well sheltered,
enjoy a mild climate and are blessed with a
rich, well-drained soil. These conditions
have been exploited for almost a century
now in one of Sussex's loveliest gardens.

Mr Ludwig Messel started planting the
property in 1885, and his son Colonel
Leonard Messel continued to nurture it
until 1954, when the gardens were
bequeathed to the National Trust. The
heart of Nymans is a Wall Garden made out
of an old orchard situated to the west of the

▲ **Topiary walls** Looking
as solid as stone
battlements, a close-
trimmed yew hedge flanks
the lawn at Nymans. Its
topiary obelisks rise
towards the roofless gable
of a grey-stone mock
medieval hall. The
mansion was destroyed
by fire in 1947, but
miraculously the flames
hardly affected the choice
plants growing against its
walls. Dressed with
flowering shrubs and
climbers, the picturesque
ruins contribute to the
romance of the gardens.

house. Some of the original apple trees still remain in the plot, but what catch the eye are the mature specimens of trees and shrubs assembled from all over the world. They were established by James Comber, head gardener for decades at Nymans, whose son Harold became a celebrated plant collector in the 1920s. James was a brilliant plantsman with a talent for coaxing the best out of delicate subjects.

The results can be seen all around the Wall Garden in the splendid specimens of magnolia, styrax and davidia, together with stewartias from the southern United States, eucryphias from the Andes and camellias and rhododendrons from the Far East. Notable features include plantings of *Cardiocrinum giganteum*, the giant Himalayan lily, which bears its drooping creamy white trumpets on stems 2.4m (8ft) tall or more. These lilies can be difficult, requiring copious feeding and a long time to settle in before they flower; they die after their spectacular display, leaving in their place young offsets. The flourishing examples at Nymans were the pride of Leonard Messel.

The main paths in the Wall Garden meet at the central Italian fountain. It is framed by four topiary yews, finely sculpted to the shape of hollow globes, while the paths themselves are lined with old-fashioned herbaceous borders. They were designed under the influence of William Robinson, a friend of the Messel family who, like the equally renowned Gertrude Jekyll, was a frequent visitor to Nymans. Between them they pioneered a whole approach to modern gardening, based on informal naturalism and cottage-garden effects. Nymans is an early – and outstanding – illustration of their principles.

There are several distinct areas, for example, the 'Top Garden', with its magnolias, styrax, cercidiphyllums and maples. The quarry from which the stone for the original paths was extracted is now full to the brim with the towering *Gunnera manicata*. There are herbaceous borders, a sunk garden and a heather garden. In the rhododendron wood, exotics from Burma, Tibet and western China clutch at the Sussex soil.

Now and again, pleasing incidents arrest the eye: here, it is a pale classical summerhouse; there, a pergola drenched in season with mauve showers of *Wisteria floribunda*. For old-world enchantment you can explore the rose garden around a bronze fountain, or admire the stone dovecote.

It would be tedious to enumerate all the interesting plants which contribute to Nymans' distinction, but special mention should be made of a few. Besides its vast range of rhododendrons, the garden is famed for its choice specimens of camellias and magnolias. Several were raised in the garden itself, as their names bear witness: the original camellias 'Leonard Messel' and 'Maud Messel', for example, and the lilac-pink *Magnolia* x *loebneri* 'Leonard Messel'.

Eucryphias, too, are well represented and include the garden's most celebrated product. This is *Eucryphia* x *nymansensis,* an evergreen raised by chance in 1915 as a hybrid of the Chilean species *E. cordifolia* and *E. glutinosa*. It blooms in late summer and early autumn, bearing white-petalled flowers with a central golden boss. The tree grows to 9m (30ft) or more, and has been widely planted in its Sussex home, along with its improved variety 'Nymansay'. More than that it has proved a gift to the whole gardening world, valued both for its hardiness and its tolerance of some lime in the soil. It flowers today in many parts of the world very far from the favoured loam of the Sussex Weald and further still from the Andean homeland of its ancestors.

Overbeck's Devon

Britain, of course, has no Mediterranean coastline, but for the feel of the Riviera you could do no better than to visit the Salcombe area. The resort is the most southerly in Devon and claims the mildest climate on the mainland. Sheltered in the Kingsbridge estuary, this favoured spot is screened from the winds which blast the Cornish headlands to the south-west. Set high above the harbour, less than 2 miles from the yachting centre, is a garden of exceptional luxury.

Overbeck's 6 acres sprawl down a steep, south-east-facing slope, commanding superb views down the inlet, out to sea and across to Prawle Point on the horizon. And the garden fully exploits the potential of its position. It was established during the early years of this century, when terraces and retaining walls were built to support a wealth of tender and unusual trees. The older surviving rarities include an aromatic camphor tree, *Cinnamomum camphora*, which is probably unique for size in the British Isles. Olives grow near by, and there are many varieties of cornus, including *C. capitata*, an evergreen from the Himalayas.

▲ **Riviera view** Palms frame a view of sunny beaches and a sail-studded blue sea in a scene reminiscent of the Mediterranean, where fruiting bananas (*Musa basjoo*) flourish in the open. But this is Devon, and the garden is Overbeck's – now under National Trust management – which looks out over the Kingsbridge estuary.

The garden is known as Overbeck's, after Mr Otto Overbeck, who owned the property from 1928 to 1937. He amassed a great collection of curios in the building, which is now maintained as a museum. His chief contribution to the garden, meanwhile, was to establish its many palm trees. The hardy Chinese Chusan palm is well represented in this pampered site, and you can also see the little *Chamaerops humilis* – a native of the western Mediterranean which is the only true palm indigenous to Europe.

Trumpets of crinum, cannas and amaryllis play from Overbeck's warm beds; tender fuchsias, hydrangeas, acacias and agapanthuses abound. A new box parterre is laid out with panels of coloured gravel and holds pot-grown orange and lemon trees in summer. But for sheer magnificence, one specimen holds pride of place. This is a large *Magnolia campbellii*, a native of the Himalayas, which was planted in 1901. It is now some 12m (40ft) tall and in March bears thousands of vivid pink chalices in a sensational display which can be seen from almost a mile away.

Oxford Botanic Gardens

In Oxford, traffic rumbles unceasingly beneath the noble tower of Magdalen College. Yet across the road is a little oasis of tranquillity. This is the Botanic Garden, whose high stone walls offer sanctuary for footsore sightseers: the shade of aged trees, the splashing of a fountain and vision of lilies in a glimmering pool.

The Botanic Garden was founded by Henry Danvers, Earl of Danby, in 1621 on the site of a medieval Jewish burial ground. It is the oldest botanic garden in Britain. The walls which enclose the original 3-acre site date from the 17th century, and you enter by a fine gate built by Nicholas Stone, master mason to James I and Charles I.

The first gardener was a German named Jacob Bobart, who had 4,000 loads of 'mucke and dunge' brought in to enrich the soil and raise it above the floodwaters of the Cherwell. A man of great energy and ingenuity, he and his son also introduced some 1,500 different plants to the garden. Among them was the yellow Oxford ragwort (*Senecio squalidus*), whose seeds were first brought to Bobart from the slopes of Mount Etna. It proved too prolific for the venerable walls to contain, and now grows wild all over England.

The garden was initially designed to accommodate medicinal plants. It formed part of the School of Medicine, and was known as the Physic Garden until 1840. Today, both medicinal herbs and culinary plants still grow in formal beds, and a yew has survived from a central avenue planted in Bobart's time. The original square design has, however, been modified and extended to include herbaceous borders and a collection of roses showing their evolution from wild ancestry to the cultured hybrid blooms of today.

College spires, perceived above the walls, are glimpsed through the foliage of the trees. Enter the complex of eight glass houses, though, and you depart from the world of stonework and scholarship. In this enclosed domain the air is aromatic and the textures exotic. In the humid, luxuriant water-lily house, for example, a splayed clump of sugar canes greets you, while bananas and papyruses flourish in the beds. The centrepiece is a swampy tank first built to house the giant Amazon water lily (*Victoria amazonica*), which Victorian visitors had to pay a shilling to see. Today, the tank holds 20 different water lilies which tinge the surface with red, pink, yellow and blue.

The succulent house has a quite different aura, like some pocket of Arizona, harbouring desert cacti and agaves. At the far end you come upon the furred gullets and tendrils of the meat-eaters: sundews, pitcher plants and Venus's flytraps. Peer into their sinister forms and the Oxonian images of sculpted bust and library fade from the mind. You are intimate here with exquisitely murderous vegetation. The sign reads CARNIVOROUS PLANTS – DO NOT TOUCH.

Packwood House Warwickshire

They rise in brooding solemnity from Packwood's lawns – scores of yews clipped as giant cones and tapering cylinders grown in some cases to 6m (20ft) in height. Who put them there and to what purpose? There is a tradition that Packwood's famous assemblage of topiaries was planted to represent the 'Multitude' at the Sermon on

▼ **City oasis** Tucked away from the roar of Oxford's traffic, the University's Botanic Gardens offer a haven of calm in the heart of the busy city. But there is more to it than that – its eight glasshouses contain a major collection of tropical plants that flourish as lushly as in their native far-away habitats.

he Mount. And the congregation does in fact stand below a raised Mount Garden crowned by a solitary cone which might be delivering some voiceless address.

Lately, the legend has been questioned. But you cannot wander among these dark abstracts without projecting animate qualities on to them. Some yews stand erect, as if spellbound; others lean slightly as if in discussion. All contribute a unique fascination to one of the most celebrated gardens in Warwickshire.

Packwood House and its 5-acre gardens lie among the fields and copses of the ancient Forest of Arden. The gabled building dates from Elizabethan times, and was built for the Fetherston family who occupied the building for some 300 years. John Fetherston enlarged the house in the 17th century, and it was he who seems to have set up the raised Mount Garden – an eminence from which he could survey his domain. The work probably took place between 1650 and 1670, and 13 of the yews are reputed to be from the original garden. Twelve flank a raised path leading up to the Mount and are known as the Apostles. A spiral path winds on up to the summit, where a single, venerable specimen known as the Master presides over the assembly.

John Fetherston lived through the English Civil War, a time of deep religious turmoil. It may well be that he had a biblical parallel in mind when he sited his 13 yews. But the Multitude assembled below are not of the original garden. They were planted in the 19th century.

There is much else at Packwood to fascinate. The main entrance in the 18th century was on the west side, where you can see a cold plunge bath, with steps leading down, which was built in 1680. The main gardens, though, extend to the south where you first enter the so-called Carolean Garden. It has gazebos at its corners. One, dating from the reign of Charles II, incorporates a furnace and flues used to heat an adjacent wall, against which peaches were grown.

Apart from a sunken garden, laid out in the present century, what next catches your eye is a wide terraced walk massed with colourful herbaceous perennials. A superb decorative gateway of 18th-century wrought ironwork leads through to the great yew garden. But before exploring their weird topiary world pause to look at the arched alcoves in the terraced wall. There are 30 of them in all, not built to house marbled busts but wicker beehives – intriguing features in this garden of curiosities.

▲ **Sermon on the Mount**
Yews play a large part in the gardens at Packwood House, a National Trust property. Brooding topiary obelisks and cones represent the Apostles and the dumbstruck Multitude in the Mount Garden. Elsewhere in the garden, thick clipped yew hedges surround formal beds with herbaceous plants and a sunken lily pool.

▲ **Gigantic geometry** The Great Garden at Pitmedden has been recreated to a 17th-century geometric design, with 3 miles of clipped box hedging, 40,000 bedding plants, traditional coloured gravel and acres of close-mown turf. At the centre is a fountain built from sculptured stones, cut by Charles II's stone mason. Clipped yew pyramids line the wide paths, and mammoth yew buttresses jut out from the massive greystone walls that surround the garden.

Pitmedden Grampian

Long ago, when dark forests were enemies and rugged rocks evoked only terror, people took no pleasure in 'wild gardening'. Raw nature was too threatening a reality to be toyed with. As far as is known, the earliest gardens were all more or less formal affairs, laid out with comforting rows of fruit trees, vegetables, flowers and herbs. From the geometrical designs of the Roman era to the elaborate knot gardens of Tudor times, styles continued to express delight in controlling nature.

The tradition reached its height in the 17th century, when vast ornamental parterres were laid out with thousands of flowers, each planted to help make up a picture – of arabesques, heraldic emblems or even written inscriptions. Spread like vast living carpets before palaces and great houses, they seem to have celebrated something more than a love of colour or design; the quality, perhaps, of sheer human cleverness.

In Britain, almost all of the great ornamental parterres were wiped out by the 18th-century landscapists. And among the few gardens which still recall the scale of 17th-century conceptions, Pitmedden is outstanding. Enclosed by massive greystone walls, the garden covers an area of 4 acres, enclosing four great rectangular beds. No fewer than 40,000 brightly coloured annuals are planted out every year to make up the intricate compositions. The sight is frankly amazing; it is as if giants had imprinted the level green turf with immaculate stamps of their grandeur.

The great floral beds at Pitmedden, though, are reconstructions, skilfully achieved by the National Trust for Scotland, which acquired the property in 1952. But the designs are traditional, and the framework is entirely authentic.

The Great Garden was founded in 1675 by Sir Alexander Seton, who was clearly influenced by the French fashions of his day. He laid out his plot by the old castle of Pitmedden, on land sloping away to the east. This permitted a split-level arrangement: an upper garden with terraced extensions to north and south looks down on the Great Garden below. Today, as in the laird's time, visitors can see the whole composition spread out at the lower level.

You come down to the parterres by imposing pillared gates and a handsome divided stairway, while matching stone pavilions rise at each corner of the main terrace wall. All these features date from the founding of the garden, but little is known of the original floral patterns. When the Trust took on the property, the whole area was being used as a kitchen garden, and records which might have shed light were destroyed in a fire of 1818. Inspiration had to be sought elsewhere, and was found in a 1647 book of engravings of Edinburgh, entitled *Bird's Eye View*.

Almost every garden represented in the book is laid out according to one geometrical design or another. Three of the Pitmedden designs are taken directly from examples in the garden at the Palace of Holyroodhouse, as shown in the book. The fourth (the north-west parterre) depicts Sir Alexander Seton's coat of arms flanked by the Scottish emblems of St Andrew's cross and thistle.

To reconstruct the parterres, the garden first had to be razed and grassed over. The designs were then marked out and planted with box hedging. In 1958 the first flowers were planted to block in the colours, and they have been planted out yearly in May ever since. The annuals used include alyssum, begonias and dwarf wallflowers – considerably gaudier subjects than would have been available to Sir Alexander Seton. They are raised in glasshouses near by, and the colour schemes are varied annually.

The Great Garden is designed to create impact from a distance. But there is much else to engage the eye. The south-east bed (displaying the inscription *Tempus Fugit* – Time Flies) has a superb 17th-century sundial at the centre; it was found in the garden and may have formed part of the original design. And if you should tire of disciplined flower and foliage there are two great billowing borders to admire. They were planned by Lady Burnett, Lady Elphinstone and Dr John M. Cowan and are massed with wands of aconitums, golden rods and red hot pokers – bold strokes which vie in high summer with the radiance of the patterned beds.

Powis Castle Powys

A traveller visiting Powis in 1784 wrote: 'In the gardens, which were laid out in the wretched taste of steps, statues and pavilions, not even the fruit is attended to; the balustrades and terraces are falling down, and the horses graze on the parterres!'

The gardens then were little cared for, and it is easy enough to understand the writer's scorn for their neglect. But no one visiting Powis today would refer to 'wretched taste' in their layout. The dramatic medieval castle, perched high on a south-east-facing bluff, commands superb views across the valley of the Severn to the line of the Breidden Hills and the flank of the Long Mountain. And the foreground frame is a quite magnificent series of steeply stepped 18th-century terraces, supported by retaining walls.

Powis has a history stretching back over 700 years, but the gardens date from the late 17th century, when construction of the great terraces with their balustrades and niches was begun under the direction of William Herbert, the 1st Marquess of Powis. Political upheaval and exile saw the gardens fall into neglect, followed over the centuries by brief periods of improvement and change.

By the time Violet, wife of the 4th Earl, took charge of the gardens in 1911, they were in a sorry state. It was her ambition to turn them into the 'most beautiful in England and Wales', with flowers, hedges, topiary and architecture. Sadly, she was killed in a car crash in 1929, but not before she had designed the Formal Garden by the Great Lawn and inspired the development of numerous other features.

The bones of Violet's designs were fleshed out after 1952 when the property was vested in the National Trust. It now contains a wealth of rare and tender shrubs not often seen at this height above sea level. The gardens reach an elevation of 137m (450ft) and the drop of the slope is immensely steep. The heavy soil contains lime and is no friend to acid-loving plants such as rhododendrons.

There are basically three levels of terracing, and the raw limestone is exposed at the highest, where it provides the setting for a rock garden at one end. At the other is a fine statue of Hercules. A 9m (30ft) high stepped and bulging yew hedge, planted early in the 18th century, marks the eastern boundary of the terraces.

Below, the second or Aviary Terrace has at its centre a handsome brick loggia clothed with a lovely *Wisteria floribunda*; tender and fragrant Himalayan rhododendrons are grown inside, in specially prepared troughs of lime-free soil. From the balustrade, delightful lead figures of shepherds and shepherdesses look out over the incomparable views.

The third or main terrace incorporates an orangery in its retaining wall. The structure was heated by a boiler in the 18th century; the orange trees would be grown in tubs and trundled outdoors during the summer months. Today, the walls are hung with roses and passion flowers, while the herbaceous borders are lavishly planted with the 'hot' colours of penstemons, alstroemerias, macleayas, dahlias and crocosmias.

Powis did not entirely escape the attentions of the landscapists. Below the main levels is a fourth or apple slope terrace leading down to the Great Lawn. Baroque fountains once played here, but were scrapped by the landscape gardener William Emes in the late 18th century. He also laid out a serpentine walk on the ridge beyond, known as The Wilderness. Its soil is acid, supporting profusions of rhododendrons and azaleas as well as exceptionally sturdy growths of trees. Powis is renowned for its oakwoods, which furnished timber for Admiral Rodney's ships in the 18th century. Many aged oaks still abound in The Wilderness, mingling with more recently planted exotics and several outstanding conifers: cedars, redwoods and giant firs.

From the east end of the Orange Terrace a serpentine Box Walk leads to the Formal Garden. Contained behind tall yew hedges and structured with straight paths, wide

▲ **Terrace gardens** Constructed in the late 17th century, the three south-facing terraces of medieval Powis Castle afford spectacular views across the Severn Valley to the Breidden Hills and down to the fourth level planted with fruit trees, and to the Great Lawn and Formal Garden designed in the 20th century. Formal balustrades, pedimented niches, huge urns and statuary lend form and substance to groups of exotic plants in the shelter of giant yew hedges.

▶ **Looking up** The sword-like leaves of dracaena make an appropriately martial pointer to the battlements of Powis Castle, perched on a crag above its terraced gardens. The 'tumps' of yew that line the topmost level have stood guard there for more than 300 years.

borders, a vine pergola, fruit tree pyramids and posts billowing with roses and scented honeysuckles, Lady Violet's formal garden is a pleasure indeed.

Near The Wilderness is a fern-edged pool overhung with the giant leaves of gunneras. A wild garden and a daffodil paddock rippling with colour in late spring are other notable features. But perhaps Powis's most memorable feature is the view back from The Wilderness to the castle, taking in the full splendour of the terraces.

Riverhill Kent

There has been a house at Riverhill since Tudor times, but the most recent remains are those of a Queen Anne-style house built by the Children family, bankers of Tonbridge, early in the 18th century. In 1840, much altered, it passed into the hands of the Rogers family, in which it has stayed ever since.

John Rogers, the first of that name to own Riverhill, was a botanist and an early member of the Royal Horticultural Society, who began a family tradition of sponsoring plant collectors in their worldwide search for new species. He bought the property because it stood on sheltered, lime-free soil, where he intended to introduce trees and shrubs brought home by plant hunters.

An archway at the garden entrance leads past a *Rhododendron* 'Nobleanum', an early-flowering pink hybrid; a Judas tree (*Cercis siliquastrum*); and a Himalayan pink tulip tree (*Magnolia campbellii*). The shrubbery here, known as The Jungle from its bamboos and pampas grass, also has pieris, and rhododendrons and azaleas

planted in the 19th century. The Rose Walk is a terraced promenade.

The Wood Garden, formerly a pheasantry consisting of natural Kentish woodland, has been planted with flowering shrubs and many varieties of Japanese maple, whose copper-bronze foliage lends warmth to the autumn scene. Rhododendrons, brought as seed from China and India and now immensely tall, are a special feature of the Wood Garden. In the Old Orchard stands a Wellingtonia planted in 1860. The rhododendrons here are even older, and are of the

▼ **Naturalised exotics** In the Wood Garden at Riverhill, introductions such as azaleas and Japanese maples are now so old-established that they blend seamlessly with swathes of bluebells and other native flowers. The replacements for casualties of the great storm of October 1987 – such as crab apples and mountain ash – appear quite at home.

pecies *arboreum*, which can reach the height of 12m (40ft) attainable in their native Himalayas. Another, *Rhododendron* 'Colonel Rogers', is a hybrid between *R. falconeri* and *R. niveum* and was named after Colonel J. M. Rogers, the present owner's grandfather.

On the bottom terrace to the south of the house are shrubs including *Clematis montana*, and, in summer, massed buddleia and petunias in urns. The West End of the garden is little changed since the house was built, except for plantings of rhododendrons and specimen trees. These include the 'Waterloo' cedar, so called because it was planted in 1815, the year of Wellington's victory. Beside a pair of limes, an 18th-century stone bridge spans a sunken way. This was an ancient track that linked the Thames with the Medway at Tonbridge, and acquired the name 'Harold's Way' from the legend that the last Saxon king of England marched along it on his last, fatal journey to Hastings in 1066.

Rousham Park Oxfordshire

In its way, Rousham Park is a time capsule, a complete and unaltered statement of the philosophy and manners of the Age of Reason – at least insofar as gardening is concerned. It was created in a style that has come to be known as classical landscaping and was the first true breakaway from the geometrical, formal style that had held Western gardeners in thrall for so long. Its inspirations were the classical education that was the birthright of every English gentleman, the wide, sunlit countryside of Italy recalled from Grand Tours, and the paintings of such French artists as Lorrain and Poussin, who depicted vast landscapes in which graceful buildings of antiquity were set in balance with trees and water and faraway hills. This should be the gardener's theme, argued writers like Alexander Pope, to supplement the landscape, not to obliterate it with flower beds:

> *To build, to plant, whatever you intend,*
> *To rear the column, or to arch the bend,*
> *To well the terrase, or to sink the Grot;*
> *In all let Nature never be forgot . . .*

Lord Burlington and Vanbrugh were in the forefront of the movement, and temples, colonnaded bridges, ruined arches and classical statuary were dotting estates all over Britain. There were several designers of talent engaged in this work, but perhaps the greatest of them was William Kent. It was he who created Rousham Park and, apart from a certain mellowing, it remains much as he planned it in 1738.

The house was built in 1635 for Sir Robert Dormer – whose descendants still live there – and was later Gothicised by Kent, who gave it a battlemented front, a cupola and lead

statues. An architect and an artist as well as a garden designer, he also refurbished the interior of Rousham Park, but it is his gardens that have excited the greatest admiration.

Kent visualised a romantic landscape with a series of idyllic scenes, meant to be seen in a particular sequence, that would link the house and its terrace with the woods and the River Cherwell. From the terrace, the visitor should wander down into Venus's Vale, with its pools, cascades and statues. Then by way of a woodland path with a little stone-lined stream running beside it to a great basin of water called the Cold Bath. Beyond is a Doric temple, named Townsend's Building after the mason who built it in 1738. From there, the path runs past a statue of Apollo to the medieval Heyford Bridge and the Temple of the Mill, a romantic ruin created from an old mill. There is the Eyecatcher, another contrived ruin on the skyline, designed to lead the eye out to the countryside. Close by is the Lime Walk, a pleasant introduction to an arcaded terrace called Praeneste, which is decorated with handsome urns and a statue of a dying gladiator. Above the river is an amphitheatre which used to contain a fountain, and across a lawn stands the Pyramid, a fine viewing-base.

▼ **Pigeons and roses** The Pigeon House Garden at Rousham Park is a maze of formal rose beds outlined by miniature hedges of box. It takes its name from the circular dovecote which was built in 1685. Close by are the walled gardens with fine herbaceous borders, parterre and a vegetable garden.

Royal National Rose Society Gardens

Hertfordshire

The Gardens of the Rose they are named, as though by some medieval troubadour. But the term is much more likely to be definitive than romantic, for this is the showplace of the Royal National Rose Society, the world arbiter of taste and fashion in all to do with that lovely flower. And what a showplace it is – 20 acres mostly of roses, 1,700 species and varieties of them, old roses, large-flowered varieties (hybrid teas), miniatures, shrubs, climbers, bushes, historical, modern, wild, and roses that so far exist nowhere else at all.

The gardens on Bone Hill, near St Albans, look as though they have been there for ever, but, in fact, they were founded only in 1960, and upon soil that is far from ideal for roses. In this part of Hertfordshire the soil is thin, with gravel not far beneath the surface, and to maintain fertility, large quantities of manure must constantly be added. But, as the society points out, this poverty of soil does have advantages as far as rose-fanciers are concerned; they will know that any plant that does well on Bone Hill could do at least as well elsewhere.

The gardens are divided into two major parts – the Display Gardens and the Trial Ground. In the Trial Ground everything is strictly regimented, with the plants in long, straight rows to facilitate observation of their behaviour and growth. Some 200 new rose varieties are submitted each year from all over the world, and trials take three years, during which the plants are awarded marks out of a possible 100 for health (the premier consideration, carrying a maximum of 20 points), vigour, habit, beauty of form, colour, continuity of flowering, general effect, fragrance and novelty. The roses actually undergoing trial are set out to the east of the gardens waiting to learn their fate, which could be anything from the good pass mark of a Trial Ground Certificate to the supreme accolade of the President's International Trophy for the champion new rose of the year. All round the Trial Ground perimeter, presumably to encourage them, are newish roses, all of which have won some award from the society since 1974.

Fascinating though the Trial Ground is, the chief attraction for most laymen is the Display Garden, which is itself divided into several parts. Near the house are several small gardens, the first of which is devised as little more than an idyllic spot in which to eat one's sandwiches, being wooed the while by the sight and scent of roses. Adjacent to this, a small enclosed garden houses a collection of early tea roses. The next is designed to show how roses can be used in a small garden. The centrepiece is a sundial and the borders around it are planted with modern floribundas in shades of yellow, white and buff. Another enclosure, a little sunken garden, is devoted to miniature roses – true miniatures, with flowers, leaves and overall size all in proportion. Around the bank are beds of herbaceous plants and bulbs providing another illustration of how well roses will mingle in a small garden.

▶ **Rose society** In spite of their infinite range of colour, size and form, even roses need the foil of other plants to point up their beauty. At the Bone Hill gardens of the Royal National Rose Society, a pond spiked by stands of iris enhances the attraction of roses massed in formal beds.

Beyond, the display becomes much grander, and is appropriately introduced by a stately brick and oak pergola that supports as many as 46 different climbing roses whose blooms tumble from the high beams in happy abundance composed of every imaginable colour. Each climbing rose has, as a companion, a clematis to complement or contrast with its host. The pergola leads to a pretty pool fed by a tinkling fountain and aswim with lilies, while on every side there are the massed phalanxes of the rose beds. All these are labelled, so that, armed with a plan obtainable at the entrance, any plant can be tracked down fairly rapidly. There are also a number of general groupings, as in the case of the 'Old Garden' roses. This is a fascinating collection, for these are the roses of history and of the poets – the Albas, Damasks, Gallicas and Mosses. Other delightful gatherings are those of the wild roses, which are dotted about the garden and provide a rich variety with their different foliage and brilliant hips when the blooming of summer is over. Then there are the great collections of the roses that everyone knows, the large-flowered, or hybrid teas, which began in the 19th century with hybrids of the China rose, *Rosa chinensis*. Among the dozens of favourites you will see 'Grandpa Dickson', 'Silver Jubilee' and the rest, as well as cluster-flowered (floribunda) roses such as 'Iceberg', 'Southampton' and 'The Times'.

Summer is obviously the most popular time to visit the Gardens of the Rose, when the whole place is vibrant with colour, but as the society itself points out a wander in the autumn is almost as rewarding.

Saltram Devonshire

The qualities of the garden at Saltram, fine though it is, tend to be overshadowed by the great house at its eastern end. Most of the house – one of the largest in Devon – was built in the 18th century by the Parker family, ennobled with the name of Boringdon and later made Earls of Morley. They were patrons of Robert Adam, who redesigned the house for them, and of Sir Joshua Reynolds, a family friend, several of whose paintings hang there.

It was John Parker, Lord Boringdon, who in the latter half of the 18th century began to give the garden its present shape. By the end of the century its setting, surrounded by hills above the estuary of the Plym, had already led Polwhele, a local historian, to call Saltram 'one of the most beautiful seats in the west of England'. The original garden was probably designed on formal lines, but today it consists for the most part of lawns and grassy glades laid out with ornamental trees and shrubs.

A great lime avenue planted in the 19th century bounds the garden on the south, and helps to screen from view the encroaching urban development of Plymouth. It is lovely in spring with old cultivars of narcissus, and in autumn with pink and white cyclamen. In the central glade grow fine specimens of stone pine and Himalayan spruce. There are Monterey and Scots pine, paperbark maple, Californian redwood, snowdrop tree (*Halesia carolina*), and Indian bean tree (*Catalpa bignonioides*). The third and fourth Earls of Morley were

◄ **The Gardens of the Rose** Beds of floribunda roses lead the eye to a pergola over which sprawl more than 40 varieties of climbing roses with their clematis companions. In all, more than 1,700 species and varieties of rose can be seen in the gardens of the Royal National Rose Society.

► **King's view** Pleached limes enclose the long formal garden which stretches out from the north side of Sandringham House. It was designed by Sir Geoffrey Jellicoe for King George VI, who liked to look down the view from his first-floor apartment. The path leads to a statue of Father Time, acquired by Queen Mary in 1950.

keen gardeners, establishing a collection that now includes azaleas, rhododendrons, camellias, magnolias and hydrangeas. Among recent plantings are hypericum, indigofera, buddleia, fuchsias and a herbaceous border near the Parker family chapel.

Typically 18th-century architectural fancies dot the garden and its neighbourhood. The little octagonal Castle was a belvedere or viewpoint, and an *al fresco* dining room. Fanny's Bower, a classical garden house, was named after the diarist Fanny Burney, who visited Saltram in 1789 in the company of George III, and was particularly taken with the spot. In winter the Orangery still shelters orange and lemon trees, which can be brought outside in South Devon's warm summers. On the banks of the Plym below Saltram Woods is the Amphitheatre, where a natural semi-circular cleft in the rocks is 'improved' with an arcaded temple façade flanked by alcove seats.

Sandringham Norfolk

Many fine gardens throughout the nation are stamped with the character of families which have loved them. To tread lawns where children have played, or come upon gravestones of favourite pets, adds a dimension of human interest which the loveliest plants cannot in themselves evoke. Sandringham has that lived-in quality – though the scale is vast and the family far from ordinary.

Rising from a windswept landscape approximately 2 miles from the Norfolk coast, Sandringham Hall was bought in 1862 as a private residence for Albert-Edward, later Edward VII. The boundaries of the estate enclosed some 7,000 acres of lean, sandy soil, with an undistinguished Georgian house as the centrepiece. But since that time the property has evolved as the much loved private home of four generations of monarchs. Edward VII held lavish shooting parties, inventing 'Sandringham Time' to extend the shooting season (all the clocks in the house were fixed half an hour fast). It was from Sandringham that George V made his first Christmas broadcast in 1932, and it is to their Norfolk home that his granddaughter and the rest of the present royal family still come to celebrate Christmas and the New Year.

No one would call the vast mansion an architectural masterpiece. Built in 1870, it is a stylistic hybrid of cupolas, turrets and gables, executed in red brick and chocolate-brown carstone. Sandringham, in fact, is one historic residence where the gardens redeem the building.

The great house is set amid lawns and gravel walks, scattered here and there with aged oaks as well as younger trees, some of them planted by royalty. The biggest of these owes its presence to Queen Victoria, who, in her diary for April 25, 1889, wrote: 'Out with Bertie (Prince of Wales), Alix (Princess of Wales), Louise (their eldest daughter) and all the children, and I planted a tree in front of the house.'

Several members of the family have been enthusiastic gardeners, among them George VI. His rooms were at the north end of the mansion, and he wanted to see flowers from his windows. Accordingly, the formal North Garden was created, a long and narrow compartment surrounded by box hedges and flanked by avenues of pleached limes. Roses

▲ **Royal Norfolk** In contrast to the formality of the northern aspect, the west front of Sandringham House looks out over the rustic surroundings of the Upper Lake to an outer shelterbelt of woodland. The margins of the lake, with a floating carpet of water lilies, are thickly planted with hostas, irises, astilbes and candelabra primulas. A path skirts through woodland between the Upper and the larger Lower Lake.

▼ **Royal favourite** Albert-Edward, Prince of Wales, and the Princess of Wales – later King Edward VII and Queen Alexandra – were the first royal residents of Sandringham. The estate was bought for the prince in 1862, and has remained a favourite residence of the royal family. King Edward first opened the gardens to the public in 1908, and they have been open ever since.

and lavenders billow from the crisply edged beds, while a central path leads to a statue of Father Time. The bearded statue wears a suitably weary air, in marked contrast to Sandringham's other memorable figure. This is 'Chinese Joss', a gold-plated bronze statue, shipped from China in 1869.

Sweeping around to the north of the house are belts of great conifers, planted to give shelter from North Sea gales. And they have served their function so well that a wealth of tender shrubs has been successfully nurtured in their half-shade: cornus, camellias and magnolias, for example, with wonderful varieties of fuchsias and hydrangeas. Swathes of polyanthus fill spaces between, and one glade in particular is flooded in spring with the colours of rhododendrons and azaleas. Their display lasts well into July, when the white rhododendron 'Polar Bear' provides a triumphant finale.

Among several choice trees, a fine pocket handkerchief tree (*Davidia involucrata*) is conspicuous, growing close to the great Norwich Gates. These were presented in 1863 to the Prince and Princess of Wales as a wedding present, forming a fittingly magnificent composition in wrought iron shaped with interlacing flowers and leaves.

'Dear old Sandringham, the place I love better than anywhere else in the world,' wrote George V. He lived from 1893 to 1926 in York Cottage, a lodge some distance from the main house which stands by the lower of two landscaped lakes.

Charm of the lakes
The lakes themselves contribute much to Sandringham's attraction, whether seen from the house or glimpsed from the woodland belt. They were excavated in the 19th century to replace an older lake lying much closer to the house. The upper is especially beautiful with rich plantings of moisture-loving marginals. At one side a dipping path leads into a dell, graced by a lovely *Magnolia denudata* which is more than 70 years old and bears hosts of white goblets in spring.

On the facing bank is a sizeable rock garden, now planted chiefly with labour-saving dwarf conifers (even royal families have to make economies; about 60 gardeners tended Sandringham before the Second World War. Today's staff numbers about 15). One interesting feature is a boathouse built like a grotto from boulders of the local brown carstone. Another is a summerhouse nestling among the conifers with lovely views over the lake. Known as the 'Nest', this charming retreat was given to Queen Alexandra in 1913 by the Comptroller of her Household. It is, of course, one small ornament in a garden of vast size and great interest. And yet, looking across the lily-strewn water and the little island set in the middle, it somehow distils that intimate quality which you might not expect in Sandringham's royal acres, and which is all the more pleasing when you meet it.

Savill Garden and Valley Garden
Surrey

William, Duke of Cumberland, the port[…] son of George II, is chiefly known to histo[…] for his victory at Culloden and for his sava[…] reprisals upon the Jacobites in its afte[…] math. A minor consequence of this was th[…] the flower Sweet William was dedicated […] him by Government sympathisers, while tl[…] Jacobites in retaliation christened tl[…] strong-smelling common ragwort Stinkir[…] Billy. That, as far as most people are awar[…] was his sole contribution to horticulture, [...] it comes as something of a surprise to lear[…]

▲ **Woodland glade** Dappled by sunlight, a group o[…] exotic foliage plants show a fantastic variety of leaf[…] forms in a woodland glade at the Savill Garden.

that among his offices was that of Ranger o[…] Windsor Great Park. With a battalion of hi[…] Culloden veterans as a workforce, h[…] created the splendid lake of Virginia Wate[…] in the park, and drained, landscaped an[…] planted with trees the surrounding swamp[…] Surrey wilderness. In 1932, the Savi[…] Garden was begun in this area, and thoug[…] it occupies no more than 35 of Windsor'[…] 4,500 acres, it is, after the castle, the park'[…] best-loved and most visited feature.

Sir Eric Savill, the Deputy Ranger of th[…] time, saw the site as perfect for a bog an[…] woodland garden. Ponds were dug, clearing[…] made, and flowering and ornamental tree[…] planted, beginning with a weeping willo[…] that can still be seen near the Temperat[…] House, and extending gradually to the north[…]

st. By 1939 the garden's perimeter had ⸱en established, as had one of its most ⸱tractive features, the alpine meadow. With ⸱e Second World War, work in the garden ⸱ded, but recommenced in 1950 with the ⸱anning and planting of the more formal ⸱art of the garden. Colour was the theme, as ⸱n be seen from the herbaceous borders ⸱brant with every hue in summer, and from ⸱e long, buttressed wall almost overwhelmed ⸱ many-hued clematis. The wall was built of ⸱icks obtained from bombed ruins in West ⸱am, in London's East End; at its foot, raised ⸱ds with a mixture of soils provide a series of ⸱bitats for bulbs and alpines.

The restaurant, built in the 1960s, pro⸱des a fine platform from which to look

withstand English frosts, are grown tender varieties of rhododendrons, mostly originating from Burma and China

Rhododendrons also provide the major theme of the Valley Garden, which occupies the slopes and valleys of the northern shore of Virginia Water, still dotted with the trees planted by the Duke of Cumberland. It contains a collection of rhododendron species gathered together over half a century at Tower Court, Ascot, before being brought here in the 1950s, and some wonderful massings of azaleas in the Punch Bowl – a large, natural amphitheatre – and in the Azalea Valley. In the midst of the garden is the Pinetum, whose collection includes some 200 dawn redwoods, among the first to

◄ **Azalea time** It is difficult to pin down azalea time in the Savill Garden – except to say that it extends over a considerable period. April and May is the main flowering period, but species and hybrids of azaleas and rhododendrons from round the world extend the flowering time into mid summer. And in autumn the deciduous azaleas dress themselves in vivid leaf colours.

⸱cross ponds and clearings fringed with ⸱hododendrons and azaleas to a beech wood ⸱arpeted with silver moss, or outwards to the ⸱ide expanse of the park. Above a little ⸱ridge near by, built in 1977 to mark the ⸱ueen's Silver Jubilee, the banks are covered ⸱ith lilies, ferns and primulas reaching out to ⸱ingle with rhododendrons and azaleas, or ⸱ith forest trees underplanted with blue ⸱ydrangeas. Climbing up a slope to the west, ⸱nd therefore less likely to be hit by spring ⸱rosts, are magnolias and camellias to bring ⸱isitors to the garden in the early part of the ⸱ear; later, they will probably return to see ⸱he roses, vivid against the dark green of ⸱onifers and handsomely displayed in large ⸱eds lapped about by neatly edged lawns.

All the same, throughout the garden the ⸱trongest accent is on rhododendrons, great ⸱arades of them flanking the walks and ⸱ides and bringing early colour indoors to ⸱he Temperate House. There, among camel⸱ias and other plants not hardy enough to

be grown in this country. The pines and cypresses make a sober introduction to the Hydrangea Garden which flanks them. There, blocks of hydrangeas with florets of blue, purple, red, pink and cream sing their colours to the sky from July to October.

On the other side of the Pinetum is the Heather Garden, ideally suited to this acid soil and, in fact, a partly natural covering that crept across a gravel pit that was abandoned before the First World War. Native heathers have been supplemented by other species and varieties so that now, among the hummocks and hollows, there is hardly a day when one cannot find a heather in bloom.

Scotney Castle Kent

Most picturesque landscapes in Britain – that is, those stately landscapes in which vistas of woodland, turf, sheets of water and artfully placed ruins are combined into a harmonious, dream-like whole – were created all of a piece by rich landowners and the great landscape artists of the 18th century. Not so at Scotney Castle. There, it all began in the 14th century, when Roger Ashburnham, probably in response to the French raids on Rye and Winchelsea, fortified his manor house; 'castle' was always a highfalutin label for Scotney. By Charles I's reign, not much of this fortification was left, apart from the moat, a small Tudor house and a sturdy tower to which the Darrells, the then owners, added a handsome mansion. Eventually the property passed to the Husseys, one of whom, Edward Hussey, when he inherited in 1836, found the old house too damp and gloomy for his taste and built a splendid Gothic Revival dwelling on a piece of level ground above. To obtain the stone for his new home he quarried deep into the hillside, so establishing the last key feature of the garden as it appears today.

Nevertheless, Edward Hussey was very much a man of his time and background, and he may well have sensed the possibilities of his estate before he engaged William Sawrey Gilpin, the veteran garden designer and arbiter of taste in all to do with the Romantic landscape. At any rate, they were in full agreement on the way the garden should develop. Where the lawn ran down to the lip of the quarry, a terrace was built to command the magical view over the old house and castle. While the yawning pit below was converted into a kind of enormous rockery filled with rhododendrons and herbaceous plants, the castle was draped with climbing roses, as was the 17th-century house, which was partially and cunningly dismantled to blend with the castle in a manner that was even more wildly Romantic than before.

Two more generations of Husseys lived long lives at Scotney before it went at last to the National Trust, who maintain it with exactly the same affection and feeling for period that was lavished upon it by the family. Many fine trees were lost in the storms of 1987, but other delights abound. On the north side of the garden the upper path is a blaze of flowering shrubs. From here there are noble prospects across the park, to Goudhurst church on the skyline. At the end of the upper path by the castle moat is an ice-house – a conical pit roofed over with heather in which ice cut from the moat in winter was kept for summer use before the introduction of refrigerators. On a spit of land in the moat lies Henry Moore's bronze sculpture *Three Piece Reclining Figure – Draped*. Having ruminated upon the Romantic and the (perhaps) incongruously modern, it is a splendid idea to wander down through the quarry where, if you look closely, the footprint of an iguanodon may be seen, pressed into the sediment of which the rock was formed, millions of years ago.

▲ **Picturesque Scotney Castle** Built in 1377, all that remains of the old Scotney Castle is one of the original four towers and some romantic, creeper-clad ruins. The moat, too, is still there, awash in summer with water lilies and bounded with lakeside plantings. Within the ancient walls are a formal rose garden and a herb garden. Dense shrubberies are as vivid in their spring flowers as in their autumn colours, and mature trees add to the romantic aura.

▲ Quarry garden Like many other features at Scotney Castle, the quarry garden was not planned – it just happened. Now a cool, green place where paths of quarry stone slabs wander between ferns and shade-loving shrubs, it was originally the pit from which stone was dug to build a new house back in the 1830s.

At the end of the shrubbery, the ruins beckon. Roses are piled everywhere, mostly old roses, and in the forecourt there is a small herb garden with an ancient well at its centre. The moat lies beyond, bright with drifts of water lilies, and on summer afternoons when the bees are about and dragonflies hover on iridescent wings, there can be few more peaceable spots on earth. One additional touch of the Picturesque remains, and that is to look back to the newer house and its terrace, seemingly piled on the top of its wonderful, stepped garden.

Sezincote Gloucestershire

'Exotic Sezincote! Stately and strange', Sir John Betjeman called it in his verse autobiography *Summoned by Bells*. As an Oxford undergraduate the poet would cycle to the house for Sunday lunch with the owners, the Dugdale family. The Cotswold lanes we[re] heavy with hawthorn scents in early summe[r] and the church towers were golden in the su[n] But his destination was no ordinary Cotswo[ld] manor. Sezincote is a Mogul palace – comple[te] with minarets, onion domes and peacock-ta[il] arches – which rises like a mirage among t[he] leafy oak woods of Gloucestershire.

The house was completed in 1805 f[or] Charles Cockerell, who had served in t[he] East India Company. With growing Britis[h] interest in the subcontinent, 'Indianesqu[e] building styles became fashionable at hom[e] But Sezincote survives as something uniq[ue] in Europe: a complete building executed i[n] the Mogul style of the 16th century, whic[h] combines both Hindu and Muslim influenc[es] And the 'Nabob's house', as Betjema[n] dubbed it, is all the more extraordinary f[or] having a purely classical interior. Thoug[h] perfectly Indian from the outside, it [is] 'coolest Greek within'.

The park and garden were landscape[d] with advice from Humphry Repton. Thoug[h] the foremost successor of 'Capability' Brow[n] he was more flexible and not averse to toyin[g] with whimsical ideas. Besides providing th[e] parkland with landscaped woods and [a] sweeping lake (made to resemble a river), h[e] also helped to select some of the Indianesqu[e] ornaments. In the main, though, thes[e] were the work of Charles Cockerell's brothe[r] the architect S. P. Cockerell, and an arti[st] named Thomas Daniell.

The ornaments are to be seen in the o[ld] garden, which lies to the north of the hous[e] Known as the Thornery, this area consists [of] a luxuriously planted pool chain. At th[e] head is a temple dedicated to the Hindu sun god Surya; below, the stream passes unde[r] an Indian bridge topped by Brahmin bull[s] Lower still is the Snake Pool, taking it[s] name from a three-headed metal serpen[t] which entwines the trunk of a dead ye[w] The snake is ingeniously devised to spou[t] water – though the stream's flow is so sligh[t] that constant use would dry it up. Th[e] Prince Regent (whose famous Pavilion a[t] Brighton was partly inspired by Sezincote[)] was once treated to an erratic display; th[e] snake is said to have stopped spouting out [of] distaste for the royal visitor's private life.

Yellow-flowering St John's wort (*Hype[r]ricum calycinum*) grows in mounds aroun[d] the Snake Pool, and the plantings becom[e] ever more lush as the water descends to th[e] Rock Pool and Island Pool. Betjeman, in hi[s] poem, recalls 'water splashing over limeston[e] rock/Under the primulas and thin bamboo[' and these plants still flourish at the water'[s] edge. Magnolias and flowering cherries con[tribute their spring colours to the Thorner[y] Irises and lilies enliven the summer scene, t[o] be succeeded by the massed blooms o[f] hydrangeas. In autumn, fiery miscellanies o[f] Japanese maples keep the colours alive. Fe[w] of these plants are specifically Indian i[n] origin, but they lend a fittingly exotic air.

Large-leaved aquatics, together with ʋeeping beeches, pears and willows, all pro-ide sculptural effects, and there are many ɡed specimens among the trees. A grove of all cedars, for example, dates from the gar-en's founding, and there is a swamp ypress which may be some 200 years old. 'here is, in addition, a huge and venerable ʋeeping horn-beam (*Carpinus betulus* Pendula'), one of the largest in England.

Sezincote suffered neglect during the econd World War, and most of the younger lantings were established by Lady leinwort, whose husband bought the estate 1944 and whose family still nurtures the arden. Lady Kleinwort also laid out a new ndian Garden to the south of the house. Its ayout is formal and emulates the traditional 'aradise Garden' favoured by Babur, the rst of the Moguls. Irish yews here accentu-te the design, rather than the sun-loving ypresses that Babur would have used. But

exotic touches are found in the orangery, where rare jasmines, passion flowers and abutilons flourish.

Presiding over all is the domed roofscape of the great house itself. It is 'stately and strange' indeed, a thing which belongs in the landscape of Rajasthan but instead looks out across Repton's lake towards Moreton-in-Marsh and the Cotswold skyline beyond.

Shakespeare Gardens
Warwickshire

I know a bank whereon the wild thyme blows,
Where oxlips and the nodding violet grows
Quite over-canopied with luscious woodbine,
With sweet musk-roses and with eglantine.

Shakespeare's love of flowers must be evi-dent to any reader of the poet's work. Lines like those quoted from *A Midsummer*

▲ **Sezincote** In the old Thornery garden, a fountain plays in the pool before a tiny temple where sits a statue of the Hindu sun-god Surya. The atmosphere of cool tranquillity is enhanced by plantings of white-flowered and silver-leaved shrubs and perennials in the raised beds flanking the temple.

Night's Dream convey an intimate affection for the woods and meadowlands of his native Warwickshire. And at Stratford-upon-Avon, the old market town where Shakespeare was born and died, five gardens in particular burst with petals and fragrances known to the poet, and which he commemorated with lyric genius.

Each of the gardens centres on a site rooted in Shakespearean lore. There is the Birthplace in Henley Street, for example, where the poet was born in 1564. In its garden you can see trees, herbs and flowers mentioned in Shakespeare's plays and sonnets. All of the Midsummer Night enchanters are represented: wild thyme, oxlips, violets, woodbines (honeysuckles), Musk roses and eglantines (sweetbriars). And scores of other Shakespearean subjects have been informally planted, from 'lady smocks all silver white' to pomegranate, wormwood and yew.

The most famous, and most photographed, of all the Shakespearean sites is Anne Hathaway's Cottage at Shottery. It was in this picturesque thatched farmhouse with its latticed windows that the poet's wife lived before her marriage. The colourful miscellany of plants is typical of those found in English cottage gardens in their heyday, at the end of the 19th century. Not every one is mentioned by Shakespeare, or even available in his time. But they provide a delectable confection; jasmine clothes the half-timbered walls while hollyhocks and foxgloves thrust their spires from crowded beds. Here you find 'hot lavender' in abundance, with rosemary 'for remembrance'. And beyond the garden is Anne Hathaway's orchard, where the gnarled trunks of venerable fruit trees seem to bend in spring under their blossom loads. Also at Shottery is the Shakespeare Tree Garden, opened in 1988, and containing examples of trees mentioned by the Bard.

The garden at Mary Arden's House surrounds the half-timbered farmstead at Wilmcote where Shakespeare's mother lived when young. Ancient box hedges and old-fashioned roses are among the memorable attractions. Hall's Croft, in the old town of Stratford itself, is very different in mood. It was here that Shakespeare's daughter, Susanna, lived with her husband Dr John Hall. The fine old house has a spacious, walled garden which was designed as recently as 1950 by the Shakespeare Birthplace Trust. The layout is formal, with a long, paved terrace, smooth lawns and herbaceous borders.

What was Shakespeare himself like as a gardener? When he retired from theatre life in London he came to New Place, one of the largest properties in Stratford. Records show that it cost him £60, and it had an orchard and kitchen garden in which the poet may well have spent many happy hours, conjuring up plots rather than gardening. New Place was already famous by the mid 18th century, and visitors would throng to see an aged mulberry tree said to have been planted by Shakespeare. The then owner was so annoyed by the intrusions that in 1756 he had the tree cut down. But one cutting was kept, and from it a new tree grew – now itself over 200 years old.

The venerable mulberry rises from a smooth expanse of lawn. From the grass below, clumps of naturalised daffodils 'come before the swallow dares', and there are long flower borders set among yew-hedged compartments. A special attraction at New Place is the knot garden, nurtured as a replica of one of those decorative plots that graced every important house in Tudor times. Just such a 'curious knotted garden' is mentioned in *Love's Labour's Lost*.

▲ **Poet's flowers** A formal knot garden, embroidered afresh each spring with flowers that Shakespeare knew, is one of the attractions at New Place, Stratford-upon-Avon.

The plot is an enclosed square, slightly sunken, and divided by paths into four patterned knots. The designs are picked out in time-honoured, sweet-scented herbs, and filled in with colourful, old-fashioned bedding plants. In effect, the knot garden is a wonderfully embroidered space, a place for lovers' dalliance whose enclosing palisade is covered with crab apples and where one oak tunnel recalls the 'pleached bower' of *Much Ado About Nothing*.

In all, the Shakespeare gardens are richly suggestive of the poet's world. Not every feature is a period piece, though there are many inspired touches – at New Place, for example, there is even a 'wild bank' where Shakespearean favourites have been naturalised. 'This garden has a world of pleasure in't', runs a line in *The Two Noble Kinsmen*. The play cannot be attributed with certainty to the Bard, but the sentiment is wholly appropriate to the garden.

▲ **Hall's Croft** Once the home of Shakespeare's daughter Susanna, Hall's Croft in Stratford-upon-Avon has a walled garden with flagstone paths and wide borders of old-fashioned perennials. A sundial counts the passage of time in a garden where the past is always present. Situated in the centre of the old town, the garden is close by the Avon and the attractive river gardens and walk that lead to Holy Trinity Church where Shakespeare is buried.

Sheffield Park Garden
East Sussex

This is gardening on the grand scale, with great seasonal sweeps of colour that seem to illuminate the very air. And what is particularly remarkable is that the displays are composed for the most part of great trees, planted with the same attention to height, grouping and colour contrast that gardeners with lesser plots devote to a flower border.

Sheffield Park Garden is, in fact, two gardens, created 200 years apart and with one superimposed upon the other; yet so well have they blended, that it is hard to imagine that the place ever looked other than it does. In 1769, John Holroyd, MP, who was shortly to become the 1st Earl of Sheffield, purchased the manor that had once belonged to Simon de Montfort and commissioned James Wyatt, a rising young architect, to build him a house. Wyatt chose the currently fashionable Gothic style, and the equally fashionable 'Capability' Brown was engaged to do something about the park.

As quite often happened, Brown left no record of his work, but it is generally agreed that he constructed at least two of the four lakes and probably the cascade, too. Humphry Repton also had a hand in designing the garden about that time. In the late 19th century the 3rd Earl of Sheffield enlarged the First and Second lakes – nearest to the house – built the waterfalls, and established the hallowed cricket ground on which for 20 years (1876-96) opening matches of Australian Test tours were always played against Lord Sheffield's XI.

In 1909 the estate was acquired by Arthur Soames, a gardener of great originality and distinction, and he it was who began the massive plantings of the exotic trees and shrubs that are the chief glory of the place today. After the Second World War, the work was continued by Captain Granville Soames and, later, by the National Trust.

The garden is organised in the most artfully casual manner possible, into walks and viewpoints, each with its special features and carefully chosen supporting casts. By First Lake, old Spanish chestnuts are surrounded by a court of rhododendrons, maples, dogwoods and pines, together with cedars and firs from western North America. At the beginning of South Garden Walk there is a large Monterey pine, one of several in the garden. And there, too, is a splendid view across the First Lake to a weeping silver-leaved pear set off by the dark column of an incense cedar.

So the parade goes on through the garden's 120 acres, along Woodland Walk, Red Walk, Queen's Walk, Women's Way – so called from the headless spectre that is said to haunt it – Big Tree Walk, with its majestic North American conifers, Palm Avenue with its startlingly tropical air, and the rest an endless parade of rarities in beautiful if bewildering array. Among them are yellow Lawson's cypress, swamp cypress from the southern USA, and two 30m (100ft) maritime pines. It must be admitted that for the layman the garden is more easily digested from one of its superb viewpoints – Top Bridge, perhaps, with its wonderful vista of tree colours, shapes and textures and, in the background, the fairy-tale battlements of the house.

Best of all, of course, is to visit the place through the seasons. To see in winter the subtly hued conifers pushing through the dark, skeletal branches of the deciduous trees, then to walk through again in spring when Lenten lilies and thousands of daffodils push through the turf. As the year advances, comes the bright snow of cherry blossom and the rhododendrons and azaleas, astonishing splashes of vivid colour against the dark green palette of their foliage. Summer is the time for water lilies and the endless stirring of foliage against the sky. But autumn is the time when Sheffield Park Garden really puts out its full panoply. Between mid October and mid November, it seemingly bursts into flame. Outstanding among all others is the soaring crimson of the maples, but their surroundings of clear yellow, russet, gold and crimson are hardly less breathtaking. Reflected in water stilled by the first frost, and arched over by the clear blue October sky, it is a scene to remember.

▼ **Forest giants** The calm mirror expanse of the lakes at Sheffield Park Garden has inspired tree plantings of majestic grandeur. Maples and dogwoods, hemlocks and birches, cypresses and gigantic rhododendrons reflect their varied colours and forms in the water.

▲ **Sheffield Park Garden** Beneath a splendid panoply of venerable forest trees, including the magnificent *Nyssa sylvatica*, the arboretum at Sheffield Park Garden is carpeted in spring with broad swathes of wild bluebells. Much later in the year, the colour is up in the sky, as the forest giants stand dressed in an autumn glory of gold, russet and scarlet.

Shugborough Staffordshire

In 1744 George Anson, commander of a naval squadron and future First Lord of the Admiralty, returned in his flagship from an epic four-year voyage round the world. He brought with him a captured Spanish galleon worth, with its cargo, some £400,000. This fortune he and his brothers used to greatly enlarge their family house at Shugborough, erecting a host of monuments in its park and garden.

Shugborough lies beside an arm of the River Sow. The broad valley is wooded, with extensive new plantings of young oaks and hybrid rhododendrons, and with massive daffodil drifts on the river banks. At the water's edge are a group of mock ruins erected for picturesque effect; a footpath runs along the bank to a Chinese House, near which grow Oriental shrubs and trees.

This delightful little house was probably the first of all the garden buildings erected by Thomas Anson. It was completed in 1747, soon after the return of his brother, the admiral. His voyage had included a long call at Canton, and the design was done from sketches made in China by one of the admiral's officers. And on an island in the river is a charming monument, said to commemorate a ship's cat which circumnavigated the globe with the flagship.

Apart from its noble ornaments, Shugborough holds much to interest garden lovers. The layout is basically 18th century, with the addition of 19th-century terraces. An Edwardian-style rose garden is full of charm, to rival that of the long herbaceous border. Shugborough also holds the Reserve National Collection of Ghent Azaleas, a tapestry of scented colours in late spring, and later rich autumn tints.

And towering around are fine beeches and cedars, which lend an air of aged grandeur. For a sense of real immensity you should not miss the great English yew (*Taxus baccata*). At 22m (72ft) it has reached a fair height. But the height is not what most impresses – it is the girth. The yew spreads its dark-green skirt at ground level to cover almost an acre of space.

Sissinghurst Kent

The story has often been told: how the Bloomsbury writers Harold Nicolson and his wife Vita Sackville-West came to Sissinghurst in 1930. The Elizabethan mansion was then in a state of appalling dereliction, as it had been for 200 years. Vita Sackville-West, scouring the Weald of Kent to find a property in which she could start a garden, came upon the estate. The 6-acre garden was cluttered with 'old iron bedsteads, old plough-shares, old cabbage stalks, old broken-down earth closets, old matted wire, and mountains of sardine tins,

▲ **Sissinghurst Garden** Looking down from the tower of Sissinghurst Castle, its 6 acres can be seen for what they are – a jewel among gardens set in the already beautiful landscape of the Kentish Weald. It is a garden of compartments, some planned for seasonal interest, others according to colour themes. An avenue of Lombardy poplars lines the approach; once inside the gatehouse, the garden becomes a complex of squares, rectangles and long walkways.

▲ **Vita Sackville-West**
Together with her husband, Sir Harold Nicolson, Vita Sackville-West created the garden at Sissinghurst from a junkyard wilderness. Harold Nicolson gave the garden its compartmental shape while Vita dressed it with flowers in enchanting associations.

all muddled up in a tangle of bindweed, nettles and ground elder'.

And yet she fell in love with Sissinghurst at first sight: the romance of the castle with its pink-brick Tudor walls, the quiet water of the moat amid the shambles. It was, she wrote, Sleeping Beauty's garden – and it cried out to be redeemed.

It took the couple three years just to clear away the rubbish, and some seven more to plan and plant the garden. But after the Second World War, when Sissinghurst was opened to the public, it became known as a wonder among British gardens – and today it has matured into a modern 'classic'.

Sissinghurst lies in the farmlands of the Weald, 40m (130ft) above sea level. And despite all the problems that the Nicolsons acquired, there were also some notable advantages. The soil, for example, was a good friable loam well worked by generations of tenant farmers. The old walls and gatehouse buildings provided both shelter and the elements of a design. It was Harold Nicolson who laid out the bones of the garden, once the mess had been cleared away.

Vita Sackville-West, meanwhile, was of a romantic temperament and infinitely sensitive to mood. Of Sissinghurst she wrote: 'Though very English, very Kentish, it had something foreign about it, a Norman manor house perhaps, a faint echo of something more southern. That was why figs and vines and roses looked so right, so inevitable. I planted them recklessly.'

Between them they aimed for a harmony: 'the strictest formality of design with the maximum informality in planting'. This was the principle pioneered at Hidcote, a garden which deeply influenced the Nicolsons. They in turn were to help shape the thinking of countless gardeners of their generation.

The garden's symmetries beautifully suit the character of the Tudor tower (in which Elizabeth I spent three nights in 1573). But for all its sophistication, Sissinghurst is no formal period piece. The loveliest of England's native wild flowers grace the garden in spring: daffodils, narcissi, blue sheets of forget-me-nots and nodding snake's head fritillaries.

Leading off the walk is The Cottage Garden set around the remnant of a wing of the Elizabethan house. Inside it is the room where Harold Nicolson used to write. Outside, the garden is filled with warm reds, orange and yellows, the narrow range of colours showing each other off to perfection. The house front is clothed with the white climbing rose 'Mme Alfred Carrière', almost unbelievable for the vast area that it covers.

Lying off the Lime Walk is the magnificent rose garden, widely famed for its old-fashioned and shrub varieties. Clematis run wild over the walls, while mingling with the roses in the plot are ceanothuses, caryopteris, lace-cap hydrangeas and a host of other shrubs. Tulips and irises surge from the beds, while pansies seem to cover every spare inch of earth. Yet, at the centre of these billowing medleys, the eye is held by the firmest of features. This is the so-called rondel, a circular patch of turf which takes its name from the round floor of Kentish oasthouses. It is framed by a mighty broken ring of yew, trimmed with austere precision.

Every compartment at Sissinghurst is a delight. There is a nuttery, whose aged nut trees are among the very few worthwhile plants which were there before the Nicolsons arrived. There is the azalea-bordered moat walk, and the paved herb garden richly stocked with aromatic plants. Artistic associations were never far from the cultured founders' minds when they planned their Wealden acres. The spring flowers in the Lime Walk, for example, were consciously nurtured to recall Botticelli's famous painting of *Spring*. Here are lime-shaded borders of clematis, anemones, forget-me-nots, scillas, grape hyacinths, fritillaries and many others.

But among all the compartments, one is an acknowledged masterpiece. This is the white garden, devoted, as its name implies, to white and grey plants and flowers. An immaculate pallor greets you here in any season. On the hottest June day, the scented

▲ **The White Garden** Cream and white flowers, with silver and grey foliage, combine to make the white garden the masterpiece of Sissinghurst.

Rosa longicuspis (syn. *R. mulliganii*) will lower your temperature. Its snowy avalanches of white, banana-scented blossom smother the central iron canopy while, later, the pale trumpets of *Lilium regale* rise through mats of grey artemisias. Wands of white delphiniums mingle with occasional heads of Scotch thistles and, as the evening draws in, baby's breath (*Gypsophila*) blows white froth around. The white garden has been called 'the most beautiful garden at Sissinghurst, and indeed in all of England'. It is not entirely white, of course: high above all rise the rose-pink walls of the castle, while, through an archway to one side, you look out to the green bosom of the Weald.

▲ **Cool white garth** Vita Sackville-West herself described her famous white garden at Sissinghurst by the old word garth, meaning a piece of enclosed ground – 'it is entirely enclosed, on one side by a high yew hedge and on the other sides by pink brick walls and a little Tudor house . . ., my grey, green, white, silver garden which looks so cool on a summer evening'. Then as now, aromatic silvery artemisias and 'Iceberg' roses laid their scent upon the air.

▲ **Border stronghold** The massive walls and 14th-century tower of Sizergh Castle today support nothing more tenacious than vigorous Boston ivies, flaming scarlet and golden in their autumn colours. Now a National Trust property, the grounds include formal gardens – species rose beds, water features, half-hardy flowering shrubs and climbers against the sheltered terrace walls – as well as informal banks clothed with native wild flowers.

Sizergh Castle Cumbria

In all the Borders, there can be few more eloquent arguments for the Union of the Crowns than Sizergh Castle. Its oldest part is a pele tower built about 1350 as a defence against marauding Scots, and very likely against quarrelsome English neighbours, too. Today, its warlike lines are blurred by a draping of Boston ivy, while below, the defences offer shelter and support to a large Turkey fig, buddleias, brooms and other flowering shrubs. At the foot of the tower is a bed of *Agapanthus* 'Isis' so startling blue as to make the late summer sky seem washed out by comparison.

From the house, an 18th-century terrace and wall run south, offering a haven to flowering shrubs and climbers – clematis, honeysuckles, vines and cotoneasters – then, below the wall, a precipitous bank falls away to a lawn. All summer long, the bank is covered by dog daisies, so that, with the old tower in the background, it looks exactly like a corner of a medieval illuminated manuscript brought to life.

The 17th-century approach to the castle was by way of a beech avenue terminating in a pair of noble, urn-crowned gate piers. The gates still stand, but the beeches have been replaced, first by limes, then by rowan trees. All the park area about the avenue has been transformed into a great lawn that is dotted with 200-year-old yews and island beds filled with roses and a dazzling variety of flowering trees and shrubs.

But the most famous – and astonishing – feature in Sizergh's surroundings is its rock garden, built of the local stone for Lord Strickland in 1926. From a pool above the house, a waterway threads its quarter of an acre, pausing at pools and little falls, before it empties into the lake. When the garden was established, a large number of dwarf conifers were included for background effect, but many are now very big dwarfs indeed. There are hummocks of spruces, 2.4m (8ft) across and 1.2m (4ft) wide, bushy pines, cypresses, yews and junipers, and a prostrate blue noble fir at least 4.5m (15ft) across. In the damp earth beside the watercourse grow primulas, polygonums, astilbes and globe flowers.

Modestly intermingled with the other plants in this lovely dell is one of the largest collections of hardy ferns in the country – more than 100 species and rare forms.

Springfields Gardens
Lincolnshire

The flat fens of Lincolnshire lie, like much of Holland, only just above the level of the sea. Ancient trading contacts connect the two flatlands, and many old houses in Lincolnshire are built in Dutch style. And in the area around Spalding, analogies with the Netherlands are even more marked. For this is Britain's 'Tulipland', where more than half of the nation's bulbs are grown. In spring the level acres surrounding the old market town come alive with vast sheets of primary colour. And the magnet for garden lovers at this time is the great show garden at Springfields.

Springfields Gardens are just outside Spalding, where the soil is a sandy loam. It is an exposed site, suffering cruel winds which no sheltering ridge helps to alleviate. The 30-acre site was established in 1964 by a branch of the National Farmers' Union.

The high season at Springfields is the six weeks in April and early May when the bulbous plants come into their own: tulips, narcissi, daffodils and hyacinths – well over a million bulbs and corms bear their blooms. The tulips, of course, hold pride of place and account for three-quarters of the plantings. They come in an astonishing range of varieties, from the smallest early flowering species to the most grandiose hybrids. Glorious battalions of yellows and reds are what first assault the eye, but Springfields' army wears a coat of many colours. Among the popular Darwin range, for example, hues range from the snowy white of 'Glacier' through a rainbow of shades to the dusky maroon of 'La Tulipe Noire'.

Although this kaleidoscope display is the traditional glory of Springfields, there are other attractions. The season now extends to September with bedding plants and shows of dahlias. New features, including a drought garden and palm house, ensure continued interest.

▲ Springfields Gardens
In Britain's own 'low country', around Spalding, a tulipland has grown up to rival that of Holland. Its showplace is Springfields Gardens, where every April and May a million bulbs burst into bloom in a vivid display of colour and form in gardens designed, fittingly, by a Dutchman, Carl van Empelen, who planted a shelterbelt of trees and shrubs and excavated a lake.

▲ **Arcadian images** The great lake at Stourhead was created in the mid 18th century by Henry Hoare, who dammed the little River Stour. A walk around the lakes reveals tantalising glimpses through venerable trees to classical buildings, temples, statues and tucked-away cascades. A rustic cottage in the ground is thought to be a lonely survivor from the days before Henry Hoare began to fulfil his dream and lay out the gardens. They are now in the care of the National Trust.

Stourhead Wiltshire

Looked at in one way, Stourhead is the Disneyland of 1744, a dream world furnished with the habitations of imaginary beings, and created purely for pleasure. In another, it is one of Britain's greatest national possessions, as important as a Turner or Constable painting, and having much in common with them – the same vistas, the same use of light and shade, the same mixture of landscape and gracious buildings. The main differences are that Stourhead is composed of real water, earth and light, and while the paintings were finished, the great garden is ever changing.

The creator of Stourhead Gardens was Henry Hoare of the London banking family, who, in 1741, inherited the house built by his father above Six Wells Bottom. He began by damming the infant Stour, so making a series of lakes, the largest of which was to be the focal point in his creation. He established about it vast plantations of trees, mainly spruce and beech, taking great care, as he said, to site them 'in large masses as the shades are in painting, to contrast the dark masses with the light ones'.

Like most English gentlemen of his time, he was not so much well versed in the classics as soaked in them, so his perfect landscape had to contain a range of Arcadian groves and pastoral vistas. Among them there gradually rose a range of buildings: the Temple of Flora, followed by the Grotto, dedicated to the River God and to the Nymph of the Grot, out of whose basin the springs of the Stour bubble. The Pantheon, with its magnificent statue of Hercules, statues and busts of other deities, was completed in 1754; the Temple of Apollo on its eminence overlooking the lake was added a decade later, as was the stone-built Turf Bridge, which carries a close-mown grassy path over a corner of the lake. About this time too, in obedience to the prevalent fancy for the Gothic, Henry Hoare added a medieval stone cross from Bristol.

Predeceased by his wife and children, he devoted the latter part of his long life entirely to the ornamentation of Stourhead, and was succeeded at last by his grandson, Sir Richard Colt Hoare, in 1785. Sir Richard respected his grandfather's overall plan, but added to it by providing gravel walks and a much greater variety of trees and shrubs. This course was followed by his descendants down to the first decades of this century, when Sir Henry Hoare, the last member of the family to live at Stourhead, planted the huge collection of azaleas and rhododendrons that are now at their somewhat overpowering peak. Thus, Stourhead is not the product of a single vision, but a grand canvas painted over nearly two and a half centuries.

Nevertheless, it is the spirit of old Henry Hoare, Stourhead's builder, that prevails.

► **Temple of Apollo** More than two centuries ago, the bleak valley at Stourhead was transformed into a series of sylvan glades, dammed lakes and classical temples, like that dedicated to Apollo, with grottoes for the lesser gods.

It was his notion that visitors should walk from the house to the lip of the valley, whence the Temple of Apollo appears to be floating between trees and water. From there, a path offering tantalising glimpses of the Pantheon crosses the northern end of the lake to the Grotto, whose mouth frames a perfect view of the Temple of Apollo on the opposite shore. The path then continues towards the Pantheon – with views of the Turf Bridge and the Bristol Cross – before climbing up to Apollo's temple and a grand panorama of the entire estate. Beyond, and by no means an anti-climax, the route then crosses the Turf Bridge to the delightful village of Stourton.

At present, most people come to Stourhead by way of the village, and thereby miss the stunning views of the landscape from above. But Stourhead never ceases to fascinate, with its walks, its architecture, its trees, shrubs and flowers, its bird life, its peace and serenity.

Stowe Buckinghamshire

In 1731, Alexander Pope wrote a number of poems on good taste in gardening style, including the following:

> *Begin with sense, of every art the soul*
> *Parts answering parts, shall slide into a whole*
> *Spontaneous beauties all around advance*
> *Start, even from difficulty, strike, from chance.*
> *Nature shall join you: time shall make it grow*
> *A work to wonder at – perhaps a Stowe.*

The advice might well be regarded as the hymn to, and the recipe for, not only Stowe, but the whole Landscape Movement.

▲ **Palladian Bridge** At Stowe, pure landscape gardening, composed of light and shade, trees, grass and water, was conceived and executed on the grandest of scales. From its zenith in the 18th century, Stowe gradually went into decline, but an ambitious restoration programme by the National Trust is recreating the philosophical designs of the Landscape Movement. Once again the Palladian Bridge over the lake rises like a fata morgana from a wintry landscape.

▲ *Templa quam dilecta*
The motto of the Temple family is illustrated throughout the gardens at Stowe with beautiful temples indeed. William Kent, who was partly responsible for the landscaping in the early 18th century, designed the Temple of Ancient Virtue.

This curious phenomenon, composed of philosophy, a thorough grounding in the classics, wistful memories of the Grand Tour in Greece and Italy and a yearning for something new, struck many 18th-century landowners like a thunderbolt. They translated their ideals into grand vistas of 'natural' landscape. So convincing are some of these landscapes that now they have matured we have almost forgotten they were created, and imagine them to be the true and ancient faces of the countryside.

It is hard to say where the movement began, for there were stirrings everywhere. But Stowe was one of the first, and is unique in showing all the phases of the movement from its beginning to the end. It is unique, too, in being the place where the movement's greatest craftsmen – Charles Bridgeman, Sir John Vanbrugh, William Kent and Lancelot 'Capability' Brown – did some of their earliest and finest work.

In 1697, Sir Richard Temple, Lord Cobham, a distinguished soldier in Marlborough's wars, inherited Stowe. The handsome brick house and formal garden were fine but in no way exceptional. Following his marriage to the heiress Ann Halsey, he was able to realise his ambition to create a memorable mansion with matching garden. Sir John Vanbrugh was engaged to expand the house and Charles Bridgeman to design the gardens. Bridgeman's first act was to do away with the wall separating the garden from the park and install in its place

a ha-ha or sunken wall, thereby bringing th surrounding countryside into the garden and drawing the eye to distant monument such as the Bourbon Tower, and Stowe Cast in the surrounding park. He also establishe parterres, walks and a canal.

Between 1715 and 1726, a huge garde was laid out; Vanbrugh designed building to embellish the formal layout, in the for of a number of temples dedicated to vagu deities. After Vanbrugh's death in 172 James Gibbs and then William Kent wer engaged to continue the expansion. Ken started the change to a more natural lan scape by designing and building the Elysia Fields, with a political overtone that can b traced throughout the garden. He manipu lated the countryside as an artist works hi oils and, in this sense, landscape gardenin was invented at Stowe. In 1741, Lancelo 'Capability' Brown came to Stowe as gardener. His talents were quickly recog nised, and promotion to head gardener an clerk of works followed. Under the directio of Lord Cobham, Brown designed th Grecian Valley.

In 1748, William Kent died, as did Lor Cobham in the following year. He was suc ceeded by his nephew, Lord Temple, wh was at least as keenly devoted to buildin and innovation as his uncle. He determine to build a house that was worthy of it surroundings and engaged the architec Robert Adam, who not so much rebuilt a encased the old house in stone, enlarged i

nd added a massive, pillared portico. Lord emple then flung landscapes and buildings ver wider, working first with Brown until e left, then with his successor, Richard oodward. By the time Lord Temple died, 1779, the gardens at Stowe were much as ney are today. The family fortunes went to decline, and only minor changes were ade to the gardens in the early 19th ntury. A rock and water garden at amport, beyond the Palladian Bridge, was ne last improvement before a financial rash in 1846.

In 1923 Stowe became a public school and till flourishes as such. In 1989 the gardens ere gifted to the National Trust, and a uge project to conserve and restore the 37 uildings and 350 acres of garden was egun. The house remains a school, but is pen to the public during the holidays. The ain state apartments give a clear idea of ne scale and wealth of its former owners.

The gardens are open to the public and ake compulsive viewing for anyone inter-sted in gardening history. Stowe is pproached from Buckingham along a 1½-ile formal avenue which leads to a riumphal Arch designed by William Pitt; ne drive goes over the Oxford Bridge with ne two Boycott Pavilions on the crest of the ill that announce the start of the garden. he present main entrance is through the xford Gate, restored in 1993.

The main garden walk starts from the recian Valley where the Temple of Concord and Victory (*c.* 1760) tops the valley, with views to Wolfe's Obelisk and the Cobham monuments, both over 24m (80ft) high, on the surrounding hills. The garden is set out as a series of scenes or pictures, with vistas, views and monuments in profusion. The family name of Temple and their motto *Templa quam dilecta* (How beautiful are thy temples) leaves little doubt that their aim was to decorate a natural garden with every type of building.

It is recommended that the visitor should turn left and descend by way of the Elysian Fields. A short way down is the Grenville Column, a monument to a Temple relative killed in action against a French frigate, and close by, most unexpectedly, a 14th-century church. This is all that remains of the 'lost' village of Stowe. 'Capability' Brown was married in the church in 1744. Near by, the temples begin. A slim waterway is crossed by the Shell Bridge, actually a dam, and close to it is a monument to Captain Cook and the now restored white marble Seasons Fountain. By the lovely Palladian Bridge, seemingly half-submerged in the lake, is the ruinous Temple of Friendship that was dedicated to Pitt the Elder and his friends in the Whig Party in 1739.

Throughout the gardens, the monuments and temples continue. Among those that should be visited is the Congreve Monument topped by a monkey gazing at itself in a mirror as a tribute to the dramatist whose speciality was the mockery of human foibles.

▲ **'Capability' Brown** It was probably at Stowe that Lancelot 'Capability' Brown founded his reputation as Britain's greatest landscape gardener.

▲ **Valley gardens** The incomparable water gardens at Studley Royal are set in the steep valley of the River Skell and laid out in a series of straight canals, geometrically-shaped pools, springs and cascades. Created early in the 18th century, the water gardens are surrounded by majestic parkland trees and velvety lawns punctuated by classical statuary. There are splendid views to the ruins of Fountains Abbey.

Studley Royal North Yorkshire

Gardens have grown out of all kinds of circumstances, but few can have odder beginnings than the lovely landscape of Studley Royal. In 1720 the South Sea Company volunteered to assume partial responsibility for the National Debt in exchange for a trading monopoly in the South Sea Islands. With such collateral, the company attracted wide, even hysterical, investment. But, alas, no trade existed, and when the South Sea 'bubble' burst the following year, thousands of people were ruined. It was one of the gravest financial disasters in the annals of the City of London, and if any single factor was to blame it was the inept, or worse, handling of the affair by the Chancellor of the Exchequer, John Aislabie. He was expelled from Parliament, which seemed to many people to be a remarkably mild penalty under the circumstances, and he prudently retired to his Yorkshire estate.

Whatever his shortcomings as a Chancellor, he was a landscape gardener of genius and, in his enforced leisure, he was able to give his talents full rein. What he sought to do was to create out of the three elements of formalism, the romantic and the picturesque, a landscape that would elevate and refresh the mind of the beholder. The canvas he used was the wild, wooded valley of the River Skell, which runs from above Fountains Abbey then through the Studley estate to join with the Ure beyond Ripon. He dammed the river to make a large lake, a canal and two other ornamental sheets of water, his Moon Pool and Half Moon Pool, overlooked by statues and the classical architecture so dear to the hearts of the period. By the Moon Pool, delicately emphasised by the surrounding velvety lawns, is the stately columned portico of the Temple of Piety and, above it, reached by a patch that runs through a grotto-like tunnel, is the Octagonal Tower, and the open rotunda of the Temple of Fame. Beyond this, suddenly revealed, is the Surprise View, the crescendo of the entire planned landscape. It is a surprise indeed, and one that never fails to take the breath away, for it is the soaring ruin of Fountains Abbey, with its great tower and gaping windows etched against the sky.

Built in the 12th and 13th centuries, and allowed to fall into ruin – and used as a quarry for nearby Fountains Hall – after its dissolution in 1539, it is one of the most perfect examples of a Cistercian monastery in Europe. John Aislabie was a true product of the Age of Reason, and it was a sense of the picturesque, rather than of piety or history, that led him to make the ruin the focal point of his garden. However, it was never actually a part of the Studley Royal estate during his lifetime, and it was not until 1768, after his son, William, had inherited, that the two estates were joined together. William

Aislabie turfed the abbey's surroundings, added some features to the joined parks and naturalised parts of the river banks in accordance with the ideas of 'Capability' Brown, whose influence in garden matters was then at its height. But the general flavour is still very much the one dictated a generation earlier by John Aislabie, and faithfully maintained today by the National Trust.

One feature, though, has nothing to do with either father or son, and that is St Mary's, the splendid Gothic church erected in the park during the 1870s by the Marchioness of Ripon. It is by no means incongruous, but from the church the visitor should look back towards the east gate. From there, another planned and astonishing vista is carried through an avenue of ancient trees and out over miles of countryside to the precisely aligned view of Ripon Cathedral's twin towers. Whatever the wrath of the 18th century, posterity cannot but be grateful to the ancient scandal and for the unseasonable retirement it brought to John Aislabie.

Syon Park Greater London

A ducal estate that time has surprised, Syon is now almost engulfed by the brick and concrete of London's western suburbs. Nevertheless, in the midst of its 55 acres it is quite possible to find the hum of insects drowning that of the traffic and to look over a landscape that wistfully reminds us what a lively county Middlesex was before commuterdom was dreamed of. In the midst of it stands Syon House, a modest term used to describe the square Tudor palace with the stiff-tailed heraldic lion of the Percys balanced above its battlements and glaring over the Thames to Kew.

It was built in the reign of the boy king Edward VI by his Protector, the Duke of Somerset, on the site of a monastic house dissolved by Henry VIII. In 1542 it served as a prison for a few months for Queen Catherine Howard, before she was rowed downriver to the Tower and execution. Five years later, Henry's corpse was kept there overnight while on its way to Windsor for burial. But the servants deserted it, leaving it to be gnawed by the dogs, thus fulfilling, so it is said, a curse put upon the king when the monks were evicted.

The Duke of Somerset was able to enjoy his new house for only five more years, before he, too, made the melancholy journey to the Tower and the block. But in that time he also constructed the terrace and, with the aid of Dr William Turner, the father of English botany, he established the first botanical garden in the country. This garden has long vanished, but the mulberry trees that were planted at the same time – about 1550 – still thrive in the private area to the east of the house.

▲ **Glass palace** Ducal gardening is, almost of necessity, on the grand scale. The Great Conservatory at Syon Park is a case in point – the area under the great dome alone, 280sq m/ 3000sq ft, is larger than many gardens.

▲ **Syon Park** The Great Conservatory, completed in 1827, was one of the wonders of the 'modern' world and used by Joseph Paxton as a model for the renowned conservatory at Chatsworth and for the Crystal Palace of 1851. Alas, none of these have survived. But at Syon Park, the impressive glasshouse remains and houses large collections of exotic plants, many chosen especially for their fragrance. In front are formal gardens and a large lily pool.

A succession of owners followed, at least two of whom also took the weary path from Syon to the Tower of London. Perhaps it was dangerous to own so grand a house so close to the capital. A number of the owners made important contributions to the gardens, but it was not until the 1st Duke of Northumberland inherited in the mid 18th century that they began to assume the appearance that they have today. Like many of his contemporaries, he was entranced – for cost-saving as well as aesthetic reasons – by the new idea of natural landscaping. In consequence, he swept away the formal Tudor beds and walled enclosures of his predecessors, and replaced them instead with vast lawns that lapped to the very windows of the house. Still not satisfied, he employed 'Capability' Brown, who, as usual, attacked the landscape with the enthusiasm of a general setting about an occupying foe. First, he excavated over a million cubic feet of earth to make a pair of lakes, and about them opened up great vistas of turf dotted with shrubberies, a botanical garden and strategic plantings of cedars, limes, oaks, chestnuts and beeches.

This was by no means the end of creativity at Syon. In the 1820s, the 3rd Duke commissioned the architect Charles Fowler to build the Riding School – now the Garden Centre – and the great, domed conservatory. Nearly 122m (400ft) long and 20m (65ft) high, it was the wonder of the horticultural world. At the same time, the 3rd Duke engaged Richard Forrest, one of the greatest gardeners of the day, to make further improvements and to supervise a collection of rare plants and trees.

Syon Park is therefore the product of many men's love and care over the centuries, which makes a pleasant reflection to accompany the visitor on a stroll about it. Many of the trees by the lake were planted by 'Capability' Brown, but among them are later plantings of weeping willows, dogwoods and swamp cypresses with their writhing, aerial roots, all united by artfully casual clumps of irises, day lilies, primulas and other moisture-loving plants. Spring bulbs, too, are a particular feature of the woodland garden, where they are naturalised among a mature and highly varied collection of trees and shrubs. Flora's Lawn – so called from a statue of the Roman goddess of flowers that stands on a 17m (55ft) plinth in its midst – was also one of Brown's creations.

By contrast, the conservatory is fronted by a garden of stately formality. There, the statue is of Mercury, forever on the point of flight from the centre of a round, still pond, while about him are shaven topiary shapes. The conservatory itself contains, as might be guessed, a fine collection of exotic plants, including ferns and cacti collections. Also at Syon is the world's largest collection of live butterflies that flutter freely among greenhouse gardens. Happily, an equally impressive collection of giant spiders and scorpions is kept enclosed.

One of the great glories of outdoor Syon is the 6-acre Rose Garden. Brown's ubiquitous hand was here, too, as may be seen by the presence of the oaks and cedars. But the original terracing and layout was planned by the Duke of Somerset more than 400 years ago. There are more than 2,000 roses in the garden, preceded in spring by an overture of massed daffodils, narcissi and crocuses.

Tatton Park Cheshire

'There is a noticeable lack of scandal and intrigue in the family history,' observes a brochure to Tatton Park. The family in question are the Egertons, an historic dynasty in Cheshire and South Lancashire who were masters at Tatton for 380 years. Apart from Maurice, the last lord (a big game hunter and pioneer of aviation), they were little given to eccentric behaviour. For colour, drama and whimsy you should not look to the family's chronicles but to their superb 60-acre gardens.

The Tatton gardens are owned today by the National Trust, and are remarkably varied in character. Set in a vast parkland landscaped by Humphry Repton, they include terraces and mixed borders, ornamental lakes, fountains, a classical temple and orangery, a complete Japanese garden and the largest fernery in Britain outside of a botanic garden.

The Egertons acquired Tatton in Elizabethan times, and occupied the site until 1958. The oldest feature of the gardens is a long, straight Beech Avenue which once formed the main approach to the house. Planted in the early 18th century, it is all that survives today of the early formal gardens. The rest were swept away by Humphry Repton, the gifted disciple of 'Capability' Brown, who was brought in to landscape Tatton in 1791. He advised breaking up the Beech Avenue to leave only informal clumps of trees. In the event the advice was ignored, though a new curving drive was introduced.

Repton's lovely parkland today provides only a background for the gardens proper. The viewing platform is a fine series of stone balustraded terraces and parterres at the south front. They were designed in the mid 19th century by Sir Joseph Paxton, famed for his work at Chatsworth and the Crystal Palace. Elaborately adorned with fountain, steps and marbled vases they are grandiose in style, but not so ornate that they clash with the misty perspectives of lake and woodland beyond.

The terrace borders are massed with perennials in pastel tones: blues, pinks, mauves and yellows mingling with fragrant lavenders and rosemary. Paxton's Italianate parterre below is equally quiet in tone; it is

▲ **Victorian survival** Ferns were a passion of the Victorians, who built elaborate glasshouses – ferneries – in which to nurture them, and displayed the green fern fronds lavishly around halls and drawing rooms. The fashion died out during the Edwardian period, and the glass-roofed fernery at Tatton Park is thought to be the last of its kind attached to a private house and still being used for its original purpose, as a unique period piece.

hard to believe that Maurice Egerton could have used it as a firing range to test out his new hunting rifles.

The fine orangery up by the house was built in 1818 and restored to the original plans in 1992. Now as then it shelters oranges and lemons. But the nearby fernery dates from Paxton's time, and may even be his design. Within the building are a gurgling pool and arrangements of mossy rockwork. The heart of the collection is formed by lofty New Zealand tree ferns (*Dicksonia antarctica*), brought to Tatton 130 years ago by a brother of the 1st Lord Egerton. Spreading their weird sheaves from truncated stems, they have an outlandish appearance. Around grows the elegant *Woodwardia radicans*, while the creeping fig (*Ficus radicans*) clothes the walls. The atmosphere is kept warm, and the mood is loaded with remembrance of a bygone taste.

The long Beech Avenue bisects the great pleasure grounds below the house, leading to a tall, narrow classical temple. At the outset of a walk down the straight way, a Brewer's spruce (*Picea breweriana*) will catch your eye. In spring the magnolias grouped around provide luminous delights. On the other side of the way is a little tower garden, named for an old brick tower from

which watch was once kept for any sheep stealers in the park. Here, among the hostas, you can see such unusual plants as the blue-podded *Decaisnea fargesii* o China, and the rare Kentucky coffee tree (*Gymnocladus dioica*).

Explore the gardens further and you wil be arrested time and again by fine specimen trees and little-seen shrubs. Banks and thickets of rhododendrons and azaleas conceal many a surprise: secret pools, a beech maze, a walled rose garden and even - improbably – a restored heather-thatched African hut which recalls the last lord's hunting days.

Perhaps the most pleasing of all these features is an authentic Japanese garden created in about 1910. It lies off the Golden Brook, a lovely stretch of water landscaped out of old marl pits, and was made by Japanese workmen brought to England specially for the task. From a small island at the centre of the lake there rises a Shinto temple, also brought from Japan, while a low and shapely arched bridge connects it with the garden itself.

The calm fantasy is watered by spring fed streams coming down from a glade of bamboos. Conspicuous features include a thatch-roofed tea-house, a miniature stone

agoda, and a steep mound of earth con-
oured to resemble Mount Fuji with white
now stones at the summit. Lanterns and
ymbolic figures are carefully grouped
round, while every plant is of Japanese
rigin. Wands of irises line the water's
dge, and cherries, plums and magnolias
se above.

The effect is more than picturesque.
risms of light in the lily-strewn water, the
uiet harmonies of flower and branch – all
ummon that tranquillity of spirit which is
e essence of Japanese gardening. The
ood, like the material, is authentic.

Threave Dumfries and Galloway

n centuries past, the great gardens of
Britain were tended by armies of gardeners.
Horticultural skills, passed on from genera-
ion to generation, provided a pool of experi-
nce for landowners to draw on. Today, very
ew gardens offer training facilities for
oungsters. But Threave in Scotland is one
f them – it was conceived from the outset
s a teaching garden.

The Threave estate covers some 1,500
cres, including five farms, extensive woods,
nd areas of wetland adjoining the River
Dee which are maintained as a wildfowl
eserve. Migrating greylag geese come here
n their hundreds every year, and whooper
wans are regular visitors. Conserving their
abitat was something that the late Major
A. F. L. Gordon had very much in mind
when, in 1948, he presented the whole
state to the National Trust for Scotland.

The major lived in the turreted mansion
until his death in 1957. Apart from one
small walled garden, his main horticultural
egacy was the planting of myriad daffodils
n the woodlands, which welcome visitors
with their radiant display in spring. But he
lso conceived the idea of making Threave
he site of a School of Practical Gardening,
o that the skills and traditions of the great
Scottish gardeners should not be lost in a
hanging world.

The school was opened in 1960, and the
55-acre gardens date from the same year.
They serve as a field of study but they are
ar from academic in their appeal. Plantings
re largely informal, and include woodland
and glade where choice shrubs have been
established among beeches, firs and larches.
Rhododendrons and azaleas are well represented and, though still young, thrive in the
heavy damp loam.

Tintinhull Somerset

The house, like Topsy of *Uncle Tom's Cabin*,
just grow'd'. In 1600 it was a Somerset
yeoman's farmhouse, then about a century
later acquired new dignity with the addition
of a rather grand west front with tall lat-

ticed windows, and a porch with pillars and
steps to enhance the front door. When, a few
years later, it was given a forecourt and
piers topped by stone eagles, it had clearly
become the residence of a country gentleman or prosperous farmer. And so it
remained until the end of the 19th century.

That it is now one of the most important
small gardens in the country is due to the
efforts of Tintinhull's last two owners, both
of whom, by happy chance, were gardeners
of considerable merit. In 1898, the house
was purchased by Dr Price, a clergyman and
distinguished botanist, who laid out the
handsome series of little gardens that
stretch out from the west front. The first of

these is the forecourt, or Eagle Court, as it
is rather splendidly called. From there, a
paved path and steps guarded by large bus-
bies of yew, run through the next area, the
azalea garden, and so to the fountain garden
with its pool and fountain surrounded by
yew hedges. At the very end there is a seat
from which one can look back down the path
and admire the softly glowing stone of the
house centred in its framing of garden.

The next owners were Captain and Mrs
Reiss, who acquired the place in 1933, and
at once set about developing and enlarging
the garden. In general, they followed the
principles of Dr Price, maintaining a series
of gardens enclosed by hedges and made to
look, in that somewhat flat part of the country, as though the whole had been created
from different levels. This is achieved by the
inclusion of a sunken garden in the plan,
and the cunning placing of steps. Other
features are a wide expanse of lawn and a
formal garden with borders, a large rectangular pool and a summerhouse.

The Reisses made many other additions
and improvements, including the building of
the terrace, but their greatest flair – and
especially Mrs Reiss's – was for planting.
She planned her borders in the manner prescribed by Gertrude Jekyll, the great garden

▲ **Tintinhull Gardens** The
rose-covered west front of
Tintinhull House, a
National Trust property,
looks out on the Eagle
Court – a walled garden
laid out on formal lines but
planted for the most part
with a lush informality.
Trim bushes of box stand
in file beside the path,
while roses, shrubs and
herbaceous plants tumble
over one another in a riot
of colour in the
surrounding beds.

▶ **Down to earth** A model of an armillary sphere – an ancient navigational aid for calculating distances between the stars – adds emphasis to the deliberate choice to 'go small' at Tintinhull. The garden is divided into many separate compartments, each with its own character, like the one glimpsed here through an arch in its enclosing hedge of yew.

designer at the turn of the century, who sought always for overall and continuing effect rather than the display of outstanding single plants or species. Thus, at Tintinhull in spring the accent is upon massed bulbs with a supporting cast of flowering cherries and a few evergreen shrubs. Then, in summer, one border is filled with bright colour such as red and white roses mixed with brilliant yellow verbascums and Spanish brooms, while another is in more muted shades, with pale yellow roses, and pale pink and mauve flowers predominating. All of the borders are mixed, an orchestration of shrubs, plants for flowers and foliage, bulbs, and even a low fronting of alpines, while each garden is brought into a pleasantly disciplined whole by its surround of dark yew. Tintinhull is a delight at any time from spring to October, but an especially good time for a visit is July, when large stone containers of Regale lilies are placed on the terrace to flaunt their white trumpets and sulphur-yellow interiors, and to fill the air with their somnolent fragrance.

Trelissick Cornwall

You expect to find hydrangeas in a Cornish garden. They are shrubs which tend to prosper in coastal areas, and especially relish the mild climate ushered in by the Gulf Stream. In summer, the common varieties seem to cluster every cottage wall with their densely flowered heads, shading from blue-mauve to pale pink according to the soil.

Trelissick Garden, above the estuary of the River Fal, is remarkable for its range of tender shrubs: choice magnolias, camellias

▲ **Ancient Cornwall** The gardens at Trelissick occupy one of the finest sites in Cornwall. From high above the Fal Estuary, Trelissick looks out to sea over green parkland and hanging woods of oak, beech and pine which run down to the water's edge. Shelterbelts of Holm oaks protect the garden's exotic plantings of choice magnolias, camellias and hydrangeas, huge Australian tree ferns, tender bulbs and, always, sweet-scented heliotropes.

and rhododendrons, for example. But if one family of plants has to be singled out as a speciality, it must be the hydrangeas. They are everywhere, from common Lace-caps and Hortensias to the rarest and least seen species. In all, over 130 different forms are represented, making the collection as complete as any in the British Isles.

Trelissick lies at the head of Falmouth Harbour, and at different points commands superb views, framed by hanging woods, down the deep-water anchorage and out to sea. But though graced with spacious lawns, the 25-acre garden is not open in every direction. It needs its protective plantings of conifers and Holm oaks to combat savage prevailing winds.

John Lawrence, a captain in the Cornwall Militia, built a house on the site in about 1750 and was remembered, enigmatically, for his 'good nature, convivial habits and wild eccentricities'. Remnants of his villa survive in the porticoed mansion seen today, though it was substantially rebuilt at different periods. The property changed hands many times over the years, and the garden grew in stages.

The Gilbert family owned Trelissick from 1844 to 1913, and their squirrel crest can be seen at the top of an old water tower in the garden. They were probably responsible for planting many of the screening trees, but the exotics were chiefly established by the Copelands, a husband and wife team who nurtured the garden from 1937 to 1955. An exotic exuberance of leaf, texture and flower form dominates the borders throughout the seasons; they include cannas, hedychium, beschornerias, agapanthus and alstromeria, while heady scent comes from lilies and the traditional Peruvian heliotropes.

Similarly luxuriant associations of plant are met throughout the garden. One magical spot is a quiet dell sheltering beneath Japanese cedars. In this lush hollow Australian tree ferns spread their green fronds among plantings of *Musa basjoo*, the hardy banana of Japan. Beneath them spreads a wild carpet of primulas, hosta and astilbes, while tall Himalayan rhododendrons loom behind.

Hydrangeas, of course, have been lavishly planted throughout the garden, lining paths with ramparts of summer colour, or planted singly as specimens. Among the host of species and cultivars there is, for example, a spectacular *Hydrangea paniculata* 'Grandiflora', which bears its freight of great white panicles throughout the summer; and a prominent mauve *H. villosa*. Among the curiosities, pride of place is probably held by *H. maritima* 'Ayesha', with its cupped clusters of lilac-grey.

North of the main garden area is a large stretch of rising ground specifically devoted to hydrangeas of the widest possible variety, planted among ornamental trees. It is reached by a bridge, and is known as Carcadden from old Cornish meaning 'fortified place'. This area was an overgrown orchard when the National Trust acquired the property in 1955. Though it has since

▶ **Blaze of scarlet** The acid soil and sheltered climate at Trelissick provide the perfect conditions for rhododendrons. Massive tree forms glow in late spring dressed in scarlet and watch with lofty superiority over matching low-growing azaleas.

een developed for decorative effect, it still retains a Victorian summerhouse which offers lovely views back from the young to the older garden.

Apart from the hydrangeas, rhododendrons have taken to Trelissick as they have to so many Cornish gardens. The coaxing climate and lime-free soil have permitted a splendid miscellany to flourish. A tall clump of the tree-like *Rhododendron* 'Cornish Red' is just one of many eye-catching plantings, and the garden also has its own rhododendron hybrids: 'Trelissick Salmon' and 'Trelissick Port Wine'.

Add the springtime freshness of camellias and magnolias, the autumn fire of maples and oxydendrums, and you have a true garden for all seasons. Nor do Trelissick's attractions end at the boundaries of the garden proper. Below the exotics are many acres of woodland where miles of carriage drives wind among the beeches and oaks. They were laid out by Ralph Allen Daniell, a tin-mining magnate of the early 19th century. Owner of the Trelissick estate, he was said to be the richest man in Cornwall in his day, and known as 'Guinea-a-minute-Daniell' after a single mine which was said to furnish him with that sum.

The walks lead down to the tide-lapped shores of the estuary, following the bank of secluded Lamouth Creek. It is a haunting inlet, evocative of a more ancient Cornwall than the garden's – of Druidic mystery and Arthurian romance, and of the smugglers, who would bring their contraband exotica by moonlit paths from the shore.

Tresco Abbey Gardens
Isles of Scilly

In a corner of Tresco Abbey Gardens is an area known as Valhalla – named for the resting place of heroes in the Norse heaven. In it you can see a collection of figureheads and other objects salvaged from ships that foundered on the Isles of Scilly. There are Saracen heads and gilded eagles, women in billowing robes – all victims of the salt gales which shriek about the islands and the wind-driven rollers which burst against their shores.

The Scillies' winds are wreckers' winds – root-wrenching, stem-snapping swashbucklers which ought to make gardening impossible. But of course it is not. Screen off the vandal air currents and you detect a special radiance in the sea-cleansed air, and a mildness of climate found nowhere on mainland Britain. Apart from tourism, flower growing is the islanders' main source of income. Bulbs, planted in sheltered, pocket-handkerchief fields, yield daffodils for Christmas.

And on Tresco, the second largest of the isles, much more than daffodils are grown. There are date palms from the Canaries and blue-plumed echiums from Australia, South African proteas and coral-red Mexican beschornerias. Strange spiky foliage, colours rich and rare – all jostle for attention in an atmosphere of unimaginable luxuriance. Tresco has been called a plant-lover's Treasure Island, and it holds Britain's most exotic paradise garden.

Tresco lies out in the Atlantic some 30

▲ **High and dry** A statue of Neptune looks out to sea from his resting place on the top terrace of Tresco Abbey Gardens. Between him and his kingdom lies a garden where 3,000 species of plants from the Southern Hemisphere flourish together in a semi-tropical paradise.

▲ **Tresco Abbey Gardens** The ruins of the old Priory of St Nicholas, which once sheltered Tresco's community of Benedictine monks, now provide support and protection for tropical climbing plants and a foothold for ferns, stonecrops and other succulents. Exotic palms and conifers jut skywards, and in every nook and cranny are self-sown mesembryanthemums, those gaudy natives of South Africa, originally introduced by Augustus Smith more than a century ago.

miles from Land's End. Though its line of latitude is fractionally to the north of the Cornish Lizard's the island is washed on all sides by the warm Gulf Stream, which accounts for its exceptionally mild climate. And it was Augustus Smith, a 19th-century Hertfordshire gentleman, who first saw Tresco's potential.

In 1834, Smith acquired the lease of all the Scillies, taking up the title of Lord Proprietor of the Isles. And he made Tresco the capital of his little Atlantic empire, building a granite house for himself on the site of Tresco's ruined Benedictine priory.

Tresco was treeless then, boasting no plant taller than a gorse bush. But Smith knew what might be done in its practically frost-free climate. Immediately on arrival he built a complex of walled garden enclosures to fend off the wind. Later, terraces were gouged out of the south-facing slopes below the abbey, and shelterbelts of conifers were established to extend the storm-proofing. By the time of his death in 1872, Tresco Abbey Gardens covered some 17 acres, with considerable woodlands around.

The purpose was, from the outset, to nurture tender exotics which would not survive on the mainland. It has been said of the Scilly Isles that they know only two seasons: spring and summer. Though slight frosts do occasionally occur at Tresco, winter temperatures vary rarely drop below 10°C (50°F); very high summer temperatures are equally uncommon. Into this balmy, ever-coaxing climate, Smith brought rare specimens from Kew as well as seeds gathered from all over the Southern Hemisphere.

The result was a garden vivid even in mid winter, a marvel among those of Smith's contemporaries. In 1851, Smith could write on Christmas Eve: 'My garden was left in high colour, the Clianthus just bursting into flower and the *Acacia lophantha* also covered with yellow blossoms.'

In Smith's day, a visit from the mainland was akin to an act of pilgrimage, and an arduous one at that. Today, it takes less effort than you might think to reach Tresco Abbey Gardens. Apart from regular ferry services, the island also claims the world's only Garden Heliport; visitors are brought from Penzance to the garden gate by a British Airways helicopter.

Whatever route is chosen, your surprise on arrival will be unfailing. The plants which flourish here with such exuberance – in spite of the damage caused by storms such as those of 1987 – might be familiar to a Maori or a Mexican; but what place have they in an English garden? Great sheaves of palms and cordylines do much to set the tone, with the sharp-leaved desert agaves, aloes and opuntias which abound. Much else contributes to the subtropical mood. Take *Kennedia nigricans*, a West Australian climber whose petals are black as ebony; dasylirions from Mexico like huge green sea urchins with their bristling spheres of spikes. Correas, puyas, gazanias and dimorphothecas . . . over 3,000 species and varieties of plants are represented.

Among the eye-catching trees in the Pebble Garden is a massive specimen of the Chilean wire palm (*Jubaea chilensis*), whose grey, barrel-like trunk is filled with its own fermented sap. This fluid is tapped in the tree's native Chile for its alcoholic properties.

Scattered about the garden are many large specimens of the Canary Island date palm (*Phoenix canariensis*). Up to 12m (40ft) high, they dominate the scene. From the island of Madeira, also in the Atlantic, comes the lily-of-the-valley-tree (*Clethra arborea*), up to 21m (70ft) tall, with its nodding, cup-shaped flowers that bloom from August to October.

Tresco has the largest specimen in Britain of the kauri pine from New Zealand (*Agathis australis*), rising to around 23m (75ft). The wood of this forest giant is highly prized as timber, and was once used by the Royal Navy for ships' spars.

The Lighthouse Way divides the garden in half. At the lower end is a 17th-century lighthouse cresset, a container in which coal fires were burned to warn passing ships of danger. At the higher end, a stone head of Neptune looks down a flight of steps flanked by Canary Island palms.

For all its luxurious diversity, Tresco is not a hard garden in which to find your way about. The sloping site is roughly rectangular, and the other main axis is a so-called Long Walk which crosses the Lighthouse Way at right-angles. Between them they divide the garden into four quarters, within each of which different areas display their own character. One, for example, is known as 'Mexico'; another is a rockery devoted to cacti and succulents from Arizona. The garden ornaments include an ancient Roman sacrificial altar which stands at the end of the Long Walk. Near by is a planting of the Chilean myrtle (*Myrtus luma*), yet another outstanding attraction. The smooth and slender orange trunks of these distinctive trees leave a memorable impression.

Ventnor Botanic Garden
Isle of Wight

Among Britain's leading Botanic Gardens, the name of Ventnor may not have the resonance of, say, a Westonbirt or a Kew. Covering some 22 acres of the Isle of Wight, the garden was only started in 1969, and it was opened as recently as 1972. It is, in fact, Britain's youngest Botanic Garden, though its maturity may make the claim hard to believe on a visit.

The Botanic Garden lies in the Undercliff – a curious 6-mile ledge in the downs. It was formed by ancient landslides, and completely protects the garden from chilly north and

east winds. Salt gales from the south and west, meanwhile, have already been largely screened by youthful shelterbelts of trees. Climatically, this warm pocket is as favoured as the Scilly and Channel Islands. Olives, pomegranates, oranges and the hardy Japanese banana (*Musa basjoo*) all fruit in the open at Ventnor.

If the south-coast sun trap has a problem it is the high alkaline content of the soil. You would not expect to find acid-loving plants in a downland setting. Yet in this, as in all else, Ventnor has been fortunate. In one area, natural deposits of peat overlie the local limestone. Camellias and magnolias thrive there, along with such rarities as the tender camphor tree (*Cinnamomum camphora*) of the Far East.

A recent attraction is the development of a temperate show house displaying a collection of plants from Australia, South Africa and the Canary Islands, and giving an extraordinary display of floral exuberance far into the year. The flamboyant Sturt's desert pea (*Cleanthus formosus*) flowers in profusion, forming a bright red carpet. Passion flowers bear masses of intricate blooms. And, to add to the gaiety of the floral show, bougainvilleas are trained to cover a large expanse of the end wall of the show house.

Ventnor includes a good selection of rare conifers, and a well-stocked rose garden. But for the most heightened tropical effects visit the Palm Garden, where many types of palms and cordylines spread their spiky fronds all around. Crotons, aspidistras and New Zealand tree ferns contribute to the mood of pampered luxury, and here, too, you can see the curious *Beschorneria yuccoides* from Mexico. It is a striking plant which seems somehow colour-schemed the wrong way round: the 1.8m (6ft) high stems are a vivid coral red, while the flowers, perversely, are a brilliant green.

Waddesdon Manor
Buckinghamshire

When Benjamin Disraeli was invited to witness the building of Waddesdon, he is said to have remarked that if only the Almighty had had a Rothschild to aid him then the Creation would have been accomplished in considerably under seven days. As it happened, it took Baron Ferdinand de Rothschild rather more than seven years, from 1875 to 1883, to build the house and the elaborate pleasure grounds surrounding it. But considering it involved lowering a 10 acre hilltop by 3m (9ft) over all, it was not too bad. A branch railway was constructed to bring the Bath stone and other materials from the main line at Quainton, while teams of Percheron mares were imported from Normandy for the last stages of the haul. Hundreds of mature trees were brought in on specially constructed carts, and tele

▲ **Ventnor Botanic Garden** Situated on the southern shore of the Isle of Wight, Ventnor has an almost Mediterranean climate thanks to a dense shelterbelt of Holm oaks. Olives, pomegranates and bananas flourish and fruit in the open, and separate sections are devoted to plants from Australia, New Zealand, Japan and South Africa. The medicinal garden is outstanding, and the large lavender-edged rose section has earned the garden international renown.

▲ Waddesdon Manor In 1875 Baron Ferdinand de Rothschild decided to bring a little bit of France to England. First he built Waddesdon Manor in the style of a French Renaissance château, then he called in a French landscape gardener to lay out the grounds. The result would fit as well into the environs of Paris as it does into the rolling landscape of Buckinghamshire.

graph wires were lowered along the roads so as not to impede their passage. The trees were then dropped by a system of chains into holes in the bare hillside. Acres of turf, paths and drives were laid, statues and fountains set up, beds planted, the aviary and pergola constructed, and there it was, the grounds virtually complete.

At its heart was the towered and turreted manor house, and there the baron lived, among his beloved collections of 18th-century art, until his sadly early death in 1898. The estate then passed to his sister, Miss Alice de Rothschild, who is still remembered in the district for her kindness and strength of character. She was also a gardener of note, and added considerably to the numbers of rare trees and shrubs. When she died in 1922, Waddesdon passed to her great-nephew, James de Rothschild, who served with distinction with the French army in the First World War, and as a junior minister in the British Government in the Second. In accordance with his grandfather's wish that the manor should never be broken up or allowed to deteriorate, he left it to the National Trust in 1957, together with all its magnificent paintings and furniture.

Waddesdon Manor is a deliberate compromise between a French château and a great Victorian country house, and a similar comment might be made about the grounds. The outlying area, with its deer pens, artfully 'genuine' caverns (for wild sheep), its apparently random distribution of grand trees and shrubs and its wonderful views

over the Chilterns to the south, is very much a Victorian adaptation of the landscape notions of the previous century. But the northern approach to the house is far more reminiscent of the great gardens of France. The introduction is a large gravel circle, in the midst of which is an awesome group of 18th-century Italian statuary Triton and the Nereids – spouting water. From there, no fewer than five parallel drives reach up, ruler-straight, to the house. All about are fine trees, for example silver limes and blue cedars, and groups of statuary depicting classical themes.

About the house are majestic terraces laid out by Baron Ferdinand de Rothschild himself. To this day, the terrace beds require some 10,000 tulips and as many wallflowers to fill them in spring; for summer colour 9,000 geraniums and 5,000 ageratums are planted. On the south terrace there is another group of fountain statuary, this one portraying Pluto and Proserpine. In the early 18th century it was united with the group by the north entrance to form, amazingly, only part of a fountain for a ducal palace near Parma.

A stroll in the grounds presents all kinds of delights. There is the vast bowl of Daffodil Valley, for instance, given extra depth by the tall conifers gathered upon its rim, and pushing forth a sea of daffodils in the spring. And certainly, no one should miss the aviary, a large semi-circle of delicate metalwork that is beautifully set off by hornbeam hedges and 'Iceberg' roses.

Wakehurst Place

West Sussex

However lovely it may be, it must still be a considerable accolade for any garden to be coveted by Kew; but so it was at Wakehurst. It is a very old place, with a robust history of abducted medieval heiresses and 18th-century rakes, but the story of its garden begins little more than 90 years ago when the estate was purchased by Gerald Loder, later Lord Wakehurst. A gardener of brilliance, he began the famous collection of trees and shrubs at Wakehurst. His work was continued by his successor, Sir Henry Price, who bequeathed the estate to the National Trust. Then, in 1965, it was acquired on a long lease by the Royal Botanic Gardens as a kind of out-of-town Kew.

The emphasis at Wakehurst is upon wild species, the botanical collections being developed along the theme of walks through the temperate woodlands of the world. They could not have a finer setting than the wooded slopes and valleys of the Sussex Weald, where so many great gardens have been created. The grounds are magnificently laid out and, in spite of severe damage in the storms of 1987, still contain landscapes which are quite extraordinary for the variety of their themes and content. Wakehurst Place offers a unique blend of the exotic and the natural, the ornamental collections blending effortlessly into the native woods and fields. Fine specimen trees include a magnolia planted in 1908, Japanese maples

and giant redwoods. Just to the west of the house is the Memorial Garden dedicated to Sir Henry Price. The Pleasaunce, near by, is another small and intimate garden with clipped yew hedges and an ornamental pond with a fountain.

One of the oldest established parts of Wakehurst is the Southern Hemisphere Garden. It was here that Gerald Loder established his collection of Australasian and temperate South American plants at the beginning of this century. There are myrtles and waratahs with flowers like red claws, beautiful white-flowering hoherias and, in late summer, the stunning white-flowering eucryphias. The Slips, not far off, is an idealised Sussex Valley, with a little stream running through it. Above the Slips is another memorial, a sundial commemorating Gerald Loder and his gardener, Alfred Coates. It bears the words:

Give fools their gold and knaves their power,
Let fortune's bubbles rise and fall,
Who sows a field or trains a flower
Or plants a tree, is more than all.

The Slips comes to an end with the Water Gardens, a series of ponds round which grow a wide variety of marsh and water-loving plants, with candelabra primulas, irises, hostas and astilbes providing an unrivalled spectacle in early June. Downhill is another valley, Westwood Valley or The Ravine, with steep, heavily wooded sides and a broad scattering of rhododendrons

▲ **Memorial garden** A walled garden, close to the house at Wakehurst Place, has been dedicated as a memorial to Sir Henry Price, who left the estate to the nation in 1964. It has been managed since then by the Royal Botanic Gardens at Kew. It is stocked with old-fashioned cottage-garden flowers in pastel shades and includes old roses, pinks and clematis.

showing through the trees. In spring, they look for all the world like an avalanche of colour breaking down the slopes. There, too, a couple of wonderful specimen trees – an 18m (60ft) tall pink-flowering magnolia, and a handkerchief tree with the curious fluttering white bracts that give it its name.

Below Rock View, a natural outcrop of the local sandstone, is the Himalayan Glade containing a collection of plants – rhododendron species, junipers and barberries – that would more normally be found about 3,000m (10,000ft) up on the shoulders of the Himalayas. Beyond is the Pinetum, a splendid, 12-acre gathering of conifers, many of which are rare in Britain. Horsebridge Woods, Bloomer's Valley and Bethlehem Wood, by contrast, seem much more like native woodland; at least at first glance. But among the more familiar trees there are also some handsome strangers, such as California redwoods, Wellingtonias, and a monkey-puzzle tree from Chile. Throughout the woods, the bluebells grow, countless thousands of them, producing in spring an acres-wide carpet of misty blue. At the head of Horsebridge Woods, the highly picturesque Rock Walk begins. A place of massive sandstone outcrops, over which writhe and flow the roots of yews, beeches and oaks.

▼ Dutch discipline Tall trees and neatly trimmed yew hedges keep untidy nature at bay in the gardens at Westbury Court. They were laid out in the late 17th century in the formal Dutch style which became popular – if not obligatory – after the accession of William of Orange. The magnificent canals and waterways are presided over by a statue of Neptune bestride a dolphin.

Westbury Court
Gloucestershire

An early 18th-century engraving show Westbury Court as a Tudor house with th tall spire of a church near by and, in th middle distance, an imposing summerhous or pavilion at the head of a long, straigh waterway. Much of the surrounding ground consist of formal flower beds, further rigidl drawn canals and row upon row of immacu lately spaced trees.

The spire still stands, and so does th summerhouse, but Westbury Court itse has long vanished as have two houses tha succeeded it. Which makes it all the mor remarkable that through a number of luck accidents, a generous and anonymous dona tion and some very hard work on the part o the National Trust the garden has survive and is now the most perfect – and the oldes – example of an enclosed Dutch-style garde in the country.

It was laid out in the closing years of th 17th century by Colonel Maynar Colchester, in response to the enthusiasr for things Dutch that swept over the coun try in the wake of William of Orange's acces sion. There were dozens of gardens like it a the time, almost all of which were to b obliterated by 'Capability' Brown and hi fellow landscape gardeners.

Westbury Court is the very antithesis o the landscape garden. Like other Dutch gar dens of its period, it depends for effect o organised prettiness close at hand. Natur was ruthlessly kept at bay by high walls an nearly 5,000 yews and hollies carved int hedges or topiary figures; babbling stream were replaced by straight-cut waterway whose limpid surfaces reflected statuary Flower beds, too, were straight-cut, outline by miniature hedges of box and interspersec with geometric shapes in topiary.

It was a place of great charm and ele gance, and its survival was due not t preservation, but neglect. For most of th 19th century it was deserted by th Colchester family, and though they move back and built another house there in 1895 they sold the estate in 1960 to a speculato who intended to build ten houses on th site. The local council refused permission however, and built a home for the elderly o the site of the old house; the garden wa offered to the National Trust.

The problems seemed insurmountable, bu thanks to a public appeal and donations fron various sources, sufficient money was raisec by 1967 for the National Trust to begin a pro gramme of restoration. All was done to con form as closely as possible with the 18th-cen tury engraving and with information gleanec from Colonel Colchester's account books anc planting records. Perhaps the most delightfu aspect is that the gardens are now replantec almost entirely with species known to have been present in England prior to 1700.

▲ **Autumn woodlands** The trees at Wakehurst Place, seemingly a natural occurrence but in reality a meticulously planned scheme of exotic and native forest species, are a delight throughout the year for garden lovers and plantsmen alike. They are perhaps at their most stunning, though, in autumn when the quiet walkways trail through a blaze of russet, scarlet and gold before the Japanese maples shed their foliage and stand naked beneath massive redwoods.

▲ **Acer Glade** Westonbirt Arboretum is sensational at any season, the mighty trunks and sheer scale of the trees providing living architecture for the scene. Visit in spring to marvel at the rhododendrons, magnolias and flowering cherries, and the anemones, primroses and bluebells in Silk Wood. But in autumn, the Acer Glade is beyond comparison – a feast of yellow and gold, pink, crimson and purple before the maples retreat into winter stillness.

Westonbirt Arboretum
Gloucestershire

King Midas, according to the old Greek myth, suffered from a curse by which everything he touched turned to gold. Visit Westonbirt in October and you may feel that autumn stalks the woodlands with the same glorious affliction. In the Acer Glade especially, fires of sensational brilliance burn all about: glowing pinks and crimsons, furious oranges and sheaves of yellow that flash so bright they seem to be lit from within.

Westonbirt is a marvel at any time of year. The cathedral spires of its mighty conifers change little month by month, and the blooms of innumerable interplanted shrubs lend colour in spring, summer and even winter. But October – the month of the Japanese maple – provides a quality of experience all its own.

The great arboretum was founded in 1829 by Robert Holford of Westonbirt House. His family had occupied the Gloucestershire estate for many generations. But what was to become the best tree collection in Europe started only when the owner began planting in pasturelands west of the park. The existing layout, with its formal avenues, broad rides and meandering paths, dates chiefly from 1855, when many oaks, beeches, pines, larches and yews were established.

The whole enterprise was designed for private pleasure and interest. From 1870 the owner's son, Sir George Holford, joined his father in amassing a wealth of ornamental trees brought to Westonbirt from all over the world. The decorative plantings were extended to cover some 247 acres in all. And the tradition established by the Holfords and their successors is now continued by the Forestry Commission, which acquired the property in 1956.

Westonbirt lies on a broad Cotswold ridge at some 120m (400ft) above sea level. But though situated in a limestone landscape, pockets of sandy loam are sufficiently free of lime to allow acid-loving plants to root comfortably. Some fine magnolias, for example, grace the woodlands in March, and by May the blossoms of rhododendrons and azaleas provide wonderful shows of colour.

The arboretum is managed today for purposes of teaching and research. But maintaining the tradition of ornamental planting has been much in the minds of the administrators. Westonbirt was after all conceived for private enjoyment. Open all the year round, it invites the public's attention. 'For us,' claims the guidebook, 'every day is an open day.'

You can wander at will throughout the entire collection with its 18,000 catalogued trees and shrubs. And the authorities are not fastidious about how you choose to view the specimens. 'For a change,' it suggests, 'put some foliage between yourself and the sun – you could not believe the colour and the

effect you will see; get down on your hands and knees if you have to, we don't mind!'

One tremendous group of old incense cedars (*Calocedrus decurrens*) is found on Holford Ride, and elsewhere all the great conifers are represented: Wellingtonias, coast redwoods and Douglas firs, for instance. But there are giants, too, among deciduous trees. The Italian alder (*Alnus cordata*), a bright green, pyramidal tree from southern Europe, regularly grows to 21m (70ft). Westonbirt's specimen easily tops that – at a height of 34m (110ft) it is the largest of its family in Britain.

There are several such record-breakers at Westonbirt. They make a fittingly diverse crew for this garden of variety, and with 17 miles of pathways winding among the woodlands the attractions are impossible to digest in one visit. The answer is to plan your explorations according to the time of year. The official guidebook suggests different areas for different seasons.

The Westonbirt calendar begins in the dark days of January and February. At a time when most English gardens are languishing, the arboretum is flecked with the colours of winter-flowering cherries; shrubs such as Christmas box (*Sarcococca humilis*) and *Viburnum farreri* scent the air.

From the bluebell days of spring through to June's lilac time, Westonbirt is radiant

▲ **Fountain Pool** Among the wonderful world of trees at Westonbirt, where deer and badgers can be glimpsed in the leafy glades, a note of formality is struck by the house and visitor centre. Here an ornate pool of classical style mirrors the sky and shimmers in summer sun with the pure white of water lilies.

with colour. In the heat of high summer you can escape to any number of cool, shady walks, and then, with September and the ripening of fruits, autumn comes with its Midas touch.

By October, the Acer Glade to the north of the entrance becomes a place of magnetic attraction. The focus of interest is a fireworks display without parallel in any English garden. The fireworks, of course, are entirely natural phenomena caused by the retreat of sap from the dying foliage of the maples. The Japanese maples (*Acer japonicum*, *A. palmatum* and their cultivars) are famed for the brilliance of their autumn colours; but the selection at Westonbirt is unique for its range and magnificence – almost every known form is represented. Several of the specimens are over 100 years old, and there are record-breakers here as elsewhere in the arboretum.

The colours are what quicken the pulse. For the most sensational effects, *A. japonicum* 'Vitifolium' holds pride of place, its foliage turning from yellow in September to a whole mosaic of tones, suffused with smoky purple as well as pink, crimson and gold – all on a single tree. In contrast, *A. palmatum* and its cultivars tend to turn colour in uniform sequence: the elegant 'Osakazuki' – a perfect scarlet – is the most prized for its purity of hue. These and a host of others, including the native field maple and common sycamore, provide one of the finest sights known to British gardeners. ·

In reality, it is more than a 'sight'. With the foliage glowing all around, shaken by gusts and carpeting the ground with their fiery leaves, you could call it an experience – a vision even – of autumn itself.

Weston Park Shropshire

The house at Weston Park dates from 1671. The family seat of the Earls of Bradford, it is one of Britain's best examples of Restoration-style architecture, and is a treasure house of pictures and tapestries. The paintings include works by Holbein, Van Dyck, Reynolds, Stubbs and Gainsborough, and there are tapestries from Aubusson and Gobelin. In a different context, admirers of P. G. Wodehouse know Weston Park as the inspiration for 'Blandings Castle'.

Some of the surrounding trees may go back as far as the house, but the rolling landscape which extends to south, east and west was contoured in the next century by 'Capability' Brown. He was commissioned in the 1760s and worked his customary magic on the terrain, filling in the middle distance with a glimmering lake, and planting trees singly and in groups to provide serpentine views towards the horizon.

A series of wide terraces looks from the house to the parkland beyond, where fallow deer and rare breeds of sheep graze.

Embellished with topiary and ornament urns, the terraces end at a beautiful balustraded arch. A Victorian oranger stands to one side of the house, with a Italianate garden spread before it.

Out in Brown's landscape there are love ly walks to be had through what Benjami Disraeli, in a letter to Selina, Countess Bradford, called Weston's 'scenes so fair'. I his 'stately woods of Weston' rhododendron and azaleas bloom in May and early Jun Temple Wood, especially, with its venerabl chestnuts and oaks, is magnificent in earl summer. Temple Wood and a Water Garde can be seen from a miniature railway. Th long, narrow woodland was laid out b Brown as a backdrop for a Temple of Dian designed by James Paine, an architect wh often collaborated with the landscapist.

The building is among the finest exam ples of Georgian garden architecture, th shapely arches of its tall glass-paned wi dows surmounted by a domed roof to th rear. But it was never designed to house shrine. The temple takes its name from dec orative panels which grace a circular te room within; they show scenes from th Roman goddess's life.

North of the building, though, is th secluded Temple Pool, overlooked by a littl domed temple of its own. This is a place c sylvan mystery, and when breezes crinkl the water and rustle among the leaves yo really can imagine that it is haunted by th woodland gods of antiquity. At the far end i Paine's Roman bridge, pale against the tree which cast long shadows on the water.

A Tropical House where bananas onc grew for the Earls of Bradford is now colourful tropical garden.

Winkworth Arboretum Surrey

The National Trust's only true arboretum Winkworth consists of 99 acres of wooded hillsides curled about a pair of still, reflec tive lakes in the Surrey 'Alps'. Most of it i the work of Dr Wilfrid Fox, a distinguishe physician and horticulturist, who bought large piece of neglected woodland in 193 and devoted the last quarter-century of hi life to making it a place of beauty that woul be enjoyed in perpetuity.

It was a magnificent accomplishment, skilful blending of exotic trees and shrub with native woodland to produce a round the-year cavalcade of colour and interes that is all the more delightful for its appar ent casualness. This is, one feels, what a British woodland might have looked lik had nature not distributed some of the mos colourful trees in other parts of the worlc instead. However, a goodly number of these have now been assembled at Winkworth among the native trees, to spring out in their seasons in wild displays of foreignness

Autumn is the crescendo, when the sky is clear and the water is polished by early frosts. Then the hillsides above flame, in the manner of the hills of New England, with the luminous yellows and oranges of snake bark maples, the deep red of American oaks and the clear, singing yellow of birches. Among them are crimson-berried cotoneasters, the coral of ornamental cherry trees, fiery Japanese maples, bronze North American sweet gums and the incredible scarlet of disanthus, a Japanese relative of hamamelis (witch hazel). At one point, there is a line of tupelo trees from the eastern United States, whose leaves flare scarlet, yellow and orange; among them, holding the brightness down, as it were, is the steely blue-grey of Atlantic cedars.

But lovely though autumn is, spring and early summer could hardly be termed an anti-climax. In May and June, mountain ashes and whitebeams put forth their white flowers – Winkworth holds the National Collection of whitebeams (Aria and Micromeles groups) – along with flowering cherries, rhododendrons, and the clear, waxy white of magnolias. This, too, is the time to visit the Azalea Steps: 93 of them climb the hillside, lined on either side by joyous masses of azaleas, giving this remarkable feature the air of a triumphal stairway. Those who prefer spring with less drama should visit the arboretum in March, when vast areas of the woodland are white with native anemones, and then again in April, when they give way to a soft ground-mist of bluebells.

In the midst of the garden there is a simple monument to Dr Fox, designed by Sir Hugh Casson and guarded by a pair of evergreen eucryphias that bear large white flowers at summer's end. Altogether a memorial that seems particularly apt.

Wisley Surrey

One of the joys of visiting any garden is to discover some plant or ornamental effect which might grace your own plot at home. Wisley, in this context, offers a range of ideas without compare in the British Isles. In these Surrey acres almost every type of gardening is practised, researched and displayed. Wisley is a great puzzle-solver – a treasury of possibilities.

If your own garden tends to go through a dull patch after June you can visit the summer garden. A host of bulbs, herbaceous plants and flowering shrubs demonstrate what a vivid palette you can draw on for colour. Suppose that some corner of your garden needs a tree for height: which has the fastest growth rate? Which offers the best tones of foliage or bark? You can visit the Jubilee arboretum, where 32 acres have been developed to answer such questions.

Wisley can advise you on what is tender, what is hardy, what to use for ground-cover

and how to clothe a wall. It has bog garden, rock garden, herb garden, heath garden, wild garden, pinetum . . . there is no space here to describe all the attractions. But there is space at Wisley – 240 acres of it – for their display on the grandest scale.

World famous today, Wisley was founded in 1878 when Mr George F. Wilson bought a 60-acre estate of neglected woodland in Surrey. He was a talented amateur gardener and former treasurer of the Royal Horticultural Society. At Wisley he quickly set to work making glades and ponds as settings for flowering shrubs, lilies, irises and a wealth of other plants. After his death, the estate was given in 1903 to the Royal Horticultural Society. It was to be developed and extended to make an experimental garden where every form of scientific and practical horticulture could be encouraged.

You approach Wisley today through a heathland lightly wooded with birches, oaks and pines. The soil is not in fact favourable to gardening, being generally lean and sandy, so that water drains swiftly away. With an average annual rainfall of only 660mm (26in), keeping the plants mulched, fed and watered is a full-time occupation for the staff. But you could be forgiven for failing to notice the difficulties on a visit. Wisley is as beautifully maintained as it is fascinating.

On entry you discover the laboratory building where subjects from propagation to pest control are studied. Near by are terraced lawns, a formal pool and pergola. The area typifies the spirit at Wisley.

Scores of gardening styles are represented, Wisley's index running from alpine meadow to winter garden. And though each holds its own fascination, some are famed in their own right as gardens of exceptional quality. The alpine meadow, for example, is a sloping expanse of grass which shimmers in early April with the tiny nodding heads of myriad yellow *Narcissus bulbocodium*, self-seeding and spreading all the time.

▲ Winkworth Arboretum
Autumn is the time to come to Winkworth, when maples, gums, oaks and birches flare into luminous imitation of a New England fall. But glorious though the Winkworth autumn is, it is almost equalled by the springtime pageant, when the azaleas put forth their near-incredible range of colours against the young green of the trees. Huge drifts line the Azalea Steps, flow down to the upper lake by The Bowl and edge the Fiona Adams Steps in Badger's Bowl.

Later, the pastels of wood anemones and dog's tooth violets will spangle the turf. Spotted orchids succeed in June and, before winter comes, purple autumn crocuses will splash the grass with colour again.

The meadow merges to one side with Wisley's celebrated rock garden, where slabs and boulders of Sussex sandstone are threaded by a chain of pools and waterfalls. Near by is the equally renowned wild garden, one of the oldest attractions at Wisley, where trees and shrubs planted by George F. Wilson have matured amid the native oaks. The soil is more moist and peaty here than is typical in the gardens. Rhododendrons, magnolias and camellias prosper in the shade, while all around rise the trunks of noble trees like the dawn redwood, a primeval conifer with its fissured red-brown bole.

These informally planted areas comprise only a part of Wisley's attraction. Elsewhere there are areas developed specifically for average gardeners with average plots. Known as the Model Gardens, they offer a wide range of imaginative ideas and practical suggestions. Situated on either side of the path to the glasshouses, the Model Gardens include fruit and herb gardens, a typical town or suburban garden, a family garden and one for disabled people. The Garden for all Seasons was created in conjunction with Reader's Digest and opened in 1991.

Simply listing the enticements does them scant justice, and that in a sense is the whole point. This, supremely, is a garden to be visited, again and again.

▲ **Hallowed hall** The offices, library and laboratory at the Royal Horticultural Society's gardens at Wisley are housed in a picturesque building. Roses, magnolias and ceanothus clothe the walls, with a formal lily pool in the foreground.

▲ **Carpet bedding** Unique for its blend of practical horticulture and inspirational vision, Wisley is a place where experienced and novice gardeners alike return time and again. Highlights include the Alpine Meadow and the rhododendrons on Battleston Hill in spring, the rose gardens and mixed borders in high summer. Guided walks throughout the year take in model gardens, practical demonstrations and trial grounds, including intricate schemes of bedding plants.

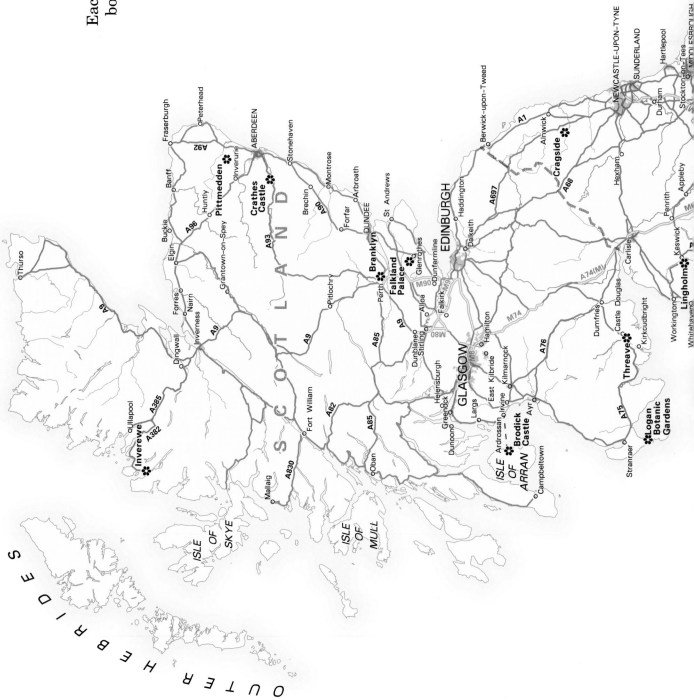

Gardens to Visit

Each of the gardens described in this book is located on the map with ❧

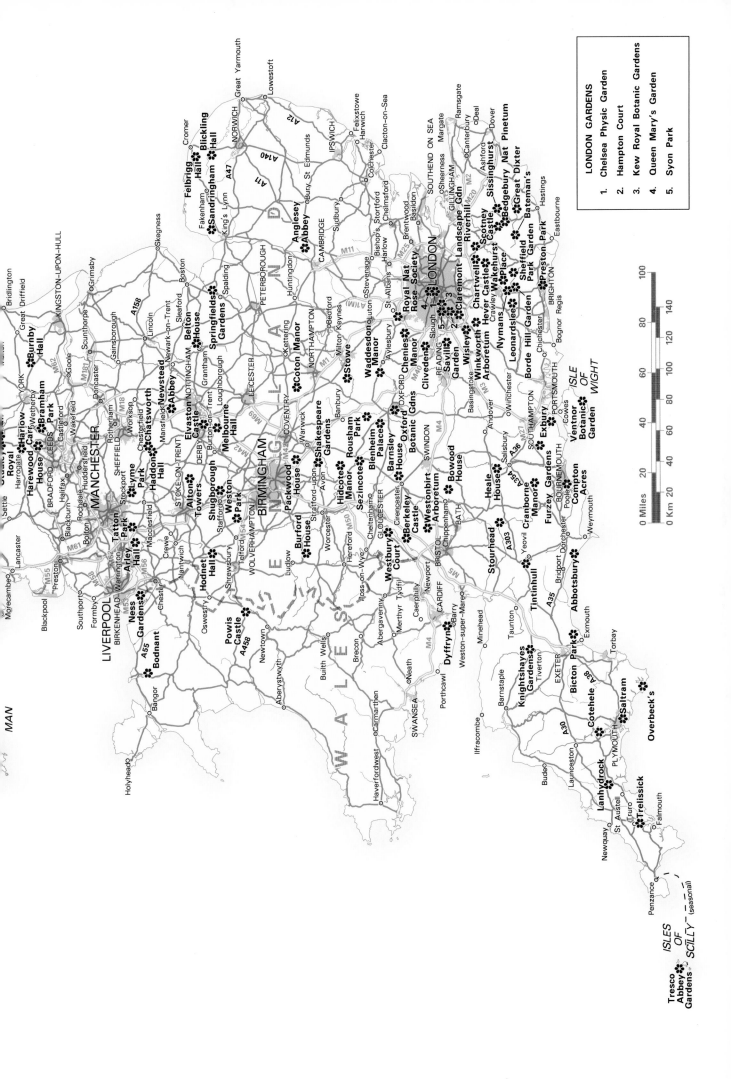

ADDRESSES

All the gardens described in this book are open to the public. Opening times vary from garden to garden, and from year to year; it is advisable to check in advance before planning a visit.

A

Abbotsbury Gardens,
Abbotsbury,
Weymouth,
Dorset, DT3 4LA.
Tel. 01305 871387

Alton Towers,
Alton,
Staffordshire, ST10 4DB.
Tel. 01538 703344

Anglesey Abbey,
Lode,
Cambridgeshire, CB5 9EJ.
Tel. 01223 812677

Arley Hall and Gardens,
nr. Northwich,
Cheshire, CW9 6NA.
Tel. 01565 777353/777284

B

Barnsley House,
Barnsley,
nr. Cirencester,
Gloucestershire, GL7 5EE.
Tel. 01285 740281/740402

Bateman's,
Burwash,
Etchingham,
East Sussex, TN19 7DS.
Tel. 01435 882302

Bedgebury National Pinetum,
nr. Goudhurst,
Cranbrook,
Kent, TN17 2SL.
Tel. 01580 211044

Belton House,
nr. Grantham,
Lincolnshire, NG32 2LS.
Tel. 01476 66116

Berkeley Castle,
Berkeley,
Gloucestershire,
GL13 9BQ.
Tel. 01453 810332

Bicton Park,
East Budleigh,
Devon, EX9 7DP.
Tel. 01395 568465

Blenheim Palace,
Woodstock,
Oxon, OX20 1PX.
Tel. 01993 811091

Blickling Hall,
Blickling,
nr. Norwich,
Norfolk, NR11 6NF.
Tel. 01263 733471

Bodnant Garden,
Tal-y-Cafn,
Colwyn Bay,
Clwyd, LL28 5RE.
Tel. 01492 650460

Borde Hill Garden,
Haywards Heath,
West Sussex,
RH16 1XP.
Tel. 01444 450326

Bowood House,
Derry Hill,
Calne,
Wiltshire, SN11 0LZ.
Tel. 01249 812102

Bramham Park,
Wetherby,
West Yorkshire,
LS23 6ND.
Tel. 01937 844265

Branklyn,
Dundee Road,
Perth,
Tayside, PH2 7BB.
Tel. 01738 625535

Brodick Castle,
Isle of Arran,
Strathclyde, KA27 8HY.
Tel. 01770 302202

Burford House Gardens,
Tenbury Wells,
Hereford and Worcester,
WR15 8HQ.
Tel. 01584 810777

Burnby Hall Gardens,
The Balk,
Pocklington,
York, YO4 2QF.
Tel. 01759 302068

C

Castle Howard,
York,
North Yorkshire, YO6 7DA.
Tel. 01653 648444

Chartwell,
Westerham,
Kent, TN16 1PS.
Tel. 01732 866368

Chatsworth,
Bakewell,
Derbyshire, DE45 1PP.
Tel. 01246 582204

Chelsea Physic Garden,
66 Royal Hospital Road,
London, SW3 4HS.
Tel. 0171 3525646

Chenies Manor,
Chenies,
Rickmansworth,
Hertfordshire, WD3 6ER.
Tel. 01494 762888

Claremont Landscape Garden,
Portsmouth Road,
Esher,
Surrey, KT10 9JG.
Tel. 01372 467806/469421

Cliveden,
Taplow,
Maidenhead,
Berkshire, SL6 0JA.
Tel. 01628 605069

Compton Acres,
Canford Cliffs,
Poole,
Dorset, BH13 7ES.
Tel. 01202 700778

Cotehele House Gardens,
St. Dominick,
Saltash,
Cornwall, PL12 6TA.
Tel. 01579 50434

Coton Manor Garden,
nr. Guilsborough,
Northampton, NN6 8RQ.
Tel. 01604 740219

Cragside House,
Rothbury,
Northumberland,
NE65 7PX.
Tel. 01669 620333

Cranborne Manor Gardens,
Cranborne,
Wimborne,
Dorset, BH21 5PP.
Tel. 01725 517248

Crathes Castle,
Banchory,
Grampian, AB31 3QJ.
Tel. 01330 844525

D

Dyffryn Gardens,
St. Nicholas,
Cardiff,
South Glamorgan, CF5 6SU.
Tel. 01222 593328

E

Elvaston Castle Country Park,
Elvaston,
nr. Derby,
Derbyshire, DE72 3EP.
Tel. 01332 571342

Exbury Gardens,
Exbury,
nr. Southampton,
Hampshire, SO45 1AZ.
Tel. 01703 891203

F

Falkland Palace Garden,
Falkland,
Fife, KY7 7BU.
Tel. 01337 857397

Felbrigg Hall,
Roughton,
Norwich,
Norfolk, NR11 8PR.
Tel. 01263 837444

Furzey Gardens,
Minstead,
nr. Lyndhurst,
Hampshire, SO43 7GL.
Tel. 01703 812464

G

Great Dixter House and Gardens,
Northiam,
nr. Rye,
East Sussex, TN31 6PH.
Tel. 01797 252878

H

Haddon Hall,
Bakewell,
Derbyshire, DE45 1LA.
Tel. 01629 812855

Hampton Court Palace,
East Molesey,
Surrey, KT8 9AU.
Tel. 0181 7819500

Harewood House,
Harewood,
Leeds,
West Yorkshire, LS17 9LQ.
Tel. 0113 2886331

Harlow Carr Botanical Gardens,
Crag Lane,
Harrogate,
North Yorkshire,
HG3 1QB.
Tel. 01423 565418

Heale Garden,
Middle Woodford,
nr. Salisbury,
Wiltshire, SP4 6NT.
Tel. 01722 782504

Hever Castle,
Hever,
Edenbridge,
Kent, TN8 7NG.
Tel. 01732 865224

Hidcote Manor Garden,
Hidcote Bartrim,
Chipping Camden,
Gloucestershire, GL55 6LR.
Tel. 01386 438333

Hodnet Hall Gardens,
Hodnet,
Market Drayton,
Shropshire, TF9 3NN.
Tel. 01630 685202

I

Inverewe Garden,
Poolewe,
Ross and Cromarty,
Highlands, IV22 2LQ.
Tel. 01445 781200

K

Kew Royal Botanic Gardens,
Kew,
Richmond,
Surrey, TW9 3AB.
Tel. 0181 3325000

Knightshayes,
Bolham,
Tiverton,
Devon, EX16 7RQ.
Tel. 01884 253264/254665

L

Lanhydrock Gardens,
Bodmin,
Cornwall, PL30 5AD.
Tel. 01208 73320

Leonardslee Gardens,
Lower Beeding,
nr. Horsham,
West Sussex,
RH13 6PP.
Tel. 01403 891212

Levens Hall,
Kendal,
Cumbria, LA8 0PD.
Tel. 015395 60321

Lingholm Gardens,
Lingholm,
Keswick,
Cumbria, CA12 5UA.
Tel. 017687 72003

Logan Botanic Gardens,
Port Logan,
by Stranraer,
Dumfries and Galloway,
DG9 9ND.
Tel. 01776 860231

Lyme Park,
Disley,
Stockport,
SK12 2NX.
Tel. 01663 762023/766492

M

Melbourne Hall,
Melbourne,
Derbyshire, DE73 1EN.
Tel. 01332 862163

N

Ness Gardens,
University of Liverpool
Botanic Gardens,
Ness,
South Wirral, L64 4AY.
Tel. 0151 3530123

Newby Hall,
Ripon,
North Yorkshire,
HG4 5AE.
Tel. 01423 322583

Newstead Abbey,
Ravenshead,
Nottinghamshire,
NG15 8GE.
Tel. 01623 793557

Nymans Gardens,
Handcross,
Haywards Heath,
West Sussex,
RH17 6EB.
Tel. 01444 400321

O

Overbeck's Museum and Garden,
Sharpitor,
Salcombe,
Devon, TQ8 8LW.
Tel. 01548 842893

Oxford Botanic Gardens,
Rose Lane,
Oxford,
Oxfordshire, OX1 4AX.
Tel. 01865 276920

P

Packwood House,
Lapworth,
Solihull,
Warwickshire, B94 6AT.
Tel. 01564 782024

Pitmedden Garden,
Pitmedden,
Ellon,
Aberdeenshire,
AB41 0PD.
Tel. 01651 842352

Powis Castle Gardens,
Welshpool,
Powys,
North Wales, SY21 8RF.
Tel. 01938 552952

Preston Park,
contact:
Brighton Borough Council,
Environmental Services
Dept.,
Tel. 01273 712932

Q

Queen Mary's Rose Garden,
Inner Circle,
Regent's Park,
London, NW1 4NR.
Tel. 0171 4867905

R

Riverhill House Gardens,
Sevenoaks,
Kent, TN15 0RR.
Tel. 01732 458802/452557

Rousham House and Garden,
Steeple Aston,
Oxfordshire, OX6 3QX.
Tel. 01869 347110

Royal National Rose Society Gardens,
Chiswell Green,
St. Albans,
Hertfordshire,
AL2 3NR.
Tel. 01727 850461

S

Saltram House,
Plympton,
Plymouth,
Devon, PL7 3UH.
Tel. 01752 336546

Sandringham House,
Sandringham,
Norfolk, PE35 6EN.
Tel. 01553 772675

Savill Garden (Windsor Great Park),
Wick Lane,
Englefield Green,
Egham,
Surrey, TW20 0UU.
Tel. 01753 860222

Scotney Castle,
Lamberhurst,
Tunbridge Wells,
Kent, TN3 8JN.
Tel. 01892 890651

Sezincote,
Moreton-in-Marsh,
Gloucestershire,
GL56 9AW.
Tel. 01386 700444

Shakespeare Gardens,
Stratford-upon-Avon,
Warwickshire,
CV37 6QW.
Tel. 01789 204016

Sheffield Park Garden,
Uckfield,
East Sussex,
TN22 3QX.
Tel. 01825 790231

Shugborough,
Milford,
nr. Stafford,
Staffordshire, ST17 OXB.
Tel. 01889 881388

Sissinghurst Garden,
Cranbrook,
Kent, TN17 2AB.
Tel. 01580 712850

Sizergh Castle,
Kendal,
Cumbria, LA8 8AE.
Tel. 015395 60070

Springfields Gardens,
Camelgate,
Spalding,
Lincolnshire, PE12 6ET.
Tel. 01775 724843

Stourhead,
Stourton,
Wiltshire, BA12 6QD.
Tel. 01747 840348

Stowe Landscape Gardens,
Buckingham,
Buckinghamshire,
MK18 5EH,
Tel. 01280 822850

Studley Royal Water Garden,
Ripon,
North Yorkshire, HG4 3DY.
Tel. 01765 608888

Syon Park,
Brentford,
Middlesex, TW8 8JF.
Tel. 0181 5600881

T

Tatton Park,
Knutsford,
Cheshire,
WA16 6QN.
Tel. 01565 654822

Threave Garden,
Castle Douglas,
Dumfries and Galloway,
DG7 1RX.
Tel. 01556 502575

Tintinhull Gardens,
11 Farm Street,
Tintinhull,
Somerset,
BA22 8PZ.
Tel. 01935 822545

Trelissick Garden,
Feock,
Truro,
Cornwall,
TR3 6QL.
Tel. 01872 862090

Tresco Abbey Gardens,
Tresco,
Isles of Scilly,
Cornwall,
TR24 0QQ.
Tel. 01720 422849

V

Ventnor Botanic Garden,
The Undercliff Drive,
Ventnor,
Isle of Wight,
PO38 1UL.
Tel. 01983 855397

W

Waddesdon Manor,
Waddesdon,
nr. Aylesbury,
Buckinghamshire,
HP18 0JH
Tel. 01296 651282

Wakehurst Place,
Ardingly,
Haywards Heath,
West Sussex,
RH17 6TN.
Tel. 01444 892701

Westbury Court Garden,
Westbury-on-Severn,
Gloucestershire, G14 1PD.
Tel. 01452 760461

Westonbirt Arboretum,
Tetbury,
Gloucestershire,
GL8 8QS.
Tel. 01666 880220

Weston Park,
Weston-under-Lizard,
Shifnal,
Shropshire,
TF11 8LE.
Tel. 01952 850207

Winkworth Arboretum,
Hascombe Road,
Godalming,
Surrey, GU8 4AD.
Tel. 01483 208477

Wisley Garden,
Wisley,
Woking,
Surrey, GU23 6QB.
Tel. 01483 224234

Details of opening times, and information about many other gardens in Britain open to the public, can be obtained from the following organisations:

National Gardens Scheme,
Hatchlands Park,
East Clandon,
Guildford,
Surrey, GU4 7RT.
Tel. 01483 211535

The National Trust,
36 Queen Anne's Gate,
London, SW1H 9AS.
Tel. 0171 222 9251

The National Trust for Scotland,
5 Charlotte Square,
Edinburgh, EH2 4DU.
Tel. 0131 2265922

Scotland's Gardens Scheme,
31 Castle Terrace,
Edinburgh, EH1 2EL.
Tel. 0131 2291870

ACKNOWLEDGEMENTS

Front Cover Garden Picture Library (JS Sira). Back Cover Clive Nichols. 1 Harry Smith Collection. 2-3 Garden Picture Library (D Askham). 4-5 Clive Nichols. 6-7 Garden Picture Library (R Hyam). 8 Bob Gibbons (Robin Fletcher). 9 Harry Smith Collection. 10 Mary Evans Picture Library. 11 Clive Nichols. 13 The National Trust (Edward Leigh). 14 John Bethell. 15 Sefton Photo Library. 17 Impact (Pamla Toler). 18 (top) Mary Evans Picture Library; (bottom) Kenneth Scowen. 18-19, 20 Bruce Coleman Ltd (Eric Crichton). 21 (top) John Bethell; (bottom) Mansell Collection. 22-23 Harry Smith Collection. 23 Mansell Collection. 24 centre National Portrait Gallery. 24-25 John Bethell. 26 Fotobank (Ray Duffurn). 27 Richard Jemmett. 28-29 British Tourist Authority. 30-31, 32 Andy Williams Photo Library. 33, 34 Tania Midgley. 35, 36 Roger Scruton. 37, 38 Harry Smith Collection. 39 Andy Williams Photo Library. 40-41 Derek Widdicombe. 42 Photos Horticultural. 43 Peter Smith, Malton. 44, 45 (left) British Tourist Authority; (right) Mansell Collection. 46 (top) Eric Crichton; (bottom) Mary Evans Picture Library. 47 Garden Picture Library (C Boursnell). 48 Garden Picture Library (J Bethell). 49 Airviews. 50 Andrew Lawson. 51 Clive Nichols. 52 Garden Picture Library (J Bethell). 53 J Allan Cash. 54-55 Adam Woolfit. 56 Neil Holmes. 57 Garden Picture Library (JS Sira). 58 Andrew Lawson. 59 Natural Image (Robin Fletcher). 60 Tony Lord. 60-61 Richard Jemmett. 62 Mansell Collection. 63 Cressida Pemberton-Pigott. 64 Roger Scruton. 65 Natural Image (Robin Fletcher). 66 Derek Forss. 67 Lucinda Lambton. 68 Exbury Gardens. 68-69 Andrew Lawson. 70 Photos Horticultural. 71 John Bethell. 72 Photos Horticultural. 73 (top) Roger Scruton; (bottom) Mary Evans Picture Library. 74 S&O Mathews. 75 British Tourist Authority. 76 Mansell Collection. 77 Colour Library International. 78 Airviews. 79 Garden Picture Library (C Boursnell). 80-81 Jerry Harpur. 82-83 Eric Crichton. 84-85 John Bethell. 86 Fotobank. 88 Harry Smith Collection. 89 Ardea (Pat Morris). 90 Mansell Collection. 90-91 Royal Botanic Gardens, Kew. 92 (top) Arcaid (Richard Bryant); (bottom left) Mary Evans Picture Library; (bottom right) Richard Bryant. 92-93 Royal Botanic Gardens, Kew. 94 Harry Smith Collections. 95 Andrew Lawson. 96 Fotobank. 97 Colour Library International. 99 Tania Midgley. 100 Janet & Colin Bord. 101 (left) Airviews; (right) Mansell Collection. 102 John Bethell. 103, 104 Garden Picture Library (C Perry). 105 (left) Mary Evans Picture Library; (right) Impact (Pamla Toler). 107 Newby Hall. 108 (left) National Portrait Gallery; (top) right Mansell Collection; (bottom right) Pat Brindley. 109 Arcaid (Richard Bryant). 110 A-Z Collection. 111 Photobank. 112 Iris Hardwick. 113 The National Trust. 114-115, 117 British Tourist Authority. 118 (top) Adam Woolfit. 119 Biofotos (Hazel le Rougetel). 120, 121 Impact (Pamla Toler). 122 Robert Harding Picture Library. 123 Bruce Coleman Ltd (Michael Freeman). 124 (right) Mansell Collection; (left) George Wright. 125 Michael Boys. 126-127 Neil Holmes. 128 Bob Gibbons. 129 Harry Smith Collection. 130, 131 Adam Woolfit. 132 Richard Bryant. 133 Andy Williams Photo Library. 134-135 George Wright. 136 top Hulton Deutsch Collection. 137 Garden Picture Library (J Miller). 138 Harry Smith Collection. 139 Photos Horticultural. 140-141 Northern Picture Library (Geoff Dore). 142 John Bethell. 142-143 Clive Nichols. 144 Harry Smith Collection. 145 (top) Garden Picture Library (N Francis); (bottom) National Portrait Gallery. 146-147 Andrew Lawson. 148 Mary Evans Picture Library. 148-149 Andy Williams Photo Library. 150 Royal Horticultural Society. 151 Impact (Pamla Toler). 152 Andrew Lawson. 153 The National Trust. 154 Iris Hardwick. 154-155 Andrew Lawson. 156 Garden Picture Library (C Perry). 157 Tania Midgley. 158-159, 161 Andy Williams Photo Library. 162, 163 John Bethell. 164 Garden Picture Library (C Boursnell). 165 Photos Horticultural. 166 Clive Nichols. 167 Garden Picture Library (J Bethell). 169 Andy Williams Photo Library. 170 Robert Harding Picture Library. 170-171 Andrew Lawson. 172-172 Map Data Management Ltd.

Printing & Binding PRINTER INDUSTRIA, GRÁFICA S.A. BARCELONA
Separations COLOURSCAN OVERSEAS CO PTE LTD, SINGAPORE; Paper PERIGORD-CONDAT, FRANCE

53-019